THE NATIONAL EVALUATION
OF SURE START

Does area-based early
intervention work?

Edited by Jay Belsky, Jacqueline Barnes and
Edward Melhuish

KH

First published in Great Britain in 2007 by

The Policy Press
University of Bristol
Fourth Floor
Beacon House
Queen's Road
Bristol BS8 1QU
UK

Tel +44 (0)117 331 4054
Fax +44 (0)117 331 4093
e-mail tpp-info@bristol.ac.uk
www.policypress.org.uk

British Library Cataloguing in Publication Data
A catalogue record for this book is available from the British Library.

Library of Congress Cataloging-in-Publication Data
A catalog record for this book has been requested.

ISBN 978 1 86134 949 1 (paperback)
ISBN 978 1 86134 950 7 (hardback)

Cover design by Qube Design Associates, Bristol.
Front cover: photograph supplied by kind permission of www.johnbirdsall.co.uk
Printed and bound in Great Britain by Hobbs the Printers, Southampton.

4/15/13

Contents

List of tables and figures

Tables

Figures

Foreword

I was delighted to be asked to write the foreword to this comprehensive story about Sure Start. There is considerable detail in the forthcoming chapters, so my particular contribution is a personal reflection on the beginnings of Sure Start and its subsequent development over the years, 1998-2006. The world of children's services in England is unrecognisable from where we were in 1998 and as is common in social policy change, we quickly forget how much worse things were, and constantly consider how much better they could be. Things for young children and their parents are infinitely better than they were nearly 10 years ago and Sure Start has been a major part of these improvements. We are not yet Sweden, but services for young children are now better in England than in most other Anglophone countries. Visitors from all over the world are now coming to England to see what we have done and how we have done it.

The beginning of the Sure Start story is the 1998 Comprehensive Spending Review (CSR) on Services for Children under Eight. This review was run by Her Majesty's Treasury and sought to find out how much was spent on young children and how effective the spending was in delivering better outcomes for children. Unsurprisingly, the review found that most of the money spent on children was spent on those of school age, five years and above, and that the system for funding services for younger children was virtually non-existent. More importantly, the CSR found that the money that was spent had no overall goals or coherent strategy and was administered from different government departments. The only universal services were midwifery and health visiting. Public funding for nursery education was left to local authorities, as was funding for day care.

The CSR also found that, particularly for children in poverty, there were enormous gains in providing services for parents and for children from pre-birth to the very early years. Several mainly American studies had found that investment in early years provision, if high quality and relevant to parents and children, pays off in reduced costs in later life: fewer teen pregnancies, less crime, better staying-on rates at school.

The Labour Party had already committed in its 1997 Manifesto to delivering universal nursery education for all three- and four-year-olds, and had committed significant investment in childcare as a critical necessity in getting lone parents back to work. So plans were already in place to greatly increase investment in early years education and childcare. The CSR was taking a different angle. It was looking at the lack of join-up across services for young children, and in particular, the need to bring together a range of services: the kind of parenting support that the best health visitors provided with the quality group play and learning provided by some local authorities and many voluntary organisations, and the kind of community development opportunities provided by local groups that worked with families. Services for young children were among a range of issues including drugs policy and youth crime, on which 'joined-up solutions' seemed to be needed.

I was at the time Chief Executive of Family Service Units, a national voluntary organisation working with some of the poorest families in Britain's inner cities. I was among a very large group of voluntary sector players whose views were sought in the review. Having worked in the voluntary sector for many years, I was used to knocking on the door of the Department of Health to argue the case for more investment in young children. It was a new experience being sought out by government, and particularly new being consulted by Her Majesty's Treasury. Norman Glass was then the key senior official leading the CSR. Many of us invited Norman to visit various programmes around the country that demonstrated the effectiveness of local community engagement in reaching poor families in very disadvantaged areas. It was a tremendous opportunity to work with someone who was new to the field of early years, was a very keen learner and, of course, had access to significant government funding. It is difficult to overestimate the sense of privilege that those of us outside government felt in having a role to play. It genuinely felt like the advice we were giving was heard.

This sense of optimism was borne out in July 1998 when Jack Straw, then Home Secretary, announced in Parliament the establishment of Sure Start with a funding package of £450 million over the first three years, 1999-2002. The funding was earmarked to set up 250 Sure Start Local Programmes (SSLPs) in the areas with very high concentrations of children under four living in poverty. Each programme would have a defined catchment area of around 'pram-pushing distance' to new services being established. The average size programme would reach around 700 children under four, with a basket of integrated health, education and social welfare services. In January 1999, Tessa Jowell, then Minister for Public Health, announced the first 60 areas to be invited to develop a plan for their local Sure Start. In February 1999, after an open competition, I was appointed Head of the new Sure Start Unit that would be overseeing the programme.

From very early on there was a strong emphasis in ensuring new investment reached poor communities, while avoiding the stigma often associated with services tightly targeted on poor families. The solution to stigma was the design of an 'area-based initiative'. That is, if you choose your area on the basis of disadvantage, you can safely make the services available to all, and feel confident that a significant proportion of those who come forward will be poor. There was also, from the very beginning, a strong emphasis on community; this involved not just consulting local parents, but also giving them a role in governance, in key decision making on what to offer and how it would be offered. Both these issues created their own challenges, which will be described later in this book.

In keeping with a still relatively new Labour government, there was real innovation in setting up the governance arrangements for Sure Start. The new Sure Start Unit would be based in the Department for Education and Employment (DfEE) (as was in 1999), and I would report to Tessa Jowell, Public Health Minister in the Department of Health. Tessa Jowell reported to David Blunkett, the Secretary of State for Education and Employment. The programme was overseen by a committee chaired by Tessa Jowell, and made up of junior ministers drawn from Home Office, Treasury, Education, Environment and Culture. Sure Start funding was firmly ringfenced. While it sat in the DfEE spending limit, it could not be used for any other purposes. My own management arrangements reflected this emphasis on cross-government working in that I had a trio of senior officials – in Health, Education and the Treasury – who were guiding and overseeing my work. Given my newness to the civil service, it took me quite a while to realise how unusual all these arrangements were. There was from the very beginning, among officials and ministers, a terrific sense of optimism. Under-fours was then a 'policy-free zone' so no department felt that their policy was being taken from them; the funding came from the Treasury so no department had to switch resources or lose out because of the creation of this new programme of highly innovative work.

From the beginning there was a strong commitment to a sophisticated, high-quality evaluation for the programme. The main debate about the evaluation was the real difficulty of a national evaluation of a programme with then 250 different local interpretations. The chapters in this book will illustrate clearly that challenge. After a detailed feasibility study, invitations to tender were invited in summer 2000 and the Birkbeck proposal was awarded the contract very early in 2001. The key debate, which still rages about Sure Start, was the commitment to local flexibility; funding based on plans to deliver specific child outcomes rather than specific services. The programmes were required to deliver a core set of services, but had considerable flexibility as long as the plans could reasonably be expected to deliver the nine Public Service Agreement targets set for the programme. These targets included birth weight, language development at age two, reduction in hospital admissions and parent satisfaction with the services. Considering those outcomes were not across a single domain, but across health, education, social well-being and parental behaviours, the evaluation was even more complex. Without having a common set of inputs, how could one learn which inputs were more successful than others in delivering such a wide range of outcomes. These issues will be discussed in more detail in later chapters in this book. Resolving them resulted in an elegant but very complex research design.

The difficulties in evaluation were compounded as the programme matured and changed. In the 2000 Spending Review the programme was doubled in size, to 500 local programmes. In the 2002 Spending Review the Sure Start Unit was merged with Early Years Division and the Childcare Unit at the Department for Education and Skills (DfES), creating a single management group to deliver SSLPs, the Neighbourhood Nursery Initiative, the National Childcare Strategy and free nursery education for all three- and four-year-olds. Significant progress on some of these policies had already been made. The task now was to bring them together into a coherent package of central government delivery commitments to families with young children, and families needing out-of-school care for older children.

The governance arrangements also changed, with the cross-government responsibility moving from the DfES and Department of Health to the DfES and the Department for Work and Pensions (DWP). As Director of this new, much larger group, I no longer reported across the two departments. The cross-departmental arrangements were ministerial, with Catherine Ashton, a Lords minister, reporting to two Secretaries of State, the DWP and DfES.

This was followed in 2003 by further radical changes in governance of children's services across Whitehall. A new post of Minister for Children was created, with Margaret Hodge as the first postholder. Children's social care was moved from the Department of Health to the DfES, and family policy was moved from the Home Office to the DfES. Combining at Cabinet level responsibility for schools and for virtually all other children's services created huge opportunities to create a coherent strategy for all children, 0 to 19 years. The Green Paper *Every child matters* (HM Government, 2003) articulated this coherent strategy. Many of the initial principles of Sure Start, the need to integrate service delivery, the need to work with parents as well as children and particularly the need to work to outcomes rather than inputs were highly influential in the emerging Every Child Matters agenda. The Every Child Matters agenda also began to address some of the main barriers that Sure Start had been experiencing at local level: the difficulties of information sharing between agencies, the absence at local level of a single senior-level responsibility for all children and the struggle in many areas to get agencies to work together.

Sure Start has continued to grow and change, and the publication in December 2004 of the report *Choice for parents, the best start for children: A ten year strategy for childcare* (HM Treasury, 2004) set the scene for what some would call the end of Sure Start, and others its future security. This document, and the 2006 Childcare Act, established the government's future policy. Sure Start Local Programmes are all now Sure Start Children's Centres. By 2010 there will be 3,500 Children's Centres, bringing together the original Sure Start principles of integrated service delivery and working with parents and children, but with much tighter performance requirements, clearer guidance on what should be delivered and how, and overall control from local authorities, not central government. Much of the guidance has been determined by learning from the National Evaluation of Sure Start and from the Effective Provision of Pre-school Education research project, co-led by Kathy Sylva and Ted Melhuish. Both research projects have been extremely useful in identifying what works, but also what does not work to improve children's outcomes. Like its sister American programmes, Head Start and Early Head Start, there have been some real disappointments and some welcome successes. The learning has justified the investment in evaluation, in that we are determined to use the evidence to inform policy and practice.

It has been a great privilege, and at times enormously stressful, to be engaged in these developments over the last nine years. We now have clear legislation that promises quality childcare for any parent wishing to work, much greater opportunities for flexible working for parents and increased flexibility in the way that childcare is delivered. We now know significantly more about the importance of quality, and what quality looks like in care for infants and toddlers as well as three- and four-year-olds. Most importantly, we now have a legislative requirement that local authorities reduce the gap in outcomes between disadvantaged children under five and the wider child population. The main vehicle for reducing the gap is the network of Sure Start Children's Centres.

These centres are not just providing childcare, but a range of locally determined support services for parents and children: health, employment advice, parenting support and early learning. What started as three very fragmented government policies – universal nursery education, childcare for working parents and Sure Start for the poorest families – is now an integrated coherent service offer for children and families, personalised to individual parent and child requirements. This book describes some of the mistakes and successes along the way. We still have a long way to go, but I am personally proud of what has been achieved.

References

HM Government (2003) *Every child matters*, Green Paper, Nottingham: Department for Education and Skills.

HM Treasury (2004) *Choice for parents, the best start for children: A ten year strategy for childcare*, London: The Stationery Office.

Naomi Eisenstadt

March 2007

List of abbreviations

ABI   area-based initiative
BCU   Basic Command Unit
BME   black and minority ethnic
BNG   British National Grid
CCDP   Comprehensive Child Development Program
CSR   Comprehensive Spending Review
DfEE   Department for Education and Employment
DfES   Department for Education and Skills
DLA   Disability Living Allowance
DWP   Department for Work and Pensions
EHS   Early Head Start program
EPPE   Effective Provision of Pre-school Education project
GCSE   General Certificate of Secondary Education
GDP   Gross Domestic Product
GIS   Geographical Information Systems
GP   general practitioner
GPS   Global Positioning System
HAZ   Health Action Zone
IGLS   iterative generalised least squares
IMD   Index of Multiple Deprivation
KS1   Key Stage One
KS2   Key Stage Two
LCA   Local Context Analysis
NDC   New Deal for Communities
NESS   National Evaluation of Sure Start
NSF   National Service Framework
OA   output area
OS   Ordnance Survey
PCA   Principal Components Analysis
PCT   primary care trust
RCT   randomised controlled trial
SD   standard deviation
SEN   special educational needs
SOA   super output area
SSLP   Sure Start Local Programme
SSU   Sure Start Unit

Notes on contributors

Debra Allnock holds an MA in Sociology and Social Research from the University of Maryland, US. She served as a researcher on the Implementation module of the National Evaluation of Sure Start (NESS) and currently works for the National Society for the Prevention of Cruelty to Children researching child protection and child sexual abuse.

Angela Anning is Emeritus Professor of Early Childhood Education at the University of Leeds, UK, and worked on the programme variation component of the Implementation module of NESS. She holds a BA (Hons) in English/Fine Art from the University of Leeds and a Masters of Education from the University of Leicester, UK. Her research interests include early childhood education, particularly in the arts, and professional knowledge and practice in services for young children and their families.

Mog Ball is a freelance writer and researcher who took responsibility for the themed studies of the Implementation module of NESS, while also working on the programme variation element of the research. She has a BA (Hons) in Latin and Greek from the University of Keele, UK. She has written many books, reports and articles on social programmes and their evaluation.

Jacqueline Barnes is Professor of Psychology at Birkbeck University of London, based at the Institute for the Study of Children, Families and Social Issues. She earned a BSc, MSc and PhD in Psychology from, respectively, University College London, the University of Wisconsin, US, and the University of London. Professor Barnes directed the Local-Context and Support-for-Local-Programmes modules of NESS. Her research interests include evaluation of early intervention programmes, community characteristics related to parenting and the use of child-care in the early years.

Jay Belsky is Professor of Psychology at Birkbeck University of London, and Director of the Institute for the Study of Children, Families and Social Issues. He holds a BA from Vassar College, US, and an MS in child development and PhD in human development from Cornell University, US. He led the team that won the competition for the NESS research grant and served as Research Director of the evaluation. His interests include infant–parent attachment and parent–child relationships, the effects of childcare, the aetiology of child maltreatment and the ecology of child development more generally.

Naomi Eisenstadt CB is a senior civil servant at the Cabinet Office. She has a Bachelors Degree in Sociology from the University of California San Diego, an MSc in Social Policy from Cranfield Institute, UK, and an honorary doctorate from the Open University, UK, for services to families and children. Two decades spent in the voluntary sector led to her seven-year civil service appointment as Director of the Sure Start programme.

Martin Frost is Reader in Geography at Birkbeck University of London. He earned his BSc in Geography and MSc and PhD in Urban and Regional Planning from the London School of Economics and Political Science. He provided geographical expertise to the Local Context Analysis module of NESS while serving as co-director of the South East Regional (Geographical) Research at Birkbeck University of London. His interests include spatial economic development, the structure of local labour markets and their relationships with public policy.

David Hall is Emeritus Professor of Community Paediatrics at the University of Sheffield. He was educated at King's College London and St Georges Hospital Medical School, University of London. His specialties include child development and its disorders, disability, child public health, developmental disorders and screening.

Gillian Harper is a Chartered Geographer who serves as a freelance geographic information systems consultant, working for the Centre for Applied Economic Geography at Birkbeck University of London, and the Royal Geographical Society. She holds a BA (Hons) in Geography from Strathclyde University and an MSc in Geographic Information Science from University College London. She worked on the Local-Context-Analysis module of NESS, specialising in geographic analysis.

Pamela Meadows is a visiting fellow at the National Institute of Economic and Social Research, UK. She has a BA in Economics from the University of Durham, UK, and an MSc from Birkbeck University of London. She is responsible for the Cost-Effectiveness module of

NESS. She was previously Director of the Policy Studies Institute and before that was Director of Economics, Research and Evaluation at the Department of Employment.

Edward Melhuish is Professor of Human Development at the Institute for the Study of Children, Families and Social Issues, School of Psychology, Birkbeck University of London and Visiting Professorial Fellow at the Institute of Education. He holds a BSc from the University of Bristol, UK, and a PhD from the University of London, both in Psychology. He served as Executive Director of NESS and has research interests in childcare, child development and social policy.

Sir Michael Rutter is Professor of Developmental Psychopathology at the Institute of Psychiatry, King's College, London. He obtained his medical degree at the University of Birmingham, UK, trained in psychiatry at the Maudsley Hospital, London, and studied child development at the Albert Einstein College of Medicine in New York. He serves on the scientific advisory board of NESS and has research interests that span epidemiology, life course development, schooling, and the interplay between genetic and environmental risk factors.

Jane Tunstill is Emeritus Professor of Social Work, Royal Holloway, University of London, and Visiting Professor, Social Care Workforce Research Unit, King's College, London. She holds a BA in Social Administration from Hull University, UK, and an MA in Public and Social Administration from Brunel University, UK. She served as Director of the Implementation module of NESS and has a long career in social work education and research into children's services.

Part One
The historical and policy context

ONE

The policy background to Sure Start

Edward Melhuish and Sir David Hall

On May Day 1997 Labour won a landslide election victory, returning to power for the first time since 1979 with a 177-seat majority. The end of 18 years of successive Conservative governments represented an opportunity to change policies that would be seen to place the improvement of people's lives at the centre of government strategy. On 6 May, Gordon Brown, the Chancellor of the Exchequer, enacted a policy at the forefront of macroeconomic thinking by giving the Bank of England operational independence from the government, including freedom to set interest rates. One consequence of this change was that a number of high-level economists at the Treasury had time to pursue other tasks. As well as being the government's foremost economic thinker, Gordon Brown also embodied its social conscience. He wanted the government to break the cycle whereby disadvantaged children relived their parents' experiences of poor education, physical ill-health and poverty. Hence, when this surfeit of economists became available he gave one of them, Norman Glass, the job of exploring what policies might fulfil this aim.

A fresh look at children's services

At this time the notion of 'joined-up' services was also in vogue within the government. Regarding services for children, Prime Minister Tony Blair (1998) commented in the Foreword to the Comprehensive Spending Review (CSR) (HM Treasury, 1998a) that 'We have looked at key problems across government. The old departmental boundaries often do not work. Provision for young children – health, childcare, support – will be co-ordinated across departments so that when children start school they are ready to learn.' In preparation for this review, which set out government spending plans for the following three years, six cross-cutting reviews were established. The need for cross-cutting reviews arose from concerns that some policy areas either might be ignored if left to a sole department or might be tackled inadequately, and such reviews were meant to facilitate 'joined-up' government. It was agreed by ministers that there should be such a review of services for young children. Provision of services appeared, in many cases, to be failing those in greatest need but there was evidence from programmes in the US such as Head Start and the Perry pre-school programme (Barnett, 1995), as well as from experimental programmes in the UK, that comprehensive early years interventions could make a difference to children's lives.

The Cross-Departmental Review of Services for Young Children was established, charged with considering all available evidence and producing policy recommendations for counteracting the cycle of disadvantage. In particular, the review was to assess whether greater emphasis on preventative action and a more integrated child-centred approach to service delivery could help cut the costs of crime and unemployment, and reduce the need for extra help for individuals at school and in later life, by helping parents, carers and communities provide the best possible start for children. The review was designed to:

- look at the policies and resources for children aged seven and under, in order to ensure effectiveness in providing preventative action and the necessary support to ensure the development of their full potential throughout their lives;
- consider whether the multiple causes of social exclusion affecting young children could be more effectively tackled at the family and community levels using an integrated approach to service provision; and
- to take account of policy developments in initiatives elsewhere (HM Treasury, 1998b).

The review involved 11 government departments together with the Social Exclusion Unit and the Number 10 Policy Unit, with a Steering Group comprised of ministers from all the departments. It gathered information through meetings with pressure groups, representatives of service providers and service users, written submissions, papers commissioned from experts, and a series of open seminars. Visits were made to various projects offering services to young children and their families and the final report to the 1998 CSR was presented by Tessa Jowell, then Minister of Public Health. It contained a wide-ranging analysis of the state of services and made a number of recommendations and conclusions including the following (HM Treasury, 1998b):

- The earliest years in life were the most important for child development, and very early development was much more vulnerable to adverse environmental influences than had previously been realised.
- Multiple disadvantage for young children was a severe and growing problem, with such disadvantage greatly enhancing the chances of social exclusion later in life.
- The quality of service provision for young children and their families varied enormously across localities and districts, with uncoordinated and patchy services being the norm in many areas. Services were particularly dislocated for the under fours – an age group that tended to get missed by other government programmes.
- The provision of a comprehensive community-based programme of early intervention and family support that built on existing services could have positive and persistent effects, not only on child and family development but also in helping break the intergenerational cycle of social exclusion, which could lead to significant long-term gain to the Exchequer.

With regard to the nature of the programme, the review argued that while there was no single blueprint for the ideal set of effective early interventions, they should be:

- two-generational, involving parents as well as children;
- non-stigmatising, avoiding labelling 'problem families';
- multifaceted, targeting a number of factors, not just, for example, education or health or parenting;
- persistent, lasting long enough to make a real difference;
- locally driven, based on consultation with and involvement of parents and local communities; and
- culturally appropriate and sensitive to the needs of children and parents.

It was argued also that a range of services should ideally be integrated to support the complex and varied physical, developmental and emotional needs of young children and families. Such services should be easily accessible – within 'pram-pushing distance' – and backed up by outreach to offer support in the home. The programme was to be *area-based*, with *all* children under four and their families living in a prescribed area being clients of the local programme, with the right to a say in the services provided. This area-based characteristic was congruent with other area-based initiatives that were a feature of much government policy.

Background to early intervention work

Considerations relevant to government policy for early interventions such as Sure Start Local Programmes (SSLPs) derive from research evidence and also from concerns that had arisen over a number of years in child health. These are considered in turn.

The use of research evidence on early child development

In an innovation for the development of policy, empirical findings of research studies were taken into account in the CSR, as described by Norman Glass (2006) in oral evidence to the House of Commons Science and Technology Committee:

> We were influenced very heavily by a series of experimental studies in the United States, many of them different but relating to early years programmes, which appeared to show significant improvements on a number of measures....We were influenced by issues of evidence from our own birth cohort studies which showed that many of the influences in people's later lives were present in the first seven years of their lives and that those were the most significant influences affecting people's lives, in so far as you could see what affected people's lives. There was a lot of evidence on the importance of things like parental attachment and so on. There was a lot of stuff around of that kind which did not point to particular programmes but nevertheless pointed in the direction of saying that early years mattered and probably mattered more than interventions you could make later on in people's lives and that there were things that appeared to be effective which were being carried out elsewhere.

The evidence from the US that particularly influenced the review included randomised controlled trials of early years interventions, demonstrating clear benefits for disadvantaged children of high-quality childcare provision, whether started in infancy (Abecedarian Project: Ramey and Campbell, 1991) or at three years of age (Perry pre-school project: Schweinhart et al, 1993). Where quasi-experimental studies had rigorous methodology, they produced similar results. Small-scale, tightly controlled interventions had produced larger effects than more extensive large-scale interventions, such as the Chicago Child-Parent Centers (Reynolds et al, 2001) and Head Start (Karoly et al, 1998). Nevertheless, the impact of large-scale interventions was still substantial, producing worthwhile benefits for children, families and communities.

Such early childhood interventions often used home visiting and parental support as a supplement to childcare, which were said to have additional benefits. There was other evidence for the benefits of home visiting provided by nurse-qualified staff, rather than by para-professionals, particularly if a highly structured approach was implemented (Olds et al, 1997, 1999). Research on early years interventions was presented to the Cross-Departmental Review (for example, Oliver et al, 1998; Pugh, 1998), since synthesised by Melhuish (2004), with conclusions similar to the earlier government review. The mounting evidence of the importance of the early years and the potential of early intervention (for example, Shonkoff and Phillips, 2000) encouraged the development of several intervention projects in the US, Australia and Canada as well as SSLPs in the UK, all setting out to address factors such as parent attitudes and mental health, childrearing, and high-quality early stimulation and education programmes. However, early results from these intervention efforts highlighted the need for caution as only sustained high-quality interventions proved to be effective (Olds, 2002; Melhuish, 2004).

Child health

Good health in the case of children enables them to (a) develop and realise their potential, (b) satisfy their needs and (c) acquire the skills and capacities that allow them to interact successfully with their biological, physical and social environments (National Research Council and Institute of Medicine, 2004). Sure Start Local Programmes were based in large measure on such a comprehensive view of child health, as well as on a clear appreciation of what was lacking in the delivery of health-related services for children. For many years it was widely acknowledged that parents found problematic the plethora of uncoordinated services (health, social services, education, voluntary sector) they had to struggle with in order to obtain diagnosis and treatment for their children. Making things additionally problematic was poor interagency collaboration among professionals in different agencies, generated in part by differences in training, culture, concepts of confidentiality and evidence, causing communication difficulties that often resulted in a lack of trust and respect.

But SSLPs were also based on basic knowledge of early development, especially with respect to disability, mental health and child maltreatment. The pathways to social exclusion include childhood disability, socially determined child mental health problems and child abuse and neglect. Although these areas of inquiry had attracted researchers from health and social sciences, little cross-fertilisation occurred either in research or in professional practice. Nevertheless, during the 1990s strands of inquiry began to converge, laying the foundation for programmes like Sure Start.

The classic concept of 'critical periods' in child development stimulated a sense of urgency in the need for services for very young children as it implied that without early intervention, a precious window of opportunity for identification and treatment would be lost for a child with abnormal brain development (Baird and Hall, 1985). Not unrelated was the emerging notion of 'brain plasticity', referring to the infant brain as rapidly developing and with great capacity for new learning, even able of using 'undamaged' areas, if needed, that were adaptable (or plastic) in their function and otherwise underutilised. These viewpoints fostered increased enthusiasm for services such as early physiotherapy and speech therapy for disabled children.

While it was necessary to identify such children as early as possible, the process of 'developmental screening' had proven much more difficult than anticipated (Sheridan, 1973). Children with major disorders such as congenital nerve deafness, classic autism or severe cerebral palsy were readily recognised without screening. However, this was not so for many children with atypical motor development that was difficult to distinguish from cerebral palsy or muscle disease and which had generally benign outcomes. Similarly, given marked variation in the rate and quality of language acquisition, it was difficult to distinguish children with serious language disorders from those who were simply 'slow starters' (Bishop, 2000).

Children with 'low prevalence but high severity' disability such as cerebral palsy, severe learning difficulties and classic autism were more easily identified. However, those with 'high prevalence but low severity' conditions like mild general learning difficulties, delayed language acquisition, dyslexia and attention deficit hyperactivity disorder were often missed in the early years – and were overrepresented in lower social classes. For society, the total burden resulting from such problems was known to be greater than that deriving from severe but low prevalence disorders.

Studies of low severity disorders, behavioural disorders, antisocial behaviour and crime indicated that precursors were often early developmental difficulties, harsh and inconsistent parenting and educational failure, together with a high incidence of child abuse and neglect, substance abuse, unemployment, parental mental health and poverty (for example, Rutter et al, 1976; Farrington, 2003). Nevertheless, while the importance of genetic influences was clear (for example, Dale et al, 1998), the follow-up of children with gross early deprivation cast new light on the concept of 'critical' or 'sensitive' periods and the sometimes remarkable degree of recovery that occurred given the right environmental conditions (Rutter and ERA, 1998).

Such evidence on the problems of early screening and the importance of social factors for low severity disability led two separate UK reviews to propose that routine developmental checks be reduced, but investment in health-promoting activities be increased (Butler, 1989; Hall, 1989). Generally, such proposals were welcomed and endorsed by the Department of Health (NHS Executive, 1996). These recommendations contributed to the focus on joined-up early child health services in SSLPs.

The problem of child abuse, which occurs disproportionately in disadvantaged families and communities, was highlighted by Kempe et al's (1962) classic description of 'battered babies'. But the full extent of emotional abuse, neglect and sexual abuse only became clear over the next 20 years. While only around 1% of parents are abusive, up to 10% provide barely adequate parenting, which is also associated with compromised development. Growing disquiet during the 1990s about the seemingly endless series of child abuse scandals, and recognition of how common child sexual and emotional abuse were, increased attention on child protection. Controversies over attribution of responsibility in child abuse cases led to health professionals in this field being criticised with often bitter campaigns to discredit them, resulting in a dramatic increase in complaints by parents against doctors working in this area. By 2000 this was having a devastating impact on doctors' willingness to be involved in child protection work. This emphasised the need for programmes like SSLPs to fully integrate medical care with the involvement of social services.

Community development

In addition to the lessons from research on early intervention and child health, Norman Glass came to believe in the importance of community involvement and thus advocated a community development approach to early years intervention. This was somewhat surprising given the nature of the evidence that was used to justify Sure Start spending, which had little, if anything, to say about community development. The emphasis placed on community development in the case of SSLPs would be an interesting tale, only part of which is known. A Treasury minister, Alastair Darling, asked Norman Glass: 'How can you assure me that this programme will not lead in 10 years' time to a lot of boarded-up, fly-blown family centres such as I have seen in my own constituency and elsewhere?', to which Glass (2005) responded as follows:

> This programme would be 'owned' by local parents, local communities and those who worked in the programme. Because those who benefited would be able to shape it to do what they wanted, rather than it being done to, or for, them, it would not be seen as just another initiative by Whitehall to do something about the feckless proles[1].

Glass (2005) subsequently recalled:

> What I learned from visits to successful early years programmes and local communities was that it was necessary, in the case of early years at any rate, to involve local people fully in the development and management of the programme if it was to take root and not simply be seen as another quick fix by middle-class social engineers.

The community development approach of Sure Start was also consistent with broader principles central to New Labour's interest in modernising government, including the view that public services should be user, not provider driven, evidence based, joined up and innovative.

The birth of Sure Start

The findings of the Cross-Departmental Review were incorporated into the 1998 CSR that delineated future government expenditure. Announcing its details to the House of Commons on 14 July 1998, the Chancellor of the Exchequer introduced the plan for what would be known as Sure Start, aiming to bring together quality services for children under four and their parents – nursery, childcare and playgroup provision, and prenatal and other health services. One new feature involved extending to parents the offer of counselling and help to prepare their children for learning and for school (HM Treasury, 1998a).

The review's final report noted that disadvantage among young children was increasing, that this could result in difficulties in later life and that the earlier intervention was undertaken, the more likely poor outcomes were to be prevented. Further, the report noted, current services were uncoordinated and patchy, young children often missed out on services that concentrated on older children and the quality of services varied. Nevertheless, there existed good practice that could inform the enhancement of programmes for young children. It was recommended, therefore, that there should be a change of approach to the design and delivery of services. They should be jointly planned by all relevant bodies, both within the local authority and outside it (HM Treasury, 1998b).

A total of £542 million became available to be spent over three years (HM Treasury, 1998b), with £452 million designated for England. England, Wales, Scotland and Northern Ireland would each develop their own Sure Start plans. In England it was decided that there would be 250 programmes up and running by 2001-02, supporting about 187,000 children, or 18% of all poor children under four. On average, a local programme was to include 800 under fours. The intention was to provide each programme with a ringfenced budget – roughly equivalent to £1,250 per annum per child – at the peak of funding. Programmes were to be funded for 10 years to ensure money was not diverted to other services and to signal a long-term commitment. Each SSLP was to run for at least seven to 10 years with government funding peaking at year three of operation and declining from year six through to zero at year 10. It was implicit that some funding would be picked up by local authorities and that some funding would no longer be needed because of the successful 'reshaping' of mainstreaming services to more appropriately meet the needs of local families. This commitment and investment utterly transformed early years services in the UK, while still representing a relatively small contribution from the perspective of the Treasury – just 0.05% of public expenditure.

The programmes were to be targeted on the 20% most deprived areas. There are no published figures on how many poor children live in such areas. However, using statistics from the Indices of Multiple Deprivation (ODPM, 2004) we have calculated that for children in families with an income 60% or less than the national median (official poverty line), 51% of all such poor children live in the 20% most deprived areas and 65% live within the 30% most deprived areas.

Joined-up government and Sure Start

The Sure Start Unit (SSU) responsible for administering the new initiative was cross-departmental, run by a ministerial steering group representing the Departments of Education and Employment; Health; Social Security; Environment, Transport and the Regions; Culture, Media and Sport; Trade and Industry; the Home Office; the Lord Chancellor's Department; and HM Treasury. The group was chaired by the Minister for Public Health (first Tessa Jowell, later Yvette Cooper), but the then Secretary of State for Education and Employment, David Blunkett, would speak for Sure Start in Cabinet. In order to underscore the cross-cutting nature of the initiative, there was an interesting constitutional innovation: in the House of Commons questions about the programme would be tabled during Education question time and answers would be provided by the Minister of Public Health. This made clear that the principal departments involved were Health and Education. Such interdepartmental cooperation could only have been achieved with the Treasury's influence.

The embryonic SSU advertised for a Head and Naomi Eisenstadt's appointment was announced in December 1998 (see Foreword). Work began on making the review's ideas a reality. Eisenstadt had a background in the voluntary sector and community development as well as early years services, and hence the aforementioned emphasis on local community autonomy was congruent with her previous experience. Also around this time government announcements became more specific about the contents of SSLPs: home visits for all families with newborn children to inform about available services and support; health, education and childcare services; toy libraries; toddler groups; and family support.

Sure Start Local Programmes were meant to bring 'joined-up' services of health, childcare and play, early education and parental support to families with a child under four years of age. Sure Start Local Programmes were to be a completely new way of working for central and local governments. It was to be the glue that would bind together a range of local services for families. It was to be based on the best evidence and on experience of what works to give children and families the very best chance to thrive.

Programmes were directed to provide outreach for difficult-to-reach families and could add extra services to suit local needs, such as debt counselling and employment and benefits advice. Community control was to be exercised through local partnerships. Initially service providers in a deprived area were invited to submit a bid for Sure Start funding.

The invitation indicated that a partnership of local stakeholders had to be constituted and that this partnership needed to draw up a plan for a Sure Start programme, nominating a lead agency. These partnerships were to be at the heart of the initiative and bring together everyone concerned with children in the local community, including health, social services, education, the private sector, the voluntary sector and parents. Thus, partnerships were to provide local community influence for the design of each SSLP and, as a consequence, even though a set of core services was required, no specification was provided of how the services would be delivered, only what they should aim to achieve. Funding was to flow from central government – the SSU – directly to programmes. Programmes could act largely independently of local government, although local government departments of education, social services and the like would typically be part of the partnership. This bypassing of local government was welcomed by a number of government ministers who viewed local government as largely failing to deal with the needs of disadvantaged communities; this belief bolstered the emphasis on community control.

Central government guidance for SSLPs

The SSU (1998) prepared guidance for local programmes, drawing on and elaborating the Cross-Departmental Review. This stipulated the key principles of the programme. Emergent SSLPs were told that services must coordinate, streamline and add value to existing services in the SSLP area, including signposting to existing services; involve parents; avoid stigma; ensure lasting support by linking effectively with services for older children; be culturally appropriate and sensitive to particular needs; be designed to achieve specific objectives relating to Sure Start's overall objectives; and promote accessibility for all local families, later changed to 'promote the participation of all local families in the design and working of the programme' (SSU, 1998, p 37). The first guidance also outlined the core services that all SSLPs were expected to provide:

* outreach and home visiting;
* support for families and parents;
* support for good-quality play, learning and childcare experiences for children;
* primary and community health care and advice about child health and development and family health; and

• support for people with special needs, including help getting access to specialised services.

Getting Sure Start started

The speed with which funding was made available for SSLPs was to some extent overwhelming, resulting in a somewhat slow start to their establishment and development to operational status. Only 6% of the millions of pounds allocated to the Sure Start scheme in 1999 was spent in that year. Of the 60 local area groups invited to form a partnership and submit programmes in January 1999, only 15 were granted full approval and allocated funds in that year. Another 44 were not approved until June 2000, after they had refined their programme plans. The 60th was delayed until the second round of programmes was announced. Despite this slower-than-expected start, and without any information pertaining to the success of the initiative, the Treasury, in its 2000 Spending Review (HM Treasury, 2000), expanded Sure Start – doubling the planned number of programmes from 250 by 2002 to over 500 by 2004, thereby more than doubling expenditure to almost £500 million by 2003-04. The expanded Sure Start initiative was to reach one third of poor children under four years of age. In return for this investment, each SSLP was expected to deliver quantified improvements (that is, specified targets) in local children's social and emotional development, health and ability to learn, as well as strengthening families and communities.

This rapid and largely unexpected rush to expand the number of SSLPs so soon after the initial setting up of the initiative was not universally welcomed, and had implications for the design of the evaluation. Some people advised that it was too early to double the number of SSLPs, but the advice was not taken. For example, Norman Glass (2006) argued against it:

> I certainly believe and I argued strongly at the time that there was sufficient evidence to have a small Sure Start programme. I think we started off with a programme of 200 which is not that small but was still small. My view – and I argued it at the time when I was in the Civil Service and I have argued it subsequently – was that we should have learned much more about the experience from those 200 before we rolled it out on any scale. I do feel that we have rolled it out on the basis of inadequate evidence about how best it should be done as much as whether it has an effect,

and being clear about the kinds of impact we wanted this programme to have.

Thus it was that SSLPs became a cornerstone of the UK government's campaign to reduce child poverty and social exclusion. Sure Start Local Programmes were to serve *all* children under four and their families in a prescribed area. This area-based strategy allowed the relatively efficient delivery of services to those living in deprived areas without stigmatising those receiving services: disadvantaged areas were targeted, but within the area the service was universal.

The autonomy of SSLPs

As a consequence of the local autonomy central to the original conceptualisation of community control of SSLPs, and as already noted, they did not have a prescribed 'protocol' of services to promote adherence to a prescribed model even though they had a set of core services to deliver. Thus, each SSLP had freedom to improve and create services in the manner it saw fit to do so, with general goals and some specified targets (for example, reduce the number of low birthweight babies, improve language development of young children), but without specification of exactly how services were to be delivered. This contrasted markedly with interventions with clear models of provision and demonstrable effectiveness that formed the basis of the research evidence justifying the creation of Sure Start (for example, Abecedarian project: Ramey and Campbell, 1991; Perry pre-school project: Schweinhart et al, 1993; Incredible Years: Webster-Stratton, 1993). It appeared that while the research evidence was critical to winning the argument for increased early years expenditure, it was largely overlooked in the detailed planning for and actual operation of programmes, despite entreaties to local programmes that their services be 'evidence based'. Indeed, the SSU published a guidance handbook offering a menu of 'evidence-based' interventions from which to choose, but there is little evidence that it was much used.

Evaluation

The Treasury's involvement with Sure Start was central to the creation of the programme and the changes to it that have occurred. One of the conditions insisted on by the Treasury was that there be a rigorous evaluation of the initiative. Following competitive tender, the National

Evaluation of Sure Start (NESS) was commissioned in early 2001 to undertake a multifaceted evaluation of SSLPs, addressing:

• the nature of the communities in which SSLPs were situated;
• the ways in which SSLPs were implemented;
• the impact of SSLPs on children, families and communities; and
• the cost-effectiveness of SSLPs.

In addition, NESS was charged with providing technical support to local programmes so that each could undertake its own local evaluation to inform the further development of the services being offered.

The great diversity among SSLPs posed a particular set of challenges for the National Evaluation in that there were not several hundred programmes delivering one well-defined intervention, but several hundred unique and multifaceted interventions operating in different places. In order to undertake the evaluation, NESS used a variety of strategies to study the first 260 SSLPs that were rolled out. These included the gathering of administrative data already available on the small geographic areas that defined SSLP communities (for example, Census data, police records and work and pension records); developing geographical information systems that allowed the collating of information in non-standard geographic units (SSLP areas); conducting surveys of SSLPs dealing with many aspects of SSLPs; carrying out face-to-face and telephone interviews with programme managers, programme employees and parents about the operation of their local programme; and conducting a large-scale survey of child and family functioning in thousands of households in SSLP areas, and in SSLP-to-be areas. In the following chapters, a summary of insights garnered across the period 2001 through 2006 from these diverse data collection strategies is presented.

Subsequent policy developments

The policy-making process did not stand still while the evaluation work presented in this volume was being carried out. The recognition of the need for even greater government coordination of children's services led, in 2003, to the creation of a Minister for Children, Young People and Families within the DfES. The first minister was Margaret Hodge. As NESS progressed, its evidence was monitored within the DfES and has influenced guidance given to SSLPs. When evidence of impact on children and families became available, discussed in Chapters Eight and Nine, this contributed to a fundamental change in the structure of SSLPs. The NESS findings indicated that SSLPs were not having the impact that had been hoped for. Also, evidence from another ongoing research project, the Effective Provision of Pre-school Education (EPPE) (see Sylva et al, 2004), indicated that a particular type of early years provision, integrated Children's Centres, was particularly beneficial to children's development. Margaret Hodge, as Minister for Children, Young People and Families, was responsible for Sure Start and she decided that this combination of evidence from these two research projects justified changing SSLPs into Children's Centres. This was announced in 2005 alongside a move to transfer the new Sure Start Children's Centres into local authority control. This transfer of control from central to local government was politically inspired to ensure that Sure Start Children's Centres became embedded within the welfare state by government statute and would thus be difficult to eradicate by any future government, but the transfer of control to local authorities has proved unpopular with many Sure Start advocates.

Also, concern about child protection that had been mounting in the 1990s reached a crisis with the horrific case of Victoria Climbié, who, despite being supposedly monitored by several agencies (health, social services, the police and so on), was tortured and murdered in 2000. This triggered a major governmental review (Laming, 2003), which emphasised the importance of high-quality work and research by all relevant professionals, so interagency collaboration and training was once again stressed (Shardlow et al, 2004). This resulted in a series of government reports, including *Every child matters* (HM Government, 2003, 2004a, 2004b), which set out plans to reform and improve children's services. These plans were incorporated into the 2004 Children Act (HM Government, 2004c), which set out a new framework for children's services, ensuring accountability and partnership at local level. The Act placed a duty on health agencies to cooperate with local authorities to improve the well-being of children, and a duty on all agencies to promote the welfare of children. It also introduced measures to support the sharing of information about children between different agencies and professionals. The term 'safeguarding' replaced 'child protection' to emphasise the responsibility of all professionals working with children to consider how their best interests, health and development could be promoted.

Within a similar timeframe, various reports on children's healthcare criticised the long-term neglect of children's services and led, in 2001, to a National Service Framework (NSF). In 2003, responsibility for policy on social services for children and young people transferred from the Department of Health to the DfES and came under the new

Minister for Children, Young People and Families. The finalised NSF (DH and DfES, 2004) thus became the joint responsibility of both departments. It was probably the most comprehensive exposition of child health policy anywhere, reflecting a very broad view of what is meant by health. It endorsed previous policy developments in the fields of early detection, child mental health and child protection, reinforcing guidance on interdisciplinary collaboration. The concepts underpinning Sure Start were strongly supported for future policy.

These changes meant that from April 2006, local authorities became the accountable body for the whole Children's Centre programme in their areas, and health agencies were legally obliged to cooperate in the provision of services within Children's Centres. The spend on Children's Centres and the associated programmes was £1.3 billion in 2005-06. For 2006-07 £1.7 billion was provided to local authorities for Children's Centres. For 2007-08, £1.8 billion was set aside. This represented almost four times the amount spent on equivalent services in 2001-02. Sure Start thus became a significant part of the welfare state. As Prime Minister Tony Blair (2006) recently stated:

> Sure Start is one of the government's greatest achievements. It is a programme that gives antenatal advice, and early-years help for children who need it. It is a vital source of learning to parents who often find work on the back of it; and a community facility that becomes a focal point for local health, childcare and educational networks. It has become a new frontier of a changing welfare state.

Note

[1] The term 'proles' derives from proletariat, referring to the working class.

References

Baird, G. and Hall, D.M.B. (1985) 'Developmental paediatrics in primary care – what should we teach?', *British Medical Journal*, vol 291, pp 583-6.

Barnett, W.S. (1995) 'Long term effects of early childhood programs on cognitive and school outcomes', *The Future of Children: Long Term Outcomes of Early Childhood Programs*, vol 5, pp 94-114.

Bishop, D.V.M. (2000) 'How does the brain learn language? Insights from the study of children with and without language impairment', *Developmental Medicine and Child Neurology*, vol 42, pp 133-42.

Blair, T. (1998) 'Foreword', in HM Treasury, *Modern public services for Britain: Investing in reform. Comprehensive Spending Review: New public spending plans 1999-2002*, London: HM Treasury, www.archive. official-documents.co.uk/document/cm40/4011/foreword.htm

Blair, T. (2006) 'A failed test of leadership', *The Guardian*, 5 October.

Butler, J. (1989) *Child health surveillance in primary care: A critical review*, London: HMSO.

Dale, P.S., Simonoff, E., Bishop, D.V.M., Eley, T.C., Oliver, B., Price, T.S., Purcell, S., Stevenson, J. and Plomin, R. (1998) 'Genetic influence on language delay in two-year-old children', *Nature Neuroscience*, vol 1, pp 324-8.

DH (Department of Health) and DfES (Department for Education and Skills) (2004) *National Service Framework for children, young people and maternity services*, London: DH, www.dh.gov.uk/ PolicyAndGuidance/HealthAndSocialCareTopics/ChildrenServices/ ChildrenServicesInformation/fs/en

Farrington, D.P. (2003) 'Developmental and life-course criminology: key theoretical and empirical issues', *Criminology*, vol 41, pp 201-35.

Glass, N. (2005) 'Surely some mistake?', *The Guardian*, 5 January.

Glass, N. (2006) *Oral evidence to House of Commons Science and Technology Committee – scientific advice, risk and evidence: How the government handles them*, 24 May, www.publications.parliament.uk/pa/cm200506/ cmselect/cmsctech/c900-ix/c90002.htm

Hall, D.M.B. (1989) *Health for all children: A programme for child health surveillance* (1st edn), Oxford: Oxford University Press.

HM Government (2003) *Every child matters*, Green Paper, Nottingham: Department for Education and Skills.

HM Government (2004a) *Every child matters: Change for children programme*, Nottingham: Department for Education and Skills.

HM Government (2004b) *Every child matters: Next steps*, Nottingham: Department for Education and Skills.

HM Government (2004c) *Children Act 2004*, London: HMSO.

HM Treasury (1998a) *Modern public services for Britain: Investing in reform. Comprehensive Spending Review: New public spending plans 1999-2002*, London: The Stationery Office, www.archive.official-documents. co.uk/document/cm40/4011/4011.htm

HM Treasury (1998b) *Comprehensive Spending Review: Cross departmental review of provision for young children*, London: The Stationery Office, www. archive.official-documents.co.uk/document/cm40/4011/401122. htm

HM Treasury (2000) *2000 Spending Review*, Cm 4196, London: The Stationery Office, www.hm-treasury.gov.uk/media/6/F/whitepaper. pdf

Karoly, L.A., Greenwood, P.W., Everingham, S.S., Hoube, J., Kilburn, M.R., Rydell, C.P., Sanders, M. and Chiesa, J. (1998) *Investing in our children: What we know and don't know about the costs and benefits of early childhood interventions*, Santa Monica, CA: RAND.

Kempe, C., Silverman, F., Steele, B., Droegmueller, W. and Silver, H. (1962) 'The battered child syndrome', *Journal of the American Medical Association*, vol 181, pp 17-24.

Laming, Lord (2003*) Inquiry into the death of Victoria Climbié*, London: HMSO.

Melhuish, E.C. (2004) *A literature review of the impact of early years provision upon young children, with emphasis given to children from disadvantaged backgrounds: Report to the Comptroller and Auditor General*, London: National Audit Office, www.nao.org.uk/publications/nao_reports/03-04/268_literaturereview.pdf

National Research Council and Institute of Medicine (2004) *Children's health, the nation's wealth: Assessing and improving child health*, Committee on Evaluation of Children's Health; Board on Children, Youth and Families; Division of Behavioural and Social Sciences and Education, Washington, DC: National Academies Press.

NHS Executive (1996) *Child health in the community: A guide to good practice*, London: Department of Health.

ODPM (Office of the Deputy Prime Minister) (2004) *The English Indices of Deprivation, 2004: Summary (revised)*, London: ODPM.

Olds, D.L. (2002) 'Prenatal and infancy home visiting by nurses: from randomized trials to community replication', *Behavioural Science*, vol 3, pp 153-72.

Olds, D.L., Kitzman, H., Henderson, C.R., Eckenrode, J. and Cole, R. (1997) 'It worked in Elmira, but will it work in Memphis? The long-term effects of nurse home visiting on mothers' lives and children's well-being', *Focus*, vol 19, pp 47-50.

Olds, D.L., Henderson, C.R., Kitzman, H., Eckenrode, J.J., Cole, R.E. and Tatelbaum, R.C. (1999) 'Prenatal and infancy home visitation by nurses: recent findings', *Future of Children*, vol 9, pp 44-66.

Oliver, C., Smith, M. and Barker, S. (1998) 'Effectiveness of early interventions', in HM Treasury, *Comprehensive Spending Review, 1998: Supporting Papers Vol. 1*, London: HM Treasury (copies available from the Public Enquiry Unit, HM Treasury, Parliament Street, London SW1P 3AG).

Pugh, G. (1998) 'Children at risk of becoming socially excluded: an introduction to the problem', in HM Treasury, *Comprehensive Spending Review, 1998: Supporting Papers Vol. 1*, London: HM Treasury (copies available from the Public Enquiry Unit, HM Treasury, Parliament Street, London SW1P 3AG).

Ramey, C.T. and Campbell, F.A. (1991) 'Poverty, early childhood education, and academic competence: the Abecedarian experiment', in A.C. Huston (ed) *Children in poverty: Child development and public policy*, Cambridge, MA: Cambridge University Press, pp 190-221.

Reynolds, A.J., Temple, J.A., Robertson, D.L. and Mann, E.A. (2001) 'Long-term effects of an early childhood intervention on educational achievement and juvenile arrest: a 15-year follow-up of low-income children in public schools', *Journal of American Medical Association*, vol 285, pp 2339-46.

Rutter, M. and ERA (English and Romanian Adoptees) study team (1998) 'Developmental catch-up, and deficit, following adoption after severe global early privation', *Journal of Child Psychology and Psychiatry and Allied Disciplines*, vol 39, pp 465-76.

Rutter, M., Tizard, J., Yule, W., Graham, P. and Whitmore, K. (1976) 'Research report: Isle of Wight studies, 1964-1974', *Psychological Medicine*, vol 62, pp 313-32.

Schweinhart, L.J., Barnes, H. and Weikart, D. (eds) (1993) *Significant benefits: The High/Scope Perry Pre-school Study through age 27*, Ypsilanti, MI: High/Scope Press.

Shardlow, S., Davis, C., Johnson, M., Long, A., Murphy, M. and Race, D. (2004) *Education and training for inter-agency working: New standards*, Salford: Salford Centre for Social Work Research, www.chssc.salford.ac.uk/scswr/

Sheridan, M.D. (1973) *From birth to five years: Children's developmental progress*, Windsor: NFER-Nelson.

Shonkoff, J.P. and Phillips, D.A. (2000) *From neurons to neighbourhoods: The science of early child development*, Washington, DC: National Academy Press.

SSU (Sure Start Unit) (1998) *Sure Start: Guide for trailblazer programmes*, London: Department for Education and Employment.

Sylva, K., Melhuish, E., Sammons, P., Siraj-Blatchford, I. and Taggart, B. (2004) *Effective pre-school provision*, London: Institute of Education.

Webster-Stratton, C. (1993) 'Strategies for helping families with young oppositional defiant or conduct-disordered children: the importance of home and school collaboration', *School Psychology Review*, vol 22, pp 437-57.

Part Two
The local context of Sure Start Local Programmes

TWO

Targeting deprived areas: the nature of the Sure Start Local Programme neighbourhoods

Jacqueline Barnes

Communities and neighbourhoods are the places in which children develop. Sure Start was, in its inception, an area-based initiative with certain types of neighbourhoods as targets – those that were among the most disadvantaged with high concentrations of families with young children. Each Sure Start Local Programme (SSLP) was expected to focus on developing and enhancing services for residents of a relatively small, disadvantaged neighbourhood that would be defined locally. As Naomi Eisenstadt notes in the Foreword, SSLP areas were conceptualised in terms of 'pram-pushing distances' and partnership boards were encouraged to think of local need and to avoid pre-existing boundaries such as electoral wards or school catchment areas when defining programme-area boundaries. Once the neighbourhood had been defined, underpinning all other aspects of service delivery and the evaluation, there needed to be a detailed picture of each area that had been selected so that it would be possible to describe not only the 'average' SSLP neighbourhood but also the extent to which there was variability among them. Only with such information could the results of the implementation, impact and cost effectiveness modules of the evaluation be fully interpreted. In addition, as described in Chapter Ten, the impact of the initiative on the communities themselves could be evaluated by looking at how the areas – that is, their characteristics – changed over time as the Sure Start programmes developed.

Accurate information about social conditions at the local level provides a powerful tool for helping local and national initiatives to pinpoint problems and target solutions, and the guidance provided by the Sure Start Unit (SSU) encouraged programmes to find out about their areas in as much detail as possible. Varied features of neighbourhoods are known to be relevant to parenting and children's development – both targets of SSLPs. The extent to which many families in an area are headed by one adult, and the number of vacant houses and the extent of poor housing in the area have also been found to predict family problems such as child abuse in the US (Coulton et al, 1996) and the UK (Sidebotham et al, 2002). Even after taking family characteristics into account, the extent of poverty and unemployment in a neighbourhood is a predictor of children's health and academic achievement, child behaviour problems and child abuse and neglect (Leventhal and Brooks-Gunn, 2000). Overall disorder and disorganisation in a neighbourhood, typified by lack of agreement between residents about appropriate behaviour and general decay of buildings and roads, has implications both for parents and for children's behaviour. It is associated with more child abuse and harsh parenting (Coulton et al, 1995; Coulton et al, 1999) and also predictive of levels of crime and delinquency (Sampson, 1992; Sampson et al, 1997). While both these types of behaviour have a common predictor, each is also associated with the other. Poor parenting is an important factor in predicting behaviour problems in children.

Not surprisingly, the extent to which information was available on the SSLP areas and the accuracy of the information were inconsistent across the country, depending to an extent on the quality of local data systems, and on the capacity of SSLP and other local staff to be able to extract information specific to SSLP areas. Investigation of the original programme plans by the Implementation module of the National Evaluation of Sure Start (NESS) revealed that some of the groups that came together to compile bids for the establishment of SSLPs had been more successful than others in collecting local area information. Many relied on data that reflected the local ward or health authority rather than the specific SSLP area. This was not surprising given how challenging it was to collate data for areas that did not fit any standard administrative unit like a ward or county. In any event, NESS needed to collect information specific to SSLP areas with accuracy and at annual intervals, for all the programme areas involved in the evaluation – the 260 SSLPs in the first four rounds and the 50 in the fifth round of programmes included in the Impact Study of NESS (see Chapter Eight). Thus it was necessary to design and implement a specially tailored data collection, one known as 'Local Context Analysis' (LCA).

The development of relevant and sensitive indicators of SSLP-specific neighbourhood features posed numerous conceptual and methodological challenges because SSLP areas were identified by each partnership board through local consensus. This had some advantages in terms of implementation of the programme, but it set limits on the range and types of data that could be collected annually for each unique SSLP area. In order to work with such non-traditional area boundaries (that is, not electoral wards), it was essential to use Geographical Information Systems (GIS) to digitise the boundaries of each SSLP area. This was accomplished for the first two rounds of SSLPs by Ordnance Survey and for subsequent rounds by the South East Regional Research Laboratory at Birkbeck, under the direction of Dr Martin Frost. Once this demanding job was completed, the digitised area data could be used to access any sources of information – such as crime in some police districts – that were based on GIS. For the majority of sources of area-based information, postcode centroids within the area could be identified, affording links with individual-level data that included postcodes – such as births or deaths, receipt of benefits, achievement in school or referral to social services. The implications of this process for data collection are discussed in detail in Chapter Three.

The present chapter deals with what SSLP areas were like when the programmes began, with some background to decisions about which indicators to select so that as many of the relevant features of the neighbourhoods as possible could be captured. First there is a description of the types of information that were collected to describe the SSLP areas. Mean values of these characteristics are then described, to determine whether the SSLP areas represented the original targets of the SSLP initiative, with information about how much variability there was around these means. Finally, groupings of SSLP areas are described, bringing together neighbourhoods that are similar to each other.

How to characterise SSLP areas

The information collected by the LCA about SSLP areas can be divided into three domains, each described in turn. The first concerns *sociodemographic features and disorder indicators*. It was essential to collect as much demographic detail as possible about the number of people residing in the areas, their age and ethnic background. With the strong association between lone parenthood and poverty, information about family structure was also relevant. Economic deprivation can be determined by the extent to which residents rely on benefits and the range (or not) of employment opportunities that are available for those seeking employment. Crime and disorder are closely related to socioeconomic deprivation, but information relevant to these topics provides additional perspective on the local area context that families and service providers experienced, as SSLPs were being established.

Second, *child health and development* indicators were considered essential to the LCA. The main aims of the SSLPs concerned enhancing young children's health and development and so many relevant measures were obtained on individual children included in the Impact Study (see Chapter Eight). Nevertheless, it was essential to describe the overall health of all children in the local SSLP areas so that any gains for individuals could be interpreted in relation to the average health and development of all children.

Finally, information about the level of *service activity* was examined, by collating child welfare activity, determining geographical access to key services for young children and their families, and collating information about the local provision of childcare services for young children. This was important because one of the aims of the SSLPs was to enhance existing services, and make them more accessible to local families.

Subsequent to garnering information that described the SSLP areas, the sociodemographic features were analysed in such a way that the variation *between* areas could be described. This was achieved by identifying subgroups of SSLP areas that were similar to each other but substantially different from other SSLP areas.

Sociodemographic indicators of deprivation and disorder

Five aspects of sociodemographics and deprivation/disorder were measured at the area level.

Population

Evidence that areas with relatively more young and older residents, but fewer of working age, are more likely to have parenting problems such as abuse and neglect (Coulton et al, 1999) made it imperative to determine how many people lived in each SSLP area, along with their relative ages. Information about the total population of each local programme area was derived in the first instance from the Indices of Multiple Deprivation (IMD) 2000 (Noble et al, 2000), based on the mid-year populations in 1998 (and therefore more up to date than the Census information, the most recent of which at the time that the LCA work was initiated was from 1991). IMD 2000 data are reported in terms of the local electoral ward, from which it proved possible to estimate the total population of SSLP areas, the total working-age population (aged 16-59 years) and the number of persons aged 60 and over. This was achieved by overlaying on the ward boundaries the digitised boundaries describing each local programme area so that ward-level information could be apportioned to SSLP areas based on the proportion of households in each ward overlapping the target programme area. The Department for Work and Pensions (DWP) Child Benefit records were the source of information about numbers of children under four and under 16, matched to lists of postcodes within each of the programme areas.

It turned out that the number of individuals resident in SSLP areas varied considerably. While the average was just under 13,000, the range was from under 3,000 to almost 32,000. SSLP areas had high concentrations of children, with 23% of residents, on average, being under 16 years, a slightly higher proportion than the 20% in England as a whole. Some 18% of the residents of SSLP areas, on average, were aged 60 or over, as compared to the England equivalent of 21%.

Government guidance to SSLPs suggested that local programme areas should include approximately 400 to 1,000 children under four years old. Taking the ratio of the number of children aged under four and the number of households, it was estimated that on average one in every eight households had a child under four. The average number of children of the target age in the areas was 687. While programme areas varied widely – from 209 to 2,098 – most (that is, 85%) met the target of between 400 and 1,000 under-fours. Many children were also being born in the SSLP areas, some 185 births per year, on average, in 2000 (range: 53-604). The birth rate in SSLP areas was notably higher than in England overall.

Family structure

Many children in SSLP areas were born to young mothers and to women unsupported by a partner. The rate of birth to mothers under the age of 18 (4%) was twice that in England overall, with the rate as high as 13% in some programme areas. On average, one quarter of births in SSLP areas in 2000 were to lone mothers compared to a national rate of 15%, the rate rising to 63% in some areas, although it was as low as 2% in others. The average rate was highest in SSLP areas in the North East Government Office region and lowest in the East, South East and South West regions.

Black and minority ethnic groups

The LCA team used the information in the 2001 Census to characterise the ethnic background of SSLP area residents. Black and minority ethnic (BME) individuals were strongly represented in a substantial proportion of SSLP areas in the first four programme rounds. Of these 260 areas, there was a minority population of 20% or more in 83 areas

(32%). Figure 2.1 shows that almost one in five SSLP areas (46, 18%) had a BME population of at least 40%. Of the 98 areas (38%) in which the BME population represented 10% or more of the local residents, 56 had residents with predominantly Indian subcontinent origins or birth, 40 had residents who were predominantly Black (African or Caribbean) and two areas had a relatively mixed BME population. Many of the SSLP areas with higher proportions of BME residents were in the London region.

Figure 2.1: Number of SSLP areas with different proportions of BME residents

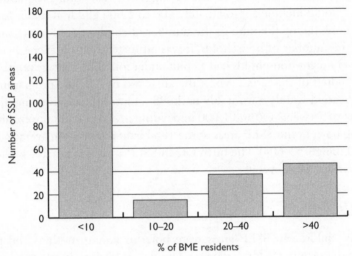

Source: 2001 Census

Deprivation

Given the targets of SSLPs – disadvantaged areas with deprived populations – it was not surprising that SSLP areas proved to have a high level of deprivation. Because IMD are available only at intervals of four or five years, they were not useful to the LCA for illuminating change over time in the SSLP areas. They did afford a basis for describing SSLP areas early on, while providing, too, a national basis for comparison. The average IMD scores for the first 260 SSLP areas were consistently higher than the England 80th percentile; falling predominantly within the 20% most deprived areas in England (see Figure 2.2). Consideration of individual components of the IMD reveals that low income and unemployment were more than double the England average, and the

Figure 2.2: IMD scores for England and SSLP areas

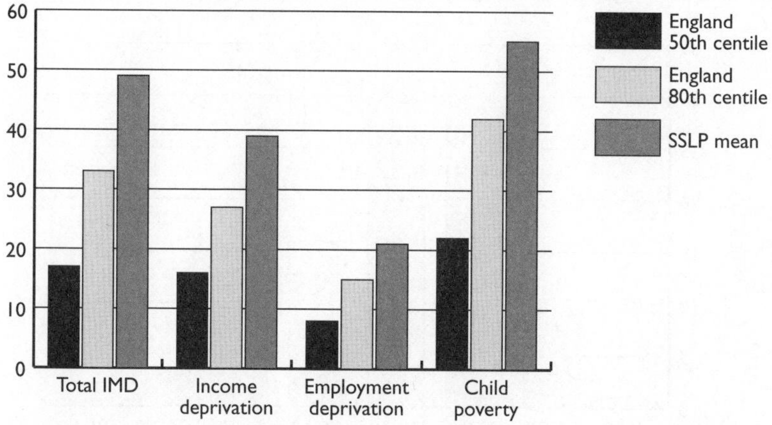

Source: 2000 IMD

same was true for levels of child poverty. For these three domains and the total IMD, the average scores for SSLP areas were equivalent to the most deprived 7-8% of wards in England.

Based on the proportion of adults receiving state benefits linked with looking for work (that is, Jobseeker's Allowance) or who were employed but earning little (Income Support), it was evident that twice as many in the SSLP areas were unemployed (7% vs 3%) or earning a low wage (15% vs 7%) in comparison with England overall. Annual statistics from the DWP allowed the LCA to calculate the proportion of young children living in households completely dependent on state benefits; in other words, households in which no one was employed. On average, 45% of children under four years old in SSLP areas lived in such 'workless' households, nearly twice the rate of England (23%). Many areas had higher rates, rising to a maximum of 81% (see Figure 2.3). SSLP areas in the North East and North West Government Office regions had the highest average rates of children in workless households (46% and 47% respectively), whereas the average was lowest in the South West (38%).

The proportion of children under the age of four in households in which a working adult's income was so low that it was supplemented by Income Support was 39% on average in SSLP areas, with a maximum of 76%. The corresponding figure for children aged four to 17 years was 35% (maximum 67%). Both of these averages were virtually double the respective national levels (20% and 18%). Thus, in some programme areas the large majority of children were in households

Figure 2.3: Percentage of SSLP areas with different proportions of children aged 0-3 living in 'workless' households

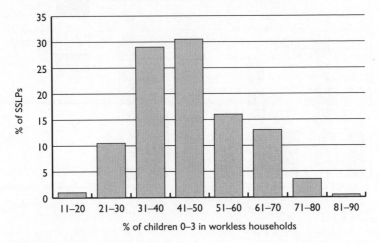

Source: DWP 2000/01

either totally or partially dependent on state benefits, and in all areas substantial proportions of the children were in economically deprived households.

A range of benefits are provided for adults with long-term health problems that mean they require assistance for their care, or they are unable to work. When it came to the proportion of adults who required assistance in looking after themselves, indicated by those of working age receiving Disability Living Allowance and those of retirement age receiving Attendance Allowance, the 2001 rate of 9% was substantially higher in SSLP areas than the 6% rate in England. Adults out of work due to ill-health may claim Severe Disability Allowance or Incapacity Benefit and the percentage receiving these benefits in SSLP areas was again higher than that for England as a whole (13% vs 8%). Finally, limiting long-term illness is recorded in the Census. The age-standardised rate per 100 population was compared (a) for the SSLP areas, (b) in the wards from the 20% most deprived without an SSLP area, and (c) in England; the SSLP area rates were higher than the other deprived wards and higher than England for females (21 vs 19 vs 15) and males (22 vs 20 vs 16).

Crime and disorder

The extent of disorder and crime can have profound implications for both residents of an area and for professionals offering services there.

High crime levels make the kind of work promoted in SSLPs, such as home visiting and other outreach, more difficult. Information was thus collected about a range of crimes – burglary from homes and from other types of building, vehicle crime, criminal damage, drug offences and violence against the person. Consistent with the deprived character, SSLP areas experienced all types of crime at levels higher than the rate for England. Burglary from homes and criminal damage were particularly high in relation to England, both approximately 60% higher, with violence against the person about 40% higher (see Figure 2.4).

Figure 2.4: Rates per 1,000 population[a] of crime in England and in SSLP areas

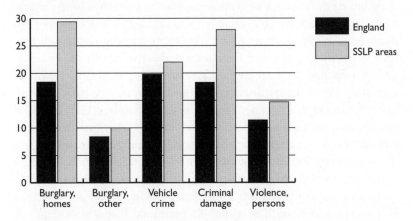

Note: [a] Burglary from homes is per 1,000 households.
Source: Police departments 2001/02

Child health and development

Information was gathered on four distinct aspects of child health and development at the area level.

Birth and the first year

Birth and the months immediately following are crucial for subsequent health and development. More vulnerable infants were born in SSLP areas than in England. Just under one tenth (9%) of births in SSLP areas were low birthweight in 2000, with a figure more than double that (22%) in one SSLP area; the corresponding figure for England was 8%. A larger proportion of infants died in SSLP areas before or right after birth, with the average perinatal mortality being 10 per 1,000 vs nine per 1,000 in England). The same pattern emerged with regard to infant death in the first month (five vs four per 1,000) and during the first year (seven vs six per 1,000). The rate per 1,000 births of perinatal mortality was as high as 50 in some areas and the rate of both neonatal and infant mortality were more than four times the national rate.

Emergency hospital admissions

One of the specific targets for SSLPs was to reduce emergency admissions to hospital of children aged under four due to three specific causes: gastroenteritis, lower respiratory infection and severe injury. Emergency admissions of young children to hospital reflect the level of child health in an area, and in addition may be indicative of the extent to which families are able to access services for young children and their families. For example, fewer admissions for common conditions such as gastroenteritis can reflect good preventive health advice being given to families about preparing and storing cooked and raw meats separately. Fewer hospitalisations for lower respiratory infection can indicate that families have accessed general practitioners (GPs) or health visitors in a timely fashion before a mild infection leads to a more serious one. More emergency admissions for such conditions can, on the other hand, indicate that family life is chaotic so that, rather than consulting local practitioners such as GPs or health visitors, a child's symptoms are not addressed until their severity leads to a visit to a hospital Accident and Emergency Department. Rates of emergency admissions for severe injury can be indicative of the level of support in an area for child safety measures in the home such as window bars, stair gates or guards to prevent saucepans from falling from the stove. They can also indicate the extent of child abuse and neglect.

Hospital Episodes Statistics collected by the Department of Health were matched to the postcodes for each SSLP area. Rates of emergency admissions per 1,000 children aged under four for gastroenteritis were on average double the national rate while admissions for severe injury and lower respiratory infection were 50% and 33% higher, respectively.

Disability and special needs

There were relatively more children with long-term disability living in SSLP areas than across England as a whole. On average, 4.4% of three-year-olds in programme areas were receiving Disability Living

Allowance in 2001, with the rate for England being 3.7%. Slightly fewer children aged four to 17 in SSLP areas were receiving Disability Living Allowance (3.2%), but again this rate was somewhat higher than that for England (2.6%). The same degree of difference was found when school records were examined to determine the proportion of children identified as having special educational needs, comparing those schools with pupils resident in SSLP areas and for all schools in England. The rate for those with special educational needs but without statements (that is, those deemed to need school action or school action plus) was 28% for SSLP area schools and 21% for England, with rates in some SSLP areas rising to more than half the children in the school. There were also more children with 'statemented'[1] special educational needs in SSLPs than in England (2.2% vs 1.7%).

Academic achievement

The academic achievement of young children targeted by SSLPs is not routinely recorded in a systematic way, although some may attend a nursery class. Nevertheless, that of older children, many of whom may be their siblings, is routinely assessed, affording comparison of SSLPs with England more generally. Thus, to gain insight into school achievement levels in SSLP areas, the performance of older children was investigated. At the time, Key Stage One (KS1) tests were administered to all seven-year-olds and Key Stage Two (KS2) tests to all 11-year-olds, although KS1 has since been replaced by teacher assessments. Children aged 15 to 16 are also assessed in a number of subjects by the General Certificate of Secondary Education (GCSE).

As can be seen in Table 2.1, the average level of achievement in schools attended by SSLP residents was lower than the overall rate in England on all these assessments.

At this first examination of the SSLP areas all such national assessments are based on children completing formal and nationally standardised activities in the areas of English, mathematics and (for the older children) science. Expected minimum standards are set by the government, level 2 or higher at KS1 and level 4 or higher at KS2. KS1 achievement was 7% lower on average for schools with SSLP pupils on their roll for writing and 4% lower for mathematics than was the case in England. The difference was more pronounced for KS2; the gap between the average percentage of children attaining the minimum standard for SSLP areas and England being 10% for English, 9% for mathematics and 5% for science. At the age of 15 or 16, after five years in secondary school, children take nationally standardised

Table 2.1: Mean rates (%) of academic achievement[a] in schools attended by pupils resident in SSLP areas (rounds 1 to 4) and in England

	SSLP (mean)	SSLP (range)	England
Level 2+ KS1 Writing	79	61-95	86
Level 2+ KS1 Mathematics	87	71-98	91
Level 4+ KS2 English	65	8-96	75
Level 4+ KS2 Mathematics	62	31-100	71
Level 4+ KS2 Science	82	45-100	87
5+ GCSE passes at grade A* to C	37	18-60	50
5+ GCSE passes at grade A* to G	87	69-97	89

Note: [a] For each examination the results are expressed in terms of the percentage of pupils reaching the government's recommended standard for their age group.

examinations in a number of different subjects (from five or six up to more than 12 for the academically gifted). The government's target is for all children to gain at least five passes at a good standard (grades A★ to C). The average proportion of children achieving five good GCSE passes in schools attended by SSLP pupils was 37%, substantially lower than the rate for England (50%), even though the rate achieving any passes (levels A★ to G) was similar.

Service provision and access

Two aspects of service provision and access were assessed by the LCA.

Health and other family services

While many SSLPs planned to develop their own buildings – which have become Children's Centres – much of the relevant work with children and families, particularly in the early stages of programme development, typically took place in other settings such as GP practices, child health clinics and libraries or arenas for exercise such as swimming pools. Comprehensive lists of addresses for local services were compiled for each of the first 260 programme areas. GP, child health clinic and library addresses were collected from local authority websites and directories; and swimming pool addresses were collected from the Sport England website (www.sportengland.org/). Almost all (93%) of the SSLP areas had at least one GP surgery within their boundary, with 40% containing two or three and a further 23% having more than four surgeries; it was not possible to determine exactly how many GPs there were per surgery. Programme areas averaged 0.5 GP surgeries per 1,000 households. More than three quarters (76%) of the areas contained at least one child health clinic, with a third having two or more, and almost three quarters (73%) had a library within their boundary, although fewer contained a swimming pool (22%).

The SSLP areas differed in size, with some much larger than a 'pram-pushing distance', so it was important to find out how far parents needed to travel on average to reach important services for themselves and their children. For each residential postcode within a programme area, the service outlet closest to it was located and its distance calculated. Few hospitals were located specifically within SSLP areas but it was important to know how far a family might have to travel in an emergency. The addresses of hospitals with Accident and Emergency services were obtained from the British Association for Accident and Emergency Medicine; the other services' addresses were collected as stated earlier. Urban areas with SSLPs were examined separately from the few in rural areas (*n*=14) because lower levels of access were expected in the latter, typically larger geographic areas.

Most households in SSLP areas had good access to GP surgeries, with more than 80% of households living within one kilometre of their nearest surgery; Table 2.2 provides details of all distances. As expected, there were differences between urban and rural areas. The proportion of households living within one kilometre of a GP surgery was 87% in urban local programme areas and only 50% in the rural areas. Although two thirds of households in the first 260 SSLP areas were within four

Table 2.2: Geographical access to services in urban (n=246) and rural (n=14) SSLP areas (% of households)

Distance	GP Urban	GP Rural	Accident & Emergency Urban	Accident & Emergency Rural	Child health clinic Urban	Child health clinic Rural	Swimming pool Urban	Swimming pool Rural	Library Urban	Library Rural
< 1 Km.	87	50	10	15	74	31	30	12	68	48
1-2 Km.	12	23	21	10	21	15	39	12	28	18
3-4 Km.	1	15	35	13	4	14	26	7	3	13
>4 Km.	0	11	34	62	1	41	5	69	1	22

kilometres of Accident and Emergency units, this service offers a comparatively low level of household access, particularly for rural SSLP areas. Almost twice as many households in rural programme areas were more than four kilometres away (62% vs 34%). Almost all (95%) of the households in urban SSLP areas were within two kilometres of a child health clinic, with 75% within one kilometre, but this was true for less than half (46%) of households in rural SSLP areas. The latter were most commonly more than four kilometres away from a clinic (41%).

Overall, two thirds of households in programme areas were within two kilometres of a swimming pool, but residents in the rural areas were not so fortunate, with only 31% of households within four kilometres. Access to libraries was slightly better, with two thirds of households within one kilometre of a library. Rural and urban households also had different levels of access to libraries, with 68% of urban but only 48% of rural of households located within one kilometre of a library.

Childcare

Increasing the number of childcare providers, enhancing the quality of care and increasing the number of places available were goals of SSLPs. Information about childcare providers and places were collated by Ofsted starting in 2000, but because their data for that year were limited, information presented here refers to the 2001/02 fiscal year. Due to the way that records were maintained and national statistics collated, information on places or providers specifically for children under four could not be obtained, so all relevant information pertains to children under eight years old. The rates of all types of childcare provision apart from crèche providers and places were lower in SSLP areas than they were in England. In particular, the number of places with childminders per 1,000 children and places in sessional childcare in SSLP areas were almost half the rates for England (see Figure 2.5).

Variability between programme areas

From the outset it was clear that while SSLP areas, on average, had substantial deprivation and the children in the areas were likely to have more health and development problems on average than those in England, it was also clear that there was a substantial range of values for each of the indicators examined across SSLP areas. To get a better handle on the nature and degree of variation, a decision was made to create a typology of areas. This was regarded as important in terms of understanding variation in the eventual implementation of SSLPs, as

Figure 2.5: Rates of childcare places per 1,000 children aged 0-7 in England and in SSLP areas

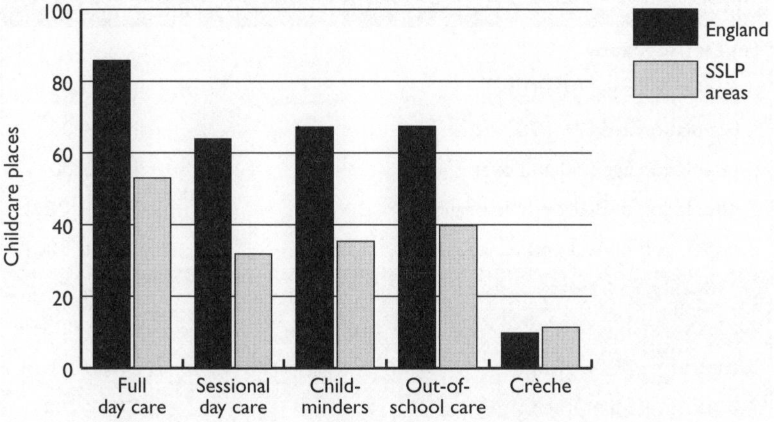

Source: Ofsted 2001/02

well as their impact on children, families and communities. After all, a fundamental goal of NESS, although not discussed further in this chapter, was to determine the conditions under which SSLPs were effectively implemented and enhanced the functioning of children and families. Creating a typology of programme areas was considered a fundamental step in the service of these long-range goals. This process involved two steps.

Principal Components Analysis (PCA) was used first to explore patterns of correlation among sociodemographic and economic indicators (see Table 2.3). This is a descriptive technique that seeks to identify a few underlying dimensions on which multiple individual measures (that is, indicators) may go together in terms of their variation. Ultimately, the aim was to reduce the number of indicators by identifying dimensions that would serve to summarise them efficiently. So, for example, applying PCA to the four indicators of adult health yielded a single underlying dimension that accounted for 80% of the variation across the four indicators and SSLPs. Similarly, for the three indicators of economic deprivation, a single underlying dimension also emerged, which explained 75% of the variation in the sample of communities on these indicators. Two other underlying dimensions were identified in a similar fashion, one reflecting demography and the other family structure.

With the resulting four dimensions in hand, cluster analysis was used in a second stage of data reduction in an effort to identify subgroups of

Table 2.3: Components of four underlying sociodemographic and deprivation dimensions used to create the SSLP area typology

	Source
(1) Demography	
% population aged 0-15	IMD 2000
% population aged 16-59	IMD 2000
% population aged 60 and over	IMD 2000
% population of Black ethnic origin	Census 2001
% population of Asian ethnic origin	Census 2001
(2) Family structure	
% births within marriage	ONS 2000
% births to women aged <18	ONS 2000
% births to lone mothers	ONS 2000
(3) Economic deprivation	
% 0-3 in 'workless' households	DWP 2001
% working-age adults receiving Income Support	DWP 2001
% 16-59 economically active	DWP 2001
(4) Adult poor health	
% adults receiving Disability Living Allowance or Attendance Allowance	DWP 2001
% adults aged 16-59 receiving Severe Disability Allowance or Incapacity Benefit	DWP 2001
Age-standardised rates, limiting long-term illness, females	Census 2001
Age-standardised rates, limiting long-term illness, males	Census 2001

communities that scored similarly across the four dimensions identified using the PCA. More specifically, following the approach employed by the Office of National Statistics to group local authorities into homogeneous clusters (Bailey et al, 1999), Ward's method was used to group SSLP areas into homogeneous subgroupings (Ward, 1963). On the basis of a cluster analysis of the four identified underlying dimensions, five area subgroups were identified. The main features of each group are identified as those for which the cluster average deviated from the overall average by at least +/- 0.5 standard deviations (SDs); those marked in bold in Table 2.4 deviate by at least one SD.

Table 2.4: Main defining characteristics of five clusters of SSLP areas in rounds 1 to 4 based on demographic and deprivation indicators[a]

Cluster	Demography	Family structure	Economic deprivation	Adult poor health
Less deprived 54 (21%)	More retired adults Fewer children Low ethnic population	Fewer lone mothers	Lower economic deprivation	Lower unemployment from ill-health Lower long-term limiting illness (females)
Typical 87 (34%)	Average	Average	Average	Average
More deprived 29 (11%)	Smaller Asian community	Higher rates of lone mothers and mothers under 18	Higher economic deprivation	Higher rates of poor health
Ethnic diversity 59 (23%)	More adults of working age Fewer retired Larger black and Asian communities	Higher rates of births inside marriage Lower rates of mothers under 18	Average	Lower rates of benefits for ill-health (Disability Living Allowance/Attendance Allowance) Lower long-term limiting illness (males)
Indian subcontinent/large families 28 (11%)	More children Fewer retired Larger black and Asian communities	Higher rates of births in marriage Lower rates of lone mothers and mothers under 18	Fewer infants in workless households Fewer adults economically active	Higher long-term limiting illness (females)

Note: [a] Under each subheading, measures for which the cluster average deviated from the overall average by at least +/- 0.5 SDs have been described; where the deviation was +/- 1.0 SDs or more, the characteristics are highlighted in bold.

41

The largest subgroups (34%) were, across all four underlying dimensions, close to the average score of SSLP areas and so this subgroup was labelled 'typical'. A second subgroup was identified that comprised about one fifth (21%) of the programme areas and these areas were, relatively speaking, less deprived than other SSLP areas with lower scores than the average; these areas were labelled 'less deprived. A third group comprised of 11% of the programme areas had more deprivation than most SSLP areas and so this group was labelled 'most deprived'. The remaining two subgroups that emerged from the cluster analysis were typified by larger minority ethnic populations and by the age and health of adults. One, representing almost a quarter of the SSLP areas (23%), had more ethnic diversity and in particular more black residents, good adult health, fewer retired adults and fewer mothers under 18 years; this grouping was labelled 'ethnic diversity'. A smaller group of programme areas (11%) had (relatively) more Asian residents, larger families, more births in marriage and poorer female health; it was labelled 'Indian subcontinent/large families'.

Conclusions

Sure Start Local Programme areas were home to substantial numbers of families with children in the target age range of under four years. The average number of such children varied, from as few as 200-300 to more than 2,000. Needless to say, different SSLPs faced rather different challenges in serving larger versus smaller communities of young children and their families. But, regardless of their size, on average the areas were experiencing some of the worst deprivation in England. Low income, unemployment and child poverty were more than double the national averages. The level of disadvantage was at the start of NESS (the year April 2000 to March 2001) consistent with or slightly higher than the average for the 20% most deprived wards in England. Many more young children lived in poverty in the first 260 SSLP areas than in England overall. Unemployment in these areas was twice the rate for England and some areas had up to one in three working-age adults receiving Income Support. Although there was a range of services in each area, many of the services being in close proximity to the residents, the health and development of children living in the areas was, on average, below that of children across England. Therefore, the extent of concentrated disadvantage and poor outcomes for children was consistent with the SSLP strategy of designing a community-based initiative that offered enhanced services to all residents with a young child in each area.

Nevertheless, SSLP areas include a great deal of variability. Whereas some areas were above average, among these deprived communities, on almost all the indicators studied, such as unemployment, children's respiratory problems or adults' reliance on benefits, a number of programme areas were above average for some indicators and below for others. Still others were well below average for all the indicators. This diversity was considered important for understanding service delivery and was therefore incorporated into subsequent work carried out by the evaluation team, as made clear in subsequent chapters of this volume.

Note

[1] The statement describes a child's special educational needs and the special help they should receive. The local authority usually makes a statement if they decide that this help cannot be provided from within a child's school.

References

Bailey, S., Charlton, J., Dollamore, G. and Fitzpatrick, J. (1999) *The ONS classification of local and health authorities of Great Britain: Revised for authorities in 1999*, London: HMSO for the Office for National Statistics.

Coulton, C., Korbin, J. and Su, M. (1996) 'Measuring neighbourhood context for young children in an urban area', *American Journal of Community Psychology*, vol 24, pp 5-32.

Coulton, C., Korbin, J. and Su, M. (1999) 'Neighbourhoods and child maltreatment: a multilevel study', *Child Abuse and Neglect*, vol 23, pp 1019-40.

Coulton, C., Korbin, J., Su, M. and Chow, J. (1995) 'Community level factors and child maltreatment rates', *Child Development*, vol 66, pp 1262-76.

Leventhal, T. and Brooks-Gunn, J. (2000) 'The neighbourhoods they live in: the effects of neighbourhood residence on child and adolescent outcomes', *Psychological Bulletin*, vol 126, pp 309-37.

Noble, M., Smith, G.A.N., Penhale, B., Wright, G., Dibben, C., Owen, T. and Lloyd, M. (2000) 'Measuring multiple deprivation at the small area level: the Indices of Deprivation 2000', *Regeneration Research Summary Number 37*, London: Department of the Environment, Transport and the Regions.

Sampson, R.J. (1992) 'Family management and child development: insights from social disorganization theory', in J. McCord (ed) *Facts, frameworks and forecasts: Advances in criminological theory, volume 3*, New Brunswick, NJ: Transaction Press, pp 63-93.

Sampson, R.J., Raudenbush, S.W. and Earls, F. (1997) 'Neighbourhoods and violent crime: a multilevel study of collective efficacy', *Science*, vol 277, pp 918-24.

Sidebotham, P., Heron, J., Golding, J. and the ALSPAC Study Team (2002) 'Child maltreatment in the "Children of the Nineties": deprivation, class and social networks in a UK sample', *Child Abuse and Neglect*, vol 26, pp 1243-59.

Ward, J.H. (1963) 'Hierarchical grouping to optimize an objective function', *Journal of the American Statistical Association*, vol 66, pp 846-50.

THREE

The challenge of profiling communities

Martin Frost and Gillian Harper

Most area-based initiatives (ABIs) – of which Sure Start Local Programmes (SSLPs) are a classic example – have needed to face the challenge of translating the concept of 'deprived areas' as targets for government intervention into actual boundaries 'on the ground'. Chapter Two explained that, in the case of SSLPs, this responsibility was largely given to the local agencies who initiated the proposals for the establishment of SSLPs. They were required to identify local communities that contained a significant number of deprived families, had a degree of social coherence and contained a sufficient number of young children to make programmes viable (Glass, 1999). In practice this meant that the boundaries of many SSLPs did not correspond to any pre-existing area boundaries that would normally be used for collecting and disseminating indicators of economic, social, health and crime conditions, such as electoral wards or police beat areas for instance. This chapter describes the use that was made of Geographical Information Systems (GIS) to identify young children living in the SSLPs to take part in the Impact Study of the National Evaluation of Sure Start (NESS), and to adapt existing data or commission new data that would allow the nature of the SSLPs to be described by the Local Context Analysis (LCA) team, while also allowing assessment of their change over the lifetime of the evaluation.

The first stage in this process was to translate programme boundaries from paper maps into a digital form that could be used within GIS software. The method used for this and the challenges faced in its application are described. The second stage was to identify a key that could link households living within an SSLP to records that would identify the presence of young children and that could be used to link the SSLP's households to other types of data that could be used to derive profiles of the SSLPs. This key was the postcode system applied to all UK addresses. Postcodes could be used within a GIS to identify households within the programme area and also to assess the degree to which other area-specific units used for data collection and dissemination, such as Census wards or police authority crime beats, overlapped with the SSLPs.

Defining and capturing boundaries

Within GIS processing, the boundaries of areas such as SSLPs are conceived as sets of points, located by their coordinates on a known map projection system, joined by straight lines (DeMers, 1997). The number of points used is a matter of choice. A choice also has to be made of the map projection system used to record the coordinates of each point. In most UK studies the British National Grid (BNG) is used for recording the boundaries of 'standard' units such as Census wards, local authority boundaries and all mapping produced by the government mapping agency, the Ordnance Survey (OS).

The proposed boundaries of all SSLPs were submitted by local agencies as part of their bids for a SSLP to be located within their area. They submitted these in paper form with their proposed boundary marked, as in Figure 3.1 (opposite). Prior to the start of NESS, some early programme boundaries were processed by OS, but all remaining boundaries for programmes in round three onwards were processed by the NESS team.

Two principal methods were used to translate the paper maps into a digital form. Both used OS maps in digital form (raster format) as the base on which to locate the boundaries of programmes. If the maps were of good quality they were scanned into images and then located directly on the underlying OS maps, as was the case with Figure 3.2. In other cases boundaries were entered manually, interpreting the paper maps submitted as part of the SSLP bids as accurately as possible. In the relatively small number of cases where programme boundaries corresponded with standard data units such as wards, they were imported from the boundary files for these units (generally produced by OS) and overlaid directly on the underlying base maps. In all, 524 SSLP areas were captured digitally to be viewed and subsequently used in a GIS framework.

This process was not without problems, however. The quality and clarity of maps submitted with SSLP proposals varied markedly. In some cases they had been prepared by the local authority GIS/mapping units and were of high quality. In other cases maps were torn out of local street guides with boundaries marked with felt-tipped pens, causing major processing difficulties. Clarification had to be sought from the programmes in a number of cases. The problems created by uncertain

Figure 3.1: Sample map of an SSLP area

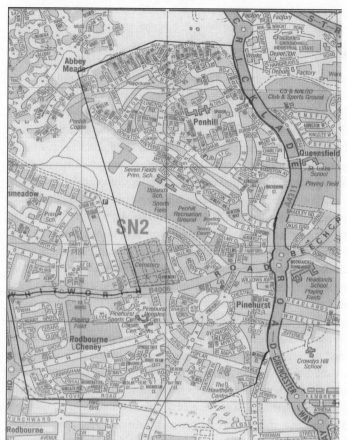

Figure 3.2: The same Sure Start area captured in GIS as a polygon in its real-life location

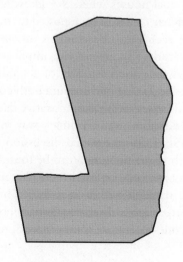

or inaccurate boundaries were particularly severe when SSLPs were adjacent to one another.

Linking programme areas to datasets

Once programme boundaries had been translated into a digital form they could be used to determine whether any other feature (for example, a house, an address or a Post Office) that also had map coordinates was inside or outside an individual SSLP area (for more discussion of the methods used to achieve this, see Longley et al, 2001, p 292). The main issue lay in finding a way of linking records in administrative databases and other sources of information to the coordinate system – in the case of NESS, the BNG. Two options were considered. The first was to identify individual dwellings within SSLPs through an OS product, Address Point, which would provide both their detailed map coordinates and their addresses. Dwellings within an SSLP could be identified by their map coordinates and their addresses could, in principle, be matched against any administrative records or the locations of local services (where these contained detailed addresses). The second option was to use the postcode system. Within the UK, the Royal Mail product, Address Manager, provides BNG coordinates for all individual postcodes. From this, the postcodes occurring within an SSLP could be determined and then matched against administrative records and the locations of relevant services where these contained postcodes identifying the location of a service or individual.

The two options differed in terms of resolution and cost. Address Point was many times more expensive but was capable of identifying individual houses whereas Address Manager could only provide the geometric centre of each postcode to an accuracy of about one metre. Since each postcode contains on average about 15 households, this was clearly less precise, the implication being that there would be cases where the boundary of an SSLP passes through an individual postcode. Taking into account both cost and the difficulty of matching full addresses to the administrative databases, it was decided to use the postcode route as the primary way in which data would be extracted for SSLPs. More detailed discussion of the structure and use of the British postcode system can be found in Raper et al (1992).

Unit postcode centroids were plotted on the SSLP areas, GIS selecting those that fell within each area. Then the relevant postcodes were exported into a database file to become the common link to attach postcode-based data from other sources (see Figure 3.3).

Figure 3.3: Illustration of how postcodes are (a) plotted, (b) selected and then (c) exported for an SSLP area

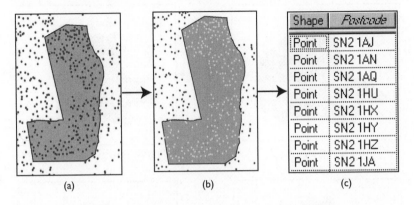

Shape	Postcode
Point	SN2 1AJ
Point	SN2 1AN
Point	SN2 1AQ
Point	SN2 1HU
Point	SN2 1HX
Point	SN2 1HY
Point	SN2 1HZ
Point	SN2 1JA

(a)   (b)   (c)

Extracting and adapting data

Once postcodes had been extracted for the SSLPs they could be used in a number of ways to extract data from administrative records that contain a postcode or by using the postcodes to estimate values for SSLPs from existing data that were released using standard units that did not necessarily correspond with SSLP boundaries. A number of the core datasets – particularly those based on the Census (both 1991 and 2001) and the government's Indices of Deprivation (DETR, 2000; ODPM, 2004) – were only disseminated using standard units such as wards, super output areas (SOAs) and output areas (OAs). To make use of these, GIS was used to calculate the proportion of each of these units that covered a SSLP area, either in terms of physical area or by an estimate of the number of residents. This process involved overlaying the boundaries of the area units (for example wards) on the SSLP areas in GIS so that the intersecting parts could be extracted. For population proportioning, postcode centroids were plotted over the intersections because they provided a count of 'delivery points' (see Figure 3.4). This was the most easily available proxy for the number of households (and therefore population) at a high resolution. The percentage of delivery points of a ward that lay in the total intersections with an SSLP area was then used to reflect the proportion of a ward that lay in an SSLP area.

Similarly, the proportion could be calculated as the percentage of the physical area of a ward that lay within an SSLP area. These percentages were then applied to the data for every ward that intersected with a given programme area and summed to give a weighted proportion.

Figure 3.4: Area proportioning, overlaying wards on an SSLP are

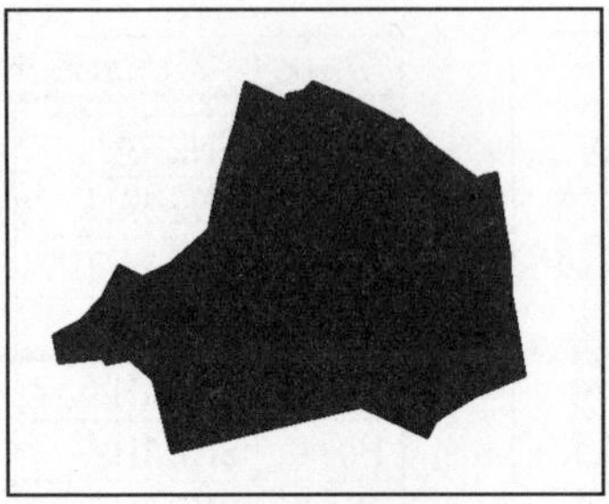

(a) A SSLP area

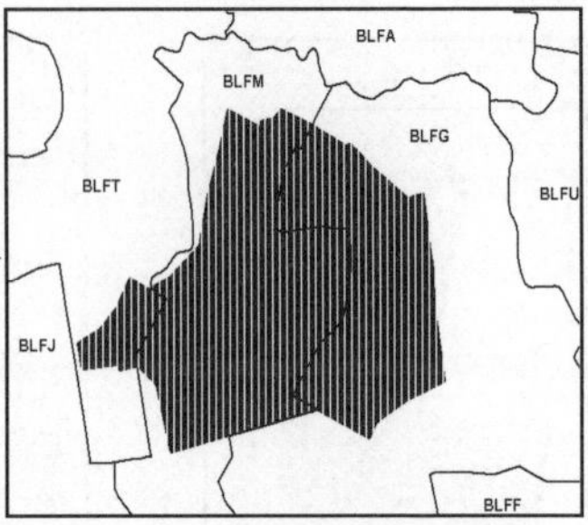

(b) Ward boundaries overlaid

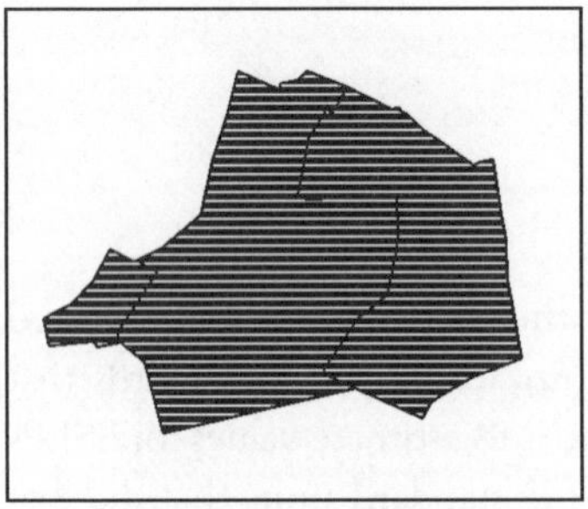

(c) Intersections created

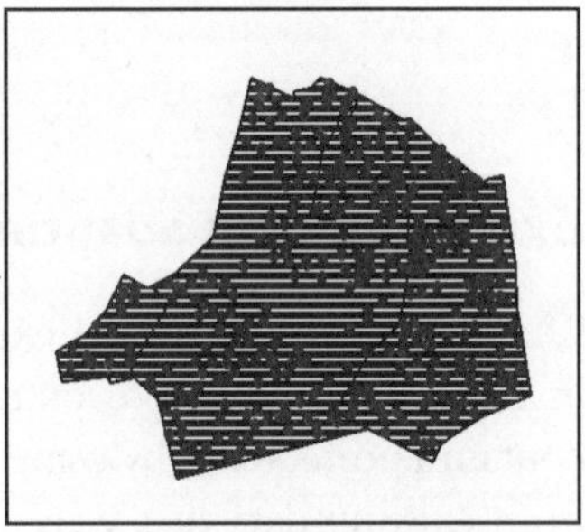

(d) Postcode centroids plotted over the intersections to calculate the number of delivery points

The above GIS methods for data capture and creation enabled data to be extracted from a number of sources, to accurately describe the SSLP areas (see Table 3.1; values of these are described in Chapter Two and changes in Chapter Ten).

Identifying children and families within SSLPs

A fundamental need of evaluation was to identify families with young children living in the SSLPs in order to conduct the NESS Impact Study data collection described in Chapter Nine. This was the first and, in some respects, the most important use of the digitally encoded SSLP boundaries and their postcodes. Potential study participants living in SSLP areas and Sure Start-to-be areas were identified with the assistance of the Child Benefit Office of (initially) the Department for Work and Pensions (DWP) and (subsequently) the Her Majesty's Revenue and Customs. Addresses of families with young children living in SSLPs were selected by the DWP in monthly cycles, linking SSLP postcode

Table 3.1: SSLP area-specific data extracted using information derived from GIS

Method	Source	Indicators
Postcode	Department for Work and Pensions	Child Benefit (counts of children)
		Income Support
		Jobseeker's Allowance
		Disability Living Allowance
		Attendance Allowance
		Severe Disability Allowance
		Incapacity Benefit
	Office of National Statistics	Births
		Births to mothers under 18 years
		Births to lone mothers
		Low birthweight
		Mortality in first year of life
	Department for Education and Skills	Achievement at Key Stages 1 and 2 and at GCSE
		Special educational needs
		Permanent exclusions
		Unauthorised absences
	Police divisions	Burglary from dwellings
		Burglary, other
		Vehicle crime
		Violence against the person
		Criminal damage
		Drug offences
	Social services departments	Referrals
		Section 47 enquiries
		Child Protection Register numbers
		Looked-after children
	Office for Standards in Education	Number of providers and places for:
		- Childminders
		- Full day care
		- Sessional day care
		- Out-of-school care
		- Crèche care

(continued)

Table 3.1: (continued)

Method	Source	Indicators
Postcode (contd)	NHS Hospital Episode Statistics	Gastroenteritis
		Lower respiratory infection
		Severe injury
	Child Health Systems	Birthweights
		Infant feeding
		Immunisations
Ward	IMD 2000	1998 population denominators
		IMD 2000 total deprivation scores
		IMD 2000 domain scores
	NOMIS	Employment opportunities
OA/SOA	Census of Population 2001	2001 population denominators
		Ethnic background of population
		Variability of disadvantage of the residents
		Variability of housing in SSLP area
		Variability of ethnic background of residents
	Annual Business Inquiry	Employment details

lists with their databases. Using Child Benefit information, relevant families were contacted by letter and given the opportunity to opt out. The DWP then checked participating families for sensitive cases or those already involved in other studies. The names and addresses of the families taking part were then released to NESS and families selected randomly from the list and passed to the fieldworkers who visited them. Geographical Information Systems information also enabled fieldworkers to be matched to their nearest SSLP.

Obtaining crime data

Crime data are predominantly collated by police beat and thus were unlikely to coincide or nest into SSLP boundaries exactly. Therefore, maps of police beats had to be requested by the LCA team and digitised in the same manner as the SSLP areas, unless they exactly matched wards. Once this was done the beat boundaries and the programme boundaries were overlaid to calculate proportions to apply to the crime data. This was done for both households and physical area to provide the most relevant proportioning for different types of crime. Some police departments used GIS themselves and this facilitated data extraction specific to SSLP areas by using the GIS boundaries.

Access by families to services

To determine the extent to which SSLP-area residents could access services such as a library, swimming pool, general practitioner (GP) surgery or a child health clinic, it was necessary to study the areas surrounding each SSLP programme. It also required knowing the exact locations of the facilities so that they could be linked to SSLP-area residents. National address lists were obtained by the LCA team for various services in England including GPs, primary schools and libraries. Other service locations had to be identified through extensive searching of local authority websites. The services were mapped as point locations in GIS, along with the SSLP boundaries. To calculate the number of services that were located within a fixed distance, buffers were produced round the programme areas and only those services that were within the SSLP areas and their buffers were selected (see Figure 3.5). For more discussion of the use of buffering in GIS analysis see DeMers (1997, p 246).

The second part of assessing access to services was based on the distance to the nearest service for all families living in the area. This was calculated as the straight-line distance between two sets of points: an SSLP child's postcode and a facility, summarised as the percentage of households with their nearest service within distance bands one kilometre, between one and two kilometres and so on. While distance by road would have been more precise, it proved too costly to obtain the road network data for England.

Travel to work and migration

The 2001 Census offered new information on the origins and destinations of people travelling to work, together with the origins and destinations of residents who changed their addresses during the year before the Census was taken. The distance of work journeys or of migrations was measured by the straight-line distance between the population-weighted centroids of the OAs of origin and destination. The range of distances of work journeys or migrations analysed for each SSLP was calculated as a median distance rather than a simple average. This is common practice in the analysis of these data because they often contain a small number of very long-distance journeys or

**Figure 3.5: Facilities mapped (as points), with the selection
of those within the SSLP area and its buffer**

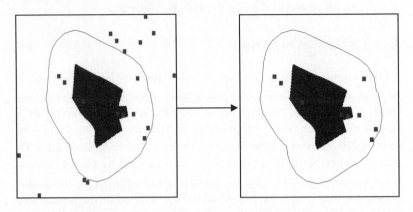

migrations that arise from inaccurate completion of Census forms. In
these circumstances the use of a median reduces the impact that a small
number of possibly false journeys has on the overall results.

Neighbourhood observations

Fieldworkers visited each SSLP area in person to fill in observational
surveys relating to aspects of the physical environment that could be
seen at particular locations and to capture qualitative information
unavailable elsewhere. Originally, postcodes were recorded to represent
the locations, but it proved difficult to always ensure that the correct
and complete postcode was used. As a result, fieldworkers were provided
with Global Positioning System (GPS) receivers to record their
locations in BNG coordinates. Three points were recorded: the start,
middle and end of the street. Once mapped in GIS and joined together
to create a street plotline, other socioeconomic data could be linked to
the street location to profile the observed areas in more detail.

Overlap between SSLPs and other ABIs

An important question for the evaluation of the impact of SSLPs was
the degree to which the programme areas were targeted by some of the
government's other ABIs. Geographical Information Systems enabled
the location of other initiatives to be overlaid onto the boundaries
of the SSLPs to assess the extent of overlap and therefore provide an
indication of the combined intensity of policy initiatives affecting

each area. The main difficulty faced by the NESS team was the lack of any centrally held records that indicated the boundaries of the areas covered by initiatives other than SSLPs in spite of plans for this to be done (Smith, 1999).

Information was collected from a combination of government departments and other evaluation teams on the presence of eight interventions or groups of interventions that were relevant to children and families (see Table 3.2), although not all the information was broken down below the broad areas 'eligible' for assistance as opposed to the specific areas 'receiving' assistance. In practice, 'presence' was not always easily defined. For many interventions only part of an SSLP area was covered. In these cases threshold rules were applied for each intervention to try to capture where the presence was 'significant'. For most, this meant that where an intervention covered more than one third of the SSLP area or more than one third of the population, it was scored as a 'significant' presence. The threshold rules and methodology for each of the eight interventions are outlined in Table 3.2. For each SSLP an index of intensity of local ABIs was produced by scoring the significant presence of an initiative as one, with the index calculated as the sum of these scores. Their distribution over the first 310 SSLP areas and 50 additional Sure Start-to-be areas selected for inclusion as part of the cross-sectional Impact Study are shown in Figure 3.6.

Very few SSLPs had no other ABI operating within their area, while a slightly larger number had as many as six. Overall, 72% of SSLPs had three or more other ABIs present. Although this index is not a comprehensive record of all ABIs – for example, it was not possible to comprehensively identify projects from the Single Regeneration Budget operating in SSLPs – the LCA team found that there was a significant relationship between the index and some indicators of local change and development within SSLPs (see Chapter Ten).

Limitations to GIS: accuracy and challenges

The constraints of translating locally defined ABIs into real boundaries on the ground and extracting data for them have associated issues of accuracy and consistency. It has already been mentioned that the standard and clarity of the source paper maps defining SSLP areas varied. Further, using unit postcode centroids as the link to datasets is prone to a degree of imprecision at the edges of areas. However, there were also other more indirect challenges that the project faced.

Table 3.2: Details of other ABIs mapped onto SSLP areas

Initiative	Threshold rules
Aim Higher, Education Action Zones and Excellence in Cities	These three were grouped together since the interventions had strong evolutionary links. All work through target schools. The National Pupil Database was used to identify pupils resident in SSLPs who attended target schools and the total number of resident pupils. Where more than 33.3% of all pupils living in an SSLP attend a target school this was coded as a significant presence
Children's Fund	A list of all wards containing Children's Fund projects was obtained from the Department for Education and Skills (DfES). This provided an approximate guide to the location of the projects. Where more than 33.3% of the area of an SSLP was contained within a ward(s) containing Children's Fund projects this was coded as a significant presence
Early Excellence Centre	A list of 112 centres was obtained from the DfES. These were coded by ward. Where more than 33.3% of the area of an SSLP was contained within a ward(s) containing an Early Excellence Centre this was coded as a significant presence
Health Action Zone (HAZ)	These were defined by local authority areas. Where an SSLP was contained within an authority defined as a Health Action Zone this was taken to be a significant presence
Neighbourhood nursery	A list of nurseries with their accompanying postcodes was obtained from the DfES. In the absence of any guidance on the extent of their actual catchment areas, circles with a radius of 1.5 kilometres were constructed around each nursery. Where more than 33.3% of the area of an SSLP was contained within one or more of these circles this was coded as a significant presence
Neighbourhood Renewal	Eligibility for Neighbourhood Renewal was determined at the level of local authorities. It was not possible to obtain a comprehensive list of local projects being conducted under the initiative so an approach similar to the HAZs was adopted – SSLPs were coded as experiencing a significant presence where they fell within an eligible local authority
New Deal for Communities (NDC)	Digital boundaries for all NDC projects were obtained from the evaluators of the initiative (through the Social Disadvantage Research Centre, University of Oxford). These were linked directly to SSLP boundaries. Given the localised nature of many NDC projects (often dealing with individual estates or parts of estates) a lower threshold of 'significance' was used. In this case, if more than 20% of the area of an SSLP fell within the boundaries of one or more NDC projects it was deemed a significant presence
On Track	A list of postcodes comprising the areas targeted by On Track was obtained from the Policy Research Bureau (evaluators of this initiative). These were allocated to SSLPs. Where more than 33.3% of all postcodes within an SSLP was part of an On Track area this was coded as a significant presence

Figure 3.6: Distribution of the number of other ABIs within SSLPs in rounds 1 to 4

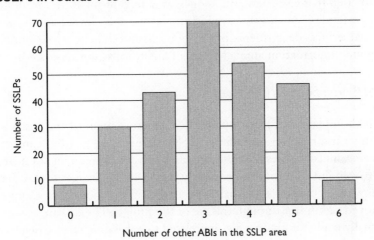

Determining denominators

In most cases the counts extracted from routine databases for each SSLP only provided a numerator, and so appropriate denominators were required to convert the counts into rates (for example, number unemployed⊠unemployment rate). Until the 2001 Census data became available, NESS used the population estimates for 1998 wards to obtain population denominators, using the previously described apportioning technique. This was replaced with population apportioning using the smaller 2001 Census OAs. Child Benefit counts were obtained from the DWP to provide denominators for those aged under 18 in single-year age bands. There was a slight discrepancy in counts between Child Benefit and the Census, but Child Benefit was selected because of problems with Census undercounts in some parts of the country.

Postcode changes

A negative feature of using postcodes extensively in the analysis was that postcodes changed over time. New codes are introduced and old ones are removed. To cope with this, the Address Manager lists are issued quarterly. In a project whose work spanned several years this required regular updating of the postcode lists for each SSLP and the archiving of all historic lists to cope with circumstances where the databases to which matching was taking place contained postcodes that had not, themselves, been updated. Data providers were sometimes surprised that each new data request was accompanied by a fresh list of postcodes, which may have influenced the delay or failure of some social services departments, police divisions and child health systems to provide information annually to the LCA team as was requested.

SSLP area boundary changes

The boundary capture and postcode extraction methodology used to extract information on individual SSLP-area residents from external sources and databases was designed on the basis of infrequent boundary changes and a controlled process by which these changes took place. However, contrary to initial expectations, SSLP boundary changes proved significant through the life of the project. These changes were usually made for sensible reasons related to enhancing service delivery or to capture more appropriate numbers of children. Nevertheless, to be able to accurately monitor change over time, NESS used a 'frozen' version of the boundaries, set to a deadline for any remaining changes to be agreed. However, boundary changes still occurred after this date and the Sure Start Unit (SSU) itself required data for the most up-to-date programme boundaries at any given time. Therefore, two different sets of boundaries and postcode lists existed and ultimately data counts for the programmes were affected. The problem that this raised was that the difference between the two counts could be attributed directly to the changed part of the programme – the additional or excluded part of the area. This is called 'differencing' (see Figure 3.7). Critically, this could be used to identify individual residents in the small area and consequently contravene the Data Protection Act 1998, something that the data agencies who were affected, mainly the DWP in this case, were concerned about. To deal with this, changes that created areas that contained less than 10 people were suppressed.

Boundary changes and looking at change in employment

Employment data from the Annual Business Inquiry provided information on places of work in and around SSLPs. At the start of the project, these data were available by ward boundaries that were current in 2000. Data from the 2004 Inquiry were, however, disseminated by SOA. Attempts to achieve the best fit of SOAs to wards current in 2000 proved impossible because the inclusion or exclusion of even one postcode could mean the incorrect inclusion or exclusion of a large employer, for example, a factory, a hospital or, in one case, a

Figure 3.7: Illustration of the problem of SSLP area boundary changes and differencing; the difference between total counts can be attributed directly to the changed part (circled)

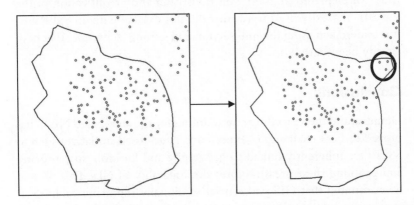

police headquarters. This made it impossible to determine if change over time was due to genuine employment changes or the boundary changes. This was the only occasion within NESS when it proved impossible to produce sensible estimates of key variables in and around the SSLPs. It illustrates a key limitation when using postcodes as a route to estimating data for non-standard boundaries or for attempting to achieve comparability over time when the spatial units for which data are available change. The method works best when the data used are based on *residents* who are reasonably dispersed over an area. Where there are single large concentrations associated with single postcodes, as is the case with workplace-based employment records, there is no alternative to working with establishment-level data.

Comparisons for SSLP areas

The majority of the LCA analyses compared SSLP area means with values of each indicator for the whole of England. However, it was also important, if possible, to compare SSLP areas to those that were similarly deprived but without a programme. For comparative purposes, a comparison group of Census wards was selected. With deprivation as the main characteristic used to determine eligibility for the SSLP initiative, scores from the Index of Deprivation 2000 were used as the basis for this selection, released with data for ward boundaries current in 1998. The challenge was to re-estimate the index for wards that were used in the release of data from the 2001 Census to allow comparative analysis of the substantial range of data available from the Census. These were wards that were in use in early 2003 (the release date for the Census), significantly different from those used for the Index of Deprivation 2000. This translation and identification of the top 20% most deprived wards that did not overlap with an SSLP area was undertaken using the intersection and joining techniques that have already been outlined.

Conclusions

Defining and then profiling communities for the area-based NESS has proved to be a challenging experience. Area-based initiatives such as SSLPs are inherently linked to geography and location, so capturing and profiling these areas requires the capability of GIS. This project demonstrated that GIS was crucial in digitally capturing each SSLP area to allow the profiling datasets required to be linked and extracted. It allowed data to be linked by any available geography, be it postcode or ward or GPS location, and created new information, such as access to services. In addition, it allowed the identification of children and families who were the focus of the NESS Impact Study.

A number of unexpected methodological complications arose through the life of the project. The boundaries of the programmes changed much more than was expected either by the project team or the SSU. The nature of crime data varied considerably between different police forces, often based on crime beats that did not match easily with other spatial units. The identification of comparator areas for the SSLPs absorbed considerable time and effort while, over the lifetime of the project, the definitions of some of the standard spatial units for the release of data (particularly wards) changed significantly. In general, the flexibility of GIS was able to cope with these issues but, in drawing lessons from the experience of the project, it is clear that much more GIS analysis and effort was needed than was anticipated in the planning stage of the evaluation. The motto of 'expect the unexpected' is appropriate for any other team planning a similar project!

References
DeMers, M.N. (1997) *Fundamentals of Geographic Information Systems*, New York: John Wiley.
DETR (Department of Environment, Transport and the Regions) (2000) *Indices of Deprivation, 2000: Regeneration Research Summary, Number 31*, London, DETR.

Glass, N. (1999) 'Origins of the Sure Start Local Programmes', *Children and Society*, vol 13, pp 257-64.

Longley, P.A., Goodchild, M.F., Maguire, D.J. and Rhind, D.W. (2001) *Geographic Information Systems and science*, Chichester: Wiley.

ODPM (Office of the Deputy Prime Minister) (2004) *The English Indices of Deprivation, 2004: Summary (revised)*, London: ODPM.

Raper, J.F., Rhind, D.W. and Shepherd, J.W. (1992) *Postcodes: The new geography*, Harlow: Longman.

Smith, G.R. (1999) *Area-based Initiatives: The rationale and options for area targeting, CASE Paper, No 25*, London: Centre for Analysis of Social Exclusion, London School of Economics and Political Science.

Part Three
The implementation of Sure Start Local Programmes

The methodologies for the evaluation of complex interventions: an ongoing debate

Pamela Meadows

The research design of the National Evaluation of Sure Start (NESS) presented many challenges. These challenges were not unique, and as this chapter shows, have been and continue to be faced by others. However, Sure Start Local Programmes (SSLPs) are both a social intervention and a complex one. There is as yet no firm consensus around the best methodologies to use to evaluate the outcomes either of social interventions or of those in which the details of the treatment can vary between individuals and may be unknown to the evaluator. The purpose of this chapter is to review some of the main issues that have arisen in the literature on both social and complex interventions and which NESS confronted. It starts with a brief history of the evaluation of social interventions. It then considers the importance in social and other policy-related interventions of the questions *why* and *how* certain interventions work, as well as the standard question of *whether* they work. Finally it discusses the recent attempts to build a consensus around approaches to the central issues of the social, cultural and political context that may be fundamental in explaining observed outcomes, however those outcomes are measured.

The development of the evaluation of social programmes

Rigorous methods for evaluating medical treatments have a long history, and were adopted in the US for looking at innovations in education during the 1950s and 1960s. The experimental or quasi-experimental evaluation of social programmes and interventions has a much more recent history. Some have suggested that it dates from 1967 with the New Jersey Negative Income Tax Experiment (Greenberg and Shroder, 2004), whereas others quote examples from earlier in the same decade (Shadish et al, 1991). Certainly, the seminal text (Campbell and Stanley,

1963) dates from the early part of the decade, which makes 1967 an unlikely date. Social programmes are generally defined as those whose *intention* is to train, educate or otherwise influence behaviour in order to achieve better outcomes for disadvantaged participants and for society more generally (Donaldson, 2003). Some health interventions have social impacts, but these are not necessarily intended, and are not always measured.

Until the late 1970s, the evaluation of social interventions followed – or at least paid lip service to the desirability of following – the 'gold-standard' medical experimental method of the randomised controlled trial (RCT). Under this system the subjects of the intervention are divided into two or more groups. Those assigned to the control group receive no treatment or an existing treatment and those assigned to the experimental/treatment group receive a new treatment (or in some cases different treatment combinations). Provided the allocation of individuals to groups is entirely random, and the sample size is large enough to minimise the impact of random events, under the right conditions any differences in the average outcomes between the treatment and control groups can be attributed to the differences in treatment. Evaluation researchers from the social sciences adopted the 'scientific' medical approach to evaluation, asking the question 'Does it work?'

The central advantage of RCTs is that they do not rely on the judgement either of the evaluator or of the practitioner who is delivering the treatment. The determination of whether an intervention or treatment is effective is based solely on standard statistical inference.[1] This is the main reason why the results of RCTs command widespread respect. These characteristics of RCTs – the internal validity and avoidance of bias on the part of the evaluator – remain their greatest strength (Campbell and Stanley, 1963; Shadish et al, 1991; Greenberg and Shroder, 2004). However, 'Does it work?' is the only question that they can answer.

During the 1980s and into the 1990s evaluators began to express concern about the reliance on the scientific experimental model to evaluate social programmes. In particular, there were concerns that findings might be particular to the circumstances and locations in which they were implemented and thus might not be able to be replicated in other locations; in other words, although they might have internal validity, they lack external validity (Rossi and Freeman, 1985; Shadish et al, 1991; Pawson and Tilley, 1997; Greenberg and Shroder, 2004). Some of those who argued that RCTs were the least worst option available nevertheless joined the critics in recognising that because social programmes are administered by institutions, there were probably aspects of the implementation that were influencing the outcomes observed. In addition, in some programmes the delivery of services was done by a key individual, and the RCT model provided no information about the nature of the relationship between the service provider and the service user, and that this might be essential to ensure the replication of outcomes in other settings (Olds, 1988; Burtless, 1995; Hollister and Hill, 1995). Thus, even if RCTs of social programmes were internally valid, they might not be externally valid.

There also were doubts about the internal validity of RCTs in relation to many social interventions, even where the nature of the intervention was clear and manualised, an issue considered in more detail later. The most common problem is control group contamination. In medical trials it is possible for the participant not to be aware of which treatment they are receiving. In social interventions that is often not possible because control group members frequently know they are not getting the services that treatment group members are getting, and they cannot be prevented from seeking out similar services from other sources. For example, recent meta-analysis of random-assignment evaluations of vocational training programmes in the US by Greenberg and Ashworth (2005) found that 54% of treatment group members had actually received vocational training, but so had 35% of control group members. Thus, the evaluations were not comparing the outcomes for vocational training against no training; instead, they were comparing the outcomes for training by one provider against training by another. Where treatment and control group members live in the same area, control group members can learn new skills and ways of behaving from treatment group members. All these features can bias the findings against the intervention.

There may also be biases the other way. For example, members of the control group may be put at a greater disadvantage by the treatment received by the treatment group or groups. This might occur when the treatment under study provides a pathway to other services that are available only in limited quantities. The treatment group may have improved access to such services, which in turn means that members of the control group are less likely to be able to access such services. This issue arose in the case of the SSLPs, as discussed in the interpretation of findings of the NESS Impact Study (see Chapter Eight).

The other important condition for internal validity is that the trial itself must not influence the behaviour of participants. In the case of medication trials, the use of placebos means that the participants are not themselves aware of whether or not they are receiving an active treatment. In the case of social interventions (and also some mental health and public health interventions), however, the participants are inevitably aware of their status as treatment or control group members, and this may influence their behaviour. The direction of this influence is not always clear. Some control group members may become demoralised by not being offered access to the services they hoped to receive. Some members of both treatment and control groups might prefer to receive an alternative treatment to the one to that they have been assigned, and may be less willing to comply with treatment protocols, or more likely to drop out of a trial. Others may become galvanised to try and find other sources of help, having had their expectations raised upon being informed of the nature of the intervention during the course of securing their informed consent. More problematically, the monitoring process might itself lead to changes in behaviour on the part of the control group and might also make treatment group members more likely to drop out of a programme than they would have been if the programme existed without the evaluation (Olds, 1988; MRC, 2000).

Another potential source of contamination comes from mainstream or alternative service providers. If the service delivery methods involved in the trial are adopted by other service providers during the course of the trial, this means that control group members have access to services that are similar to those available to treatment group members. This risk becomes particularly acute if the new service is seen to represent 'good practice' by practitioners (MRC, 2000).

There are also worries about the need for programme participants to be volunteers and provide informed consent to taking part (although this applies equally to medical research). If volunteers have stronger motivation or confidence than non-volunteers, it is not possible to draw general conclusions from the outcome for that population (Rossi and Freeman, 1985). Pawson and Tilley (1997) have presented an illustration drawn from an intervention for prisoners, where the outcome for those who volunteered for the programme but did not receive the treatment was significantly better than the outcome for those who did not volunteer at all (and was only slightly worse than the outcome for the treatment group). The key driver of the observed outcome appeared to be the motivation that led to volunteering rather than the treatment itself.

Attempts to build a new consensus

From the late 1980s onwards, evaluators of social programmes recognised the need to develop approaches to the evaluation of social programmes that both provided rigour in measuring outcomes and answered the questions that really mattered for policy makers, and which RCTs do not touch on:

- If the intervention makes a difference, how or why does it do so?
- If the intervention makes a difference on average, is this difference larger for, or confined to, certain subgroups within the population, and are there any groups for whom the impact is negative?
- Will it make a difference to a wider group of people if implemented more widely?
- Is the number of potential beneficiaries large or small?

In the UK this methodological debate should also be seen in the context of the wider debate about evidence-based policy making in government more generally (Davies et al, 2000; Walker, 2001; Coote et al, 2004).

As Pawson and Tilley (1997, p xiii) have argued:

> Evaluation, perhaps above all, needs to be realistic. The whole point is that it is a form of applied research, not performed for the benefit of science as such, but pursued in order to inform the thinking of policy makers, practitioners, programme participants and public.

Pawson and Tilley's work is widely regarded as seminal, but they were building on that of others, particularly Rossi and Freeman (1985) and Shadish et al (1991). There have also been other major contributions to the debate such as Donaldson and Scriven (2003). The emphasis of those arguing for a new approach was on the idea that evaluation should be driven by theories of *how* an intervention could be expected to make a difference, with a particular emphasis on ensuring that the evaluation addresses the kinds of questions that would allow replication. Is there something about a particular community, a particular local authority or a particular part of the implementation process that facilitates positive outcomes? However, perhaps the key contribution of Pawson and Tilley (1997) to the debate was their argument that in practice it may be impossible to disentangle outcomes from the social and cultural contexts within which implementation takes place. By contrast, the RCT seeks as far as possible to decontextualise the impact of an intervention.

This does not rule out an RCT in the case of social interventions, but does mean that it should not be conducted in isolation from other elements of the evaluation that address these additional questions. However, if an intervention is intended to influence the outcomes for people who are not direct recipients of services or treatment, then an RCT alone (without supporting evidence about processes and where appropriate qualitative research to provide contextual information) is unlikely to provide an accurate assessment of impact. Murphy and associates (1998) provide an extensive literature review of work on combining qualitative and quantitative methods, Crawford and associates (2002) provide clear examples of such an approach in a clinical context, Rychetnik and associates (2002) do so for public health and Plewis and Mason (2005) do the same for a social intervention.

Analysis of the impact on subgroups is an important element for policy replication. For instance, an intervention might have a large effect on a very small group, but be of no benefit to the majority of recipients. Alternatively, an intervention might have a relatively small effect, but the potential number of beneficiaries might be very large. Both these outcomes could produce identical group averages in an RCT, but the social (and possibly the cost) implications would be very different. For a fuller discussion of this issue, see NIMH (2000, Appendix E, pp 73-6).

Complex interventions: a different type of problem

In general, established evaluation methodologies, particularly RCTs, rest on the assumption that the intervention itself is clearly defined, that the population receiving the treatment or service is known, and that the intervention does not have an indirect effect on those not (directly) receiving the service or treatment. In the case of SSLPs none of these conditions applied. Thus, the National Evaluation of SSLPs confronted major methodological challenges.

The intervention was complex, in that the 'treatment' involved the provision of a range of services for young children and their parents by staff and volunteers with varying skills and occupational backgrounds, varying from trained professionals (for example, health visitors, speech and language therapists, social workers) to community members recruited and trained specially. Part of the purpose of the intervention was to change the nature of the relationship between service providers and service users, and in particular to inform and empower users. Moreover, within a very broad framework, each of the 260 SSLPs included in the evaluation was free to choose the exact nature of the services they provided and the mechanisms for delivering those services. As Weiss and Jacobs (1988, p 5) said of earlier attempts to evaluate programmes of this kind, 'There is widespread agreement that the evaluation of family support and education programmes has been straining and stimulating measurement and evaluation technology'.

The services provided by SSLPs had a variety of objectives, including the health and cognitive, emotional and social development of the children; the health and social, emotional and economic well-being of the parents; and the general well-being of the wider community. In point of fact, then, the need to look simultaneously at social and emotional as well as cognitive outcomes for children, and to also look at outcomes for parents and the wider community, and the impact on local services could not easily be addressed by a strict RCT approach. Also complicating matters was the fact that SSLPs were area-based interventions, with the services provided intended to be of *direct* benefit to service recipients, but also to have an *indirect* impact on other members of the wider community within the area. This feature is common to other area-based initiatives such as Health Action Zones (Bonner, 2003), New Deal for Communities, On Track (Hine, 2005) and Employment Zones. It is also a common feature in health promotion and other public health interventions (Rychetnik et al, 2002). The problem of determining the causality of any observed outcomes was thus confounded by the fact that most SSLP areas had several other area-based initiatives operating within them at the same time.

The heterogeneity and the complexity of the intervention itself, the range of intended beneficiaries and the range of potential outcomes for each group of beneficiaries meant that the design of the National Evaluation was never going to be straightforward. Although standard texts on evaluation methodology recognise the practical challenges confronted by evaluators of complex interventions (for example, Scriven, 1991), much of the recent debate on the best approaches to adopt has taken place among researchers who have practical experience of designing and undertaking evaluations of complex interventions in both health and social policy fields (for example, Weiss and Jacobs, 1988; Wolff, 2001; Crawford et al, 2002; Bonner, 2003).

In recognition of the challenges faced by evaluators, several organisations have produced guidance, including the Medical Research Council (MRC, 2000) and the US National Institute for Mental Health (NIMH, 2000). This guidance, aimed mainly at those undertaking complex health interventions, is in fact equally relevant to those designing evaluations of complex social interventions. For example, the MRC definition of a complex intervention could apply equally to social interventions:

> Complex interventions are built up from a number of components, which may act both independently and inter-dependently. The components usually include behaviours, parameters of behaviours (e.g. frequency, timing), and methods of organising and delivering those behaviours (e.g. type(s) of practitioner, setting and location). It is not easy precisely to define the 'active ingredients' of a complex intervention. (MRC, 2000, p 2)

In the US the Aspen Institute has taken a particular interest in the issue, organising the discussions that led to the publication of Connell and associates' (1995) path-breaking book and co-funding the work of Coote et al (2004) in the UK.

The main features that can influence outcomes are integral to the implementation process. They include issues of leadership, organisation, interagency working (both historically and in the context of the particular intervention under scrutiny) and access to services or the engagement with users (see Pawson, 2004; France and Crow, 2005; Hine, 2005; Mason et al, 2005; Tunstill et al, 2005). They also include the details of the service provided (for example, what the background of the staff delivering the service is, how they are trained, whether they use a manual or clearly defined protocol or whether they can use their own judgement in delivering the service). These issues are common features of social interventions, but are also found in interventions for people with mental health problems, for example. Moreover, part of the service delivery in complex interventions is the social relationship between the person delivering the service and the service recipient and their family, and the wider social and cultural context within which that relationship takes place (Wolff, 2001; Crawford et al, 2002; Pawson, 2004).

In addition to the multiplicity of services in SSLPs, there was also the issue of widely differing services being offered under the same service heading and the difficulty of generating research tools to capture complex concepts such as outreach, team working or multidisciplinarity. Other evaluators have encountered similar difficulties (for example, Campbell, 2003). Unless these factors are controlled for, or standardised across the trial, the results of an RCT cannot be regarded as a reliable indicator of replicability. The capture of this information is particularly important in the case of interventions that appear not to be effective. This is because apparently ineffective interventions could be the result of a failure of theory (that is, the intervention does not actually work in the way it was expected to work) or a failure of implementation (that is, the intervention does work, but only if properly implemented) (Rychetnik et al, 2002).

The Medical Research Council guidance (MRC, 2000) provides examples of how qualitative research may be an essential adjunct of an RCT. However, in terms of the complexity of the intervention itself, it argues that within the RCT it may be feasible to vary the method of delivery or the content of what is being delivered, and to allow limited practitioner discretion *within carefully defined limits*. It had clearly not occurred to the authors that anyone might be asked to evaluate an intervention – such as SSLPs – in which *both* the method and the content varied across delivery sites, and where a wide range of practitioners had a great deal of autonomy over the style and content of what was delivered.

In the case of SSLPs, one of the central issues was location. Within each SSLP area all the children who met the age criteria and their families were eligible to receive services. This 'bounded universality' was a core feature of the design of the programme, intended to address the issue of stigma in services targeted at disadvantaged individuals. This feature was incompatible with an evaluation design involving random assignment of individuals within the area, however. This is a common problem for community-wide initiatives (for example, Hollister and Hill, 1995). Thus, the only feasible RCT option would have been one in which geographically defined areas were themselves randomly assigned to treatment or control status. This would have had the potential advantage of providing a mixture in both treatment and control areas of attributes related to service delivery, including the history of interagency working, the local social environment and the level and quality of existing services for young children and their families (Wolff, 2001). Unfortunately, by the time the evaluation was commissioned the first 260 areas that had applied to be SSLPs had been selected for service delivery, and during the final design stage of the evaluation the number of areas designated to receive services was increased to 524. This made it more or less impossible to identify areas of deprivation like SSLP areas that were not going to receive SSLPs. In practice if not in theory, then, government decision making had ruled out the prospect of an RCT in which areas would be randomly assigned to have – or not have – an SSLP.

There are UK government precedents for area-based comparisons, although these have generally been quasi-experimental rather than true random-assignment experiments. They include the Earnings Top-Up for unemployed people without dependants (Marsh, 2001), the Education Maintenance Allowance (Middleton et al, 2005) and community policing (Bennett, 1991). However, even if the government had been willing in the case of SSLPs to engage in an area-based experiment, the timing of the commissioning of the evaluation relative to the selection of areas for service delivery meant that this was not a practical option. Doubts ultimately remain as to whether genuine random allocation experiments are politically or practically feasible, given the pressure on governments to be seen to allocate resources fairly between areas, and the small sample sizes (WHO, 2001; Greenberg and Shroder, 2004), however useful they are for evaluators.

The NESS was developed after many local programmes had been launched. It was not therefore possible to prescribe or standardise any elements of the delivery of services. It had to deal with all the methodological difficulties that are standard in complex interventions. Its potential value ultimately resides in its ability to indicate whether, how and why changes in the level and type of services for children and families and the way in which they are delivered might affect the long-term life chances of disadvantaged children. Because of problems inherent in quasi-experimental evaluations such as the one reported in this volume, questions will probably always be raised as to whether effects detected were truly causal in nature; or even whether effects that actually occurred simply proved undetectable.

Note

[1] There is actually some debate around the appropriate cut-off point for determining whether a result is statistically significant. The conventional cut-off is based on a 5% probability of a result having come about by chance, but some argue that this means that potentially beneficial interventions may be rejected. Alternatively, if a treatment carries a risk to patients as some new medical treatments do, then a more stringent test (say a 1% probability of the result being observed by chance) might be appropriate. This determination of the cut-off point is one where evaluators have some discretion.

References

Bennett, T. (1991) 'The effectiveness of a police-initiated fear-reducing strategy', *British Journal of Criminology*, vol 31, pp 1-14.

Bonner, L. (2003) 'Using theory-based evaluation to build evidence-based health and social care policy and practice', *Critical Public Health*, vol 13, pp 77-92.

Burtless, G. (1995) 'The case for randomized field trials in economic and policy research', *Journal of Economic Perspectives*, vol 92, pp 63-84.

Campbell, A. (2003) 'Developing and evaluating Early Excellence Centres in the UK: some issues in promoting integrated and "joined-up" services', *International Journal of Early Years Education*, vol 11, pp 235-44.

Campbell, D. and Stanley, J. (1963) *Experimental and quasi-experimental evaluations in social research*, Chicago, IL: Rand McNally.

Connell, J.P., Kubisch, A.C., Schorr, L.B. and Weiss, C.H. (eds) (1995) *New approaches to evaluating community initiatives: Vol. 1: Concepts, methods and contexts*, Washington, DC: Aspen Institute.

Coote, A., Allen, J. and Woodhead, D. (2004) *Finding out what works: Understanding complex community-based initiatives*, London: King's Fund.

Crawford, M.J., Weaver, T., Rutter, D., Sensky, T. and Tyrer, P. (2002) 'Evaluating new treatments in psychiatry: the potential value of combining qualitative and quantitative methods', *International Review of Psychiatry*, vol 14, pp 6-11.

Davies, H.T.O., Nutley, S.M. and Smith, P.C. (eds) (2000) *What works? Evidence-based policy and practice in public services*, Bristol: The Policy Press.

Donaldson, S.I. (2003) 'Theory-driven program evaluation', in S.I. Donaldson and M. Scriven (eds) *Evaluating social programs and problems: Visions for the new millennium*, Mahwhah, NJ: Lawrence Erlbaum Associates, pp 3-16.

Donaldson, S.I. and Scriven, M. (eds) (2003) *Evaluating social programs and problems: Visions for the new millennium*, Mahwhah, NJ: Lawrence Erlbaum Associates.

France, A. and Crow, I. (2005) 'Using the 'Risk Factor Paradigm' in prevention: lessons from the evaluation of Communities that Care', *Children and Society*, vol 19, pp 172-84.

Greenberg, D. and Ashworth, K. (2005) 'Workfare evaluations and meta-analysis', in A. Cebulla, K. Ashworth, D. Greenberg and R. Walker (eds) *Welfare to work: New Labour and the US experience*, Aldershot: Ashgate, pp 52-72.

Greenberg, D. and Shroder, M. (2004) *The digest of social experiments* (3rd edn), Washington, DC: The Urban Institute Press.

Hine, J. (2005) 'Early multiple intervention: a view from On Track', *Children and Society*, vol 19, pp 117-30.

Hollister, R. and Hill, J. (1995) 'Problems in the evaluation of community-wide initiatives', in J.P. Connell, A.C. Kubisch, L.B. Schorr and C.H. Weiss (eds) *New approaches to evaluating community initiatives: Vol. 1: Concepts, methods and contexts,* Washington, DC: Aspen Institute, pp 127-72.

Marsh, A. (2001) *Earnings top-up evaluation: Synthesis report,* Department of Social Security Research Report No 135, Leeds: Corporate Document Services, www.dwp.gov.uk/asd/asd5/rrep135.asp

Mason, P., Morris, K. and Smith, P. (2005) 'A complex solution to a complicated problem', *Children and Society,* vol 19, pp 131-43.

Middleton, S., Perren, K., Maguire, S., Rennison, J., Battistin, E., Emmerson, C. and Fitzsimons, E. (2005) *Evaluation of Education Maintenance Allowance pilots: Young people aged 16 to 19 years: Final report of the quantitative evaluation,* Department for Education and Skills Research Report No RB678, Nottingham: DfES.

MRC (Medical Research Council) (2000) *A Framework for development and evaluation of RCTs for complex interventions to improve health,* Swindon: MRC.

Murphy, E., Dingwall, R., Greatbach, D., Parker, S. and Watson, P. (1998) *Qualitative research methods in health technology assessment: A review of the literature,* Health Technology Assessment 2, York: York Publishing Services, www.hta.ac.uk/fullmono/mon216.pdf

NIMH (National Institute of Mental Health) (2000) *Translating behavioural science into action: Report of the National Advisory Mental Health Council Behavioural Science Workgroup,* Publication no 00-4699, Bethesda: National Institutes of Health, www.nimh.nih.gov/publicat/nimhtranslating.pdf

Olds, D. (1988) 'Common design and methodological problems encountered in evaluating family support services: illustrations from the prenatal/early infancy project', in H.B. Weiss and F. Jacobs (eds) *Evaluating family programs,* New York: Aldine de Gruyter, pp 239-65.

Pawson, R. (2004) 'Evidence-based policy: in search of a method', *Evaluation,* vol 8, pp 157-81.

Pawson, R. and Tilley, N. (1997) *Realistic evaluation,* London: Sage Publications.

Plewis, I. and Mason, P. (2005) 'What works and why: combining quantitative and qualitative approaches in large-scale evaluations', *International Journal of Social Research Methodology,* vol 8, pp 185-94.

Rossi, P. and Freeman, H. (1985) *Evaluation: A systematic approach,* Beverley Hills, CA: Sage Publications.

Rychetnik, L., Frommer, M., Hawe, P., and Shiell, A. (2002) 'Criteria for evaluating evidence on public health interventions', *Journal of Epidemiology and Community Health*, vol 56, pp 119-27.

Scriven, M. (1991) *Evaluation thesaurus* (4th edn), Newbury Park, CA: Sage Publications.

Shadish, W.R., Cook, T.D. and Levinton, D.C. (1991) *Foundations of program evaluation*, Newbury Park, CA: Sage Publications.

Tunstill, J., Allnock, D., Akhurst, S., Garbers, C. and the NESS research team (2005) 'Sure Start Local Programmes: implications of case study data from the National Evaluation of Sure Start', *Children and Society*, vol 19, pp 158-71.

Walker, R. (2001) 'Great expectations: can social science evaluate New Labour's policies?', *Evaluation*, vol 7, pp 305-30.

Weiss, H.B. and Jacobs, F. (eds) (1988) *Evaluating family programs*, New York: Aldine de Gruyter.

WHO (World Health Organization) (2001) *Evaluation in health promotion: Principles and perspectives*, WHO Regional Publications European Series No 92, Copenhagen: WHO.

Wolff, N. (2001) 'Randomised trials of socially complex interventions: promise or peril', *Journal of Health Services Research and Policy*, vol 6, pp 123-6.

FIVE

Sure Start Local Programmes: an overview of the implementation task

Jane Tunstill and Debra Allnock

Sure Start Local Programmes (SSLPs) have enjoyed one of the highest ever profiles of any UK government initiative concerning children and families. Such visibility carried both advantages and disadvantages and also affected the task of evaluation. While the main advantage was that SSLPs were, from the outset, of interest at the highest levels of government, this led to the major disadvantage: the short-term perspective often adopted by politicians in search of signs of its positive impact (Glass, 2006; Jack, 2006;) and, closely related, the attendant high level of publicity granted by commentators to *some* although not *all* of the evaluation findings. Perhaps inevitably, therefore, early findings of rather modest *impact* on individual children (see Chapters Eight and Nine) received widespread coverage and other results, including those pertaining to the process of implementing SSLPs and addressed in this chapter, were often neglected.

The research team studying SSLP implementation had two key purposes – to provide data that could inform the Impact Study of the National Evaluation of Sure Start (NESS) and to generate insights into increasing the smooth and effective functioning of SSLPs (see Foreword). In other words, the data collected by the team studying implementation were intended, from the very start, to provide insights for policy makers *and* practitioners on the ground, *during the course of the initiative*, not only *at its completion*. The contribution of the implementation team to the Impact Study is reflected in the conclusions about programme variability presented in Chapter Nine of this volume. However, the particular focus of *this* chapter is on the existing and future implications of findings pertaining to implementation for the development of community-based services for young children and their families.

As set out in Chapter One, a set of policy drivers determined the original objectives of SSLPs and, as of this writing in early 2007, continue to influence the development of services for children and families. The three key *imperatives* of SSLPs were to facilitate increased access to services; encourage and stimulate better collaboration between agencies and professionals; and develop new ways of working. Therefore, in spite of the limited life of SSLPs as separate entities, following their incorporation since 2005 into Children's Centres, their experiences remain likely to be of relevance to the task of designing and delivering improved services to children and families in community-based settings.

This chapter highlights key lessons learned about the trio of imperatives just mentioned. Following a brief resume of the methodology used to study implementation, an integrated overview of the implementation process is provided in terms of three major foci. The first concerns *transcending organisational and professional boundaries* and describes the work undertaken by SSLPs to 'create the right network' – by establishing relationships among service providers at every level and 'exploiting' the network to underpin multidisciplinary working. The second concerns the *continuum of access* and provides an overview of the ways in which SSLPs undertook the task of engaging the community. This subsection describes how they established a profile in the community through consultation and outreach. It also highlights specific strategies employed to identify the most vulnerable groups. The third and final subsection concerns *a new approach to service delivery for children and parents* and describes the way in which the SSLP principles were applied to service planning, including the relationship between group-based and individually-based services; the role of childcare as a means to access other services; and the relative roles of centre-based and outreach service delivery.

Studying programme implementation

The case for studying the process and outputs of implementation as an integral part of any evaluation is the subject of an ever-growing literature (Patton, 1990; Ghate, 2001; Plewis and Mason, 2005). Many commentators have echoed the views of King et al (1987, p 9):

> To consider only questions of program outcomes may limit the usefulness of an evaluation ... unless you have taken care to describe the details of the program's operations, you may be unable to answer a question that logically follows such a judgement of success: 'what worked?' If you cannot answer that, you will have wasted the effort measuring the

outcomes of events that cannot be described and therefore remain a mystery....

Some key issues explored in research include the need to acknowledge the impact on service evaluation design of current government priorities (Ghate, 2001; Tunstill, 2003; Tunstill et al, 2005a). For example, the emphasis in government policy on the theoretical framework of *'prevention'* (Schweinhart et al, 1993), as well as the concern to *address 'cross-cutting' social problems through 'joined-up' policy initiatives* (Sanderson, 2002), had implications for the design of the NESS implementation methodology. It was essential to focus on a wide range of diverse agencies; be sensitive to data collection on referrals; and at least attempt to access the views of low-intensity/infrequent service users. *Preventive ways of working* and a *stress on early intervention* also put a particular premium on getting data about possible obstacles/barriers to service in the first place. (For a fuller account of some of these interrelationships, see Allnock et al, 2006; Garbers et al, 2006.)

The implementation methodology

There were three interlinked methodological components in NESS' study of implementation. First, a national survey of SSLPs was repeated at annual intervals over a three-year period, except in the case of programmes that were initiated later, which were only surveyed twice. Second, a set of in-depth case studies of a representative 10% sample of the first 260 programmes was undertaken (see Tunstill et al, 2005b). Finally, a series of themed studies focused on topics meriting qualitative investigation and including diverse subsamples of these 260 SSLPs were carried out (see Chapter Six). In the course of conducting this work, it was essential that the researchers build positive and sustainable relationships with the key stakeholders in the local programmes and the local authorities. In particular, it was critically important to forge good relationships with programme managers, as it was these individuals who played a central role in determining the success of the implementation team in getting questionnaires answered and face-to-face interviews set up.

Transcending organisational and professional boundaries

As explained in Chapter One, the original vision of SSLPs reflected the emphasis placed on multi-agency or interagency working in the

UK over the past two decades (for example, DH, 1997, 2001; Cabinet Office, 1999; DfES, 2004). Despite extensive empirical work on such in a range of settings (Wilson and Pirrie, 2000; Cameron and Lart, 2003; Atkinson et al, 2005), little of it has concerned outcomes for children (Glisson and Hemmelgarn, 1998). Data collected by the implementation module adds to this knowledge base by providing an overview of the experiences of SSLPs in the construction of working partnerships to deliver services for children and families, identifying a number of factors that facilitated or undermined joined-up working.

Research on joined-up working highlights three sets of challenges faced in realising this ambition (Cameron and Lart, 2003, p 9). *Organisational challenges* include clarity of aims and objectives; differences in organisational processes and clearly defined roles and responsibilities; equal levels of strategic commitment; and good communication resources. *Cultural and professional obstacles* include negative professional stereotyping; lack of trust and respect among partner agencies; and diverse professional philosophies or ideologies. *Contextual barriers* can involve varying geographical areas of responsibility; and financial uncertainty (Frost, 2005). The NESS implementation examined all of these in its effort to understand how SSLPs were trying to enhance interagency collaboration. Five factors, each discussed in turn, emerged as crucial to their subsequent success – or lack thereof: (1) partnership history; (2) clarity of purpose; (3) degree of strategic commitment at the highest levels; (4) trust among partners; and (5) characteristics of the national workforce.

Partnership history

Pre-existing good interagency relationships proved important to achieving success in establishing the partnerships envisaged in the government guidance to SSLPs. However, while some SSLPs had inherited well-functioning local linkages, others had not. Where there were few previously established – and well-functioning – interagency links, the most important compensatory factor turned out to be having the right programme manager, discovered to be one who would make *sustained high-profile* efforts to overcome partner indifference. Such proactive networking could balance even a 'lean' inheritance of services by alerting staff to the urgency of the task of building better partnerships and convincing the programme team that the construction of partnerships really was a feasible goal.

Clarity of purpose

Having shared or complementary objectives and targets was perceived to be helpful by many SSLPs, despite being criticised in the wider social policy context (Cutler and Waine, 2000; Tilbury, 2004). But targets could also be a source of tension in partnership boards because they were often seen as *not the right ones, at least for a particular agency involved with the SSLP*. For example, targets for preventive work were not regarded as pertinent to social services as they were to health. When supposedly collaborating agency partners did not share objectives, or at least not with comparable enthusiasm, staff in mainstream services tended to be wary about committing time and effort to work that they did not see as contributing directly to their own organisation's targets. Clarity around *accountability* was also important, especially given that the lead body could be a statutory agency (predominantly the local council, sometimes the primary care trust, PCT), or more rarely, a voluntary agency. When the PCT was the lead, tensions sometimes arose in trying to distinguish – and separate – narrower PCT objectives from wider SSLP ones.

Sure Start Local Partnerships sought to overcome these tensions by fostering a sense of shared purpose. They held Open Days, for example, to enable different agencies to meet their respective targets. Thus, local further education colleges could fill training places; the Early Years Development and Childcare Partnership (EYDCP) could recruit parents onto training courses such as those for childcare jobs; and local employers could make contact with potential employees among the community, all in pursuit of the SSLP goal of reducing the number of children living in workless households.

Strategic-level commitment

The key factor in developing good relationships among agencies proved to be a strategic commitment at the most senior level of each partner organisation. Local authority chief executives, for example, could positively influence the profile of SSLPs and increase the morale of programme staff. There was, however, great awareness of the difficulty of working in partnership with all agencies and sectors. In the end, failure to establish visible high-level commitment had a corrosive effect on already tense relationships.

Nevertheless, the broad picture was one of enthusiasm at most levels of the programme, but this depended to a great extent on the programme manager. They needed to address, on an ongoing basis, the tension between the bureaucratic burden of managing resources – including money, staff and time – and their strategic programme responsibilities for partnership building. When partnership members got 'bogged down' in the management of resources, this tended to sap morale, leading ultimately to the withdrawal of some agencies and a reduction in parent participation.

Trust among partners

Three perceived 'status-inequality issues' affected the development of trust within programmes. First, relationships with health agencies were often cited as problematic given the structure of health trusts; the high status of many health professionals; and the perceived inappropriateness of the 'medical model' for a preventative programme such as the SSLP. Second, problems arose when SSLP partnerships were disproportionately weighted – or seen to be – towards the lead partner. Finally, tensions arose when a single agency was viewed as securing too many resources.

The existence of trust was crucial to the task of information sharing. But establishing trust was often difficult because staff trained in different professions operated according to varying codes of practice, including procedures for protecting client confidentiality. Referrals between agencies proved to be a particular source of tension, in part because the concept of referral meant different things to different professionals. Whereas some programmes succeeded in developing a shared referral system for service providers, this remained a 'work in progress' for others, requiring ever-continuing negotiations. The matter was only complicated by unresolved confusions in this area of national policy (Cleaver et al, 2004). Also making information sharing challenging was the absence of appropriate hardware and software for clear and consistent record keeping.

Characteristics of the national workforce

Workforce issues exerted a major influence on partnership building. Three issues were particularly important, having to do with recruitment and retention of staff, the secondment of staff from one agency to another and the achievement of the 'right mix' of staff and skills.

As a result of an often very small pool of qualified professionals in the local area, SSLPs often competed with each other, with mainstream agencies and with other national government initiatives, for staff. The nature of employment contracts often did not facilitate the smooth running of SSLPs either, as short-term attachments sometimes led to good staff leaving in search of better salaries and employment conditions. This created a vicious circle of higher workloads for remaining staff, leading to lower job satisfaction and higher turnover rates. A common SSLP response was to recruit staff from a variety of backgrounds, including parents and other community members, train them to work as befrienders and in crèches and drop-ins, while ensuring that they were managed by a professional staff member. In these cases, care had to be taken not to exacerbate underlying tensions among professional staff who, understandably, saw themselves as having considerable and specific expertise.

The temporary transfer of an employee from one agency to another – secondment – often proved to be a mixed blessing. This system had clear advantages for bringing in a variety of professionals with existing skills and experience while simultaneously providing job security for seconded staff. Having staff from mainstream services working in the SSLP produced the additional bonus of readymade links with mainstream agencies, links that often enhanced levels of confidence in the SSLP when agencies saw their own staff working there. Staff viewed secondment as good for their own career development, enabling them to return to their home agencies with new skills. Issues such as pay, grading and conditions of employment often had to be dealt with, however, in order to prevent – or deal with – tensions arising from different conditions and terms of employment across agencies.

The task of getting skills right was complicated by workforce shortages and finite finances. To enhance the skill mix under these conditions, SSLPs developed their own workers, employed expensive specialists only when they were absolutely essential, and looked beyond the immediate community to recruit staff. This was proved particularly useful when it came to obtaining specific cultural and ethnic expertise.

The three issues considered provide insight into some of the implementation challenges involved in facilitating collaborative working relationships among agencies in the small geographical areas served by SSLPs. However complex the task and however much the task was made more difficult due to national issues such as workforce deficits, compensatory strategies often proved effective when sufficient enthusiasm for the SSLP mission was evident. Thus, even though a history of limited interagency working could not be rewritten and proved an impediment to successful realisation of the SSLP mission, committed programme managers made a positive difference when it came to local working relationships.

The continuum of access

Facilitating access to services is a longstanding theme in policy literature, and a universal challenge for policy makers and practitioners who are responsible for designing and delivering services for children and families in the community (Philo et al, 1995; Kempson and Whyley, 1999; Sanderson, 2002). Services can only foster positive outcomes if they are actually *used* (Statham, 1994). The government Sure Start Unit (SSU) sharpened the focus on access in each new edition of SSLP guidance. Indeed, the first principle of SSLPs, as highlighted on the Sure Start website, stipulated that 'every family should get access to a range of services that will deliver better outcomes for both children and parents, meeting their needs and stretching their aspirations' (DfES, 2005a).

Programmes faced well-established challenges in facilitating access to services and the actual figures for 'reach' remained disappointing (see Garbers et al, 2006). Insight into the process of facilitating reach came from parental accounts of their experience with their local programme and staff descriptions of strategies for making contact with families. Analysis of these data revealed 'a continuum of access' regarding how programmes sought to reach out to families and diverse 'parental styles of service use'.

The *continuum of access* highlights five steps in linking families with SSLP services that programmes seemed to use, to greater or lesser extent, although families could enter this sequence at other than the first point and not pass through all points:

(1) making initial contact with a parent;
(2) introducing a family to the service;
(3) facilitating the autonomous take-up of at least one SSLP service;
(4) facilitating autonomous take-up of more than one service; and
(5) facilitating the autonomous take-up of services other than those provided by the SSLP.

Important to appreciate is that reaching parents was rarely a one-off event.

No matter how imaginative and extensive the range of services offered by an SSLP, not all parents wanted to engage with them in an identical fashion. Indeed, three *parental styles of service use* were identified. *Autonomous* parents were those who, upon learning about their local programme from another parent or a leaflet through their letterbox, visited the programme of their own accord. *Facilitated* parents might have been reluctant to do so for a variety of reasons (for example due to cultural/language barriers, having the status of lone/teen parent or mental/physical illness), including previous negative encounters with a service. Such parents needed encouragement to use an SSLP service and this was facilitated, for example, by a programme advocate or 'befriender' or through the provision of assistance (for example, crèche facilities, transport and interpreters). Finally, *conditional* parents were those for whom any of these forms of encouragement proved inadequate. This might be due to their own personal circumstances, including physical illness, depression, agoraphobia or negative experiences such as racist abuse in the local area. In addition, religious/cultural norms could preclude a woman from leaving her house alone. Such parents only used SSLP services on very specific conditions set by themselves. Their needs were most likely to be met through a targeted outreach strategy.

Two examples of activity subsumed within the five-point continuum of access are provided below, taking into account the range of parental styles of service use (the full continuum and its implications are described in Garbers et al, 2006).

Making initial contact

Contact between a local programme and a family occurred in a variety of ways, including consultation; outreach activity; highly visible centre-based and drop-in venues; and an effort focused specifically on special groups of potential clients (for example, asylum seekers, depressed mothers). The task of consultation could involve leafleting campaigns; face-to-face outreach work; and community events organised to build relationships with the community and ascertain their needs about the services they wanted.

Outreach emerged as a key strategy for taking both programme promotion and services themselves out into the community. This often served its intended purposes of attracting parents who were not aware of the programme. Health visitors and midwives were key players in this effort, ones who not only identified families with new babies, but who promoted relevant services and signed up families for 'membership.' Door-knocking campaigns serving the same ends often involved a programme's entire staff.

Alongside these proactive outreach strategies, multi-purpose SSLP centres and more limited 'shop-front' offices constituted an important route by which families were identified. Parents were encouraged to use them as meeting places and an information point, especially when they included a community café or were located near other amenities.

These more or less 'standard' approaches were not enough to ensure contact with some especially hard-to-reach families, including those with drug/alcohol problems, problems with domestic violence or having special medical needs (for example, disabled child, depressed mother), to name but a few examples. Reaching these families was facilitated best when SSLPs had a worker designated as specifically responsible for establishing contact with the hard-to-reach group in question. Such targeted outreach might be undertaken by a bilingual key worker, a male staff member engaging fathers (Lloyd et al, 2003) or a worker with specific knowledge of asylum seekers. Holding community events targeted at particular groups also proved useful in attracting community members with particular needs.

Introducing parents to a 'service'

Ensuring that parents and children *want* to attend a service is a key component of a community-based open-access policy (Statham, 1994). As well as feeling comfortable about using services, they needed to have confidence in the professionals providing them. SSLPs had to spend time gaining and maintaining parental trust; and acknowledge the complex relationship between the perceived benefits of professional expertise and status on the one hand, and experiencing a friendly way of working, on the other.

Often parents were introduced to a particular service in order to facilitate their engagement of the programme more generally. For example, some SSLPs provided a free session of day care as a 'taster' to highlight their friendly atmosphere and high-quality facilities.

Always crucial to families was the question of service relevance. For parents to take up services, services had to be the right ones. The 'menu' of services across SSLPs addressed a range of different issues and developmental stages for children. (For a full account of the range of services in SSLPs, see Allnock et al, [2005].) To 'get the services right' SSLPs adopted strategies such as questionnaires to parents; informal chats and anonymous 'drop boxes' with parents; and parent forums and panels designed to provide the chance for parents to voice their views. A few programmes even set up 'parental commissioning panels' where parents themselves were in charge of commissioning new services. Where there was parental interest in a specific service but there were not sufficient means to run the service in question, SSLPs looked to alternative funding streams.

These examples illuminate the variety of strategies used to facilitate access to SSLP services, while illuminating different styles of parental engagement of services. In so doing they highlight the variety of ways in which programmes operated. Issues around the detailed design of services are explored in the next section.

A new approach to service delivery for children and parents

Sure Start Local Programmes were required to deliver services in new and innovative ways in order to maximise child well-being – 'putting the child at the centre of services' – while at the same time supporting the family. They did so against a backdrop of longstanding and unresolved tensions that bedevilled community-based services for children and families. These included the issues of selectivity versus universality; local versus central determination of need; needs and rights of children versus those of parents; and evidence-based versus entitlement-based services (Tunstill, 2000). Sure Start Local Programme services were required to be (1) high quality (for example, increased training, new equipment, attractive buildings and so on); (2) responsive (for example, consulting parents, striving to meet the needs of minority groups, overcoming cultural and language barriers and so on); (3) flexible (for example, out-of-hours services, sessional provision, delivered in people's own homes and so on); and (4) proactive (that is, not waiting for parents to approach the programme).

The NESS implementation team discovered that programmes sought to achieve a balance – or series of balances – when planning services. This resulted in the development both of new services and new ways of delivering existing services. The following three examples highlight the balancing required between individual need and parental preference: (1) outreach and centre-based provision; (2) group versus individual service provision; and (3) childcare provision.

Outreach and centre-based provision

A key task for programmes was to maintain a balance between outreach and centre-based provision. The quality and quantity of *outreach* was frequently an indicator of wider programme quality, responsiveness, flexibility and proactivity. Outreach was central to the SSLP mission and could be seen as (a) a service in its own right, (b) a method of delivering other services or (c) a means of facilitating and encouraging access to services delivered elsewhere. Sure Start Local Programme outreach work encompassed five, sometimes overlapping, activities:

(1) raising awareness of SSLP services;
(2) befriending parents/carers and introducing them to the programme;
(3) exploiting existing networks (for example, health visiting services);
(4) providing a gateway to other services; and
(5) delivering outreach provision of specialist services.

Outreach and home visiting services were sometimes universal, sometimes targeted; they were sometimes regular, sometimes occasional. They involved, depending on the programme and the service, visits by the same or different people.

Outreach work co-existed with centre-based service provision. Sure Start Local Programme premises comprised a variety of configurations, including single buildings and multi-venue sites. Over time, SSLPs endeavoured to have one 'flagship' building, often referred to as the 'Sure Start Centre'. This building was intended to focus community interest and engagement with the SSLP, by signifying to the local community that the SSLP was 'here to stay'. Centres also symbolised the multi-agency aspect of the programme, because they often were central to (physically) joined-up working, providing easy access to a range of services (see Chapter Six; Ball and Niven, 2005; Tunstill et al, 2005c).

Group versus individual service provision

Group-based services were often helpful in building relationships among parents and reducing the isolation often experienced by parents of young children. They served a range of other functions, including learning opportunities related to parenting skills as part of a more general 'parenting support' package; 'confidence building', to help parents embark on local training or job opportunities; and skills development (that is, basic skills, English for Speakers of Other Languages [ESOL], information technology, CV writing and interviewing) (Meadows and Garbers, 2004).

Group provision was not the right approach for everyone. Some types of provision were best delivered on a one-to-one basis, as in the case of intensive support and work with parents requiring extra encouragement to take up services initially. Such parents typically were intimidated by the prospect of joining a group. Their anxiety could be compounded by other circumstances such as having a problem about which they were self-conscious and reluctant to discuss in a group (for example substance abuse). There were also cultural issues that meant that one-to-one provision was more attractive than group activities (for example post-natal depression) (Kurtz et al, 2005). Where English was not the parent's first language, one-to-one provision was often the most appropriate, and in these cases, programmes used interpreters and translation services.

High-quality, accessible childcare

Access to high-quality childcare was central to the government's 10-year childcare strategy (HM Treasury, 2004) and the experiences of SSLPs anticipated many of the challenges still evident in early 2007 when this chapter was written: quality, diversity and affordability of provision; relevance to local needs in terms of relationships with local employment opportunities; the enhancement of interagency working (for example, childminders and social services departments); the delivery of culturally appropriate services; and accessibility to parents in terms of information, publicity and entry to services.

Good-quality childcare provision serves multiple functions (Brannen and Moss, 2003; Melhuish, 2004). In addition to the obvious benefit for children, day care can be an important source of support for parents in employment, training or in need of respite. Childcare can remove a key barrier for parents who wish to join the labour market.

Despite these potential benefits to children and their parents, the provision by SSLPs of formal childcare for working parents was low (Early Years Study 2004: Anning et al, 2005; Employability Study 2004: Meadows and Garbers, 2004; National Survey, 2002-2004: Tunstill et al, 2005a; see also Chapter Ten). There were a number of contributing factors to this. Some SSLPs co-existed with the Neighbourhood Nursery Initiative so this other area-based initiative was regarded as having responsibility in this area of service delivery (National Survey, 2002-2004: Tunstill et al, 2005a). But low levels of provision in many SSLP areas also reflected low demand from parents, who were reluctant to use non-family members for childcare. Crucially, childcare for children under school age is expensive, even with the childcare element of the Working Tax Credit, and parents who consulted benefits advisors often found that they were not any better off financially in work after paying their residual childcare costs (Meadows and Garbers, 2004).

Less formal childcare provision could, however, play a vital role in enabling parents to engage in group-based activities and training courses both in SSLP venues and outside (for example local colleges) by providing crèche facilities for parents. Many SSLPs improved crèche provision by increasing the staff in crèches; improved quality by providing additional training for crèche staff; increased the availability of crèche sessions during the week and at weekends; and improved linkages with other agencies by encouraging them to use the crèche also (see Chapter Ten).

This section provided insight into approaches SSLPs adopted to (re)configure services. For most programmes, outreach remained a challenge. But SSLPs were in the fortunate position of having substantial funds available to support service development, even if this could not overcome structural factors such as workforce shortages. In most communities, they succeeded in developing a new service menu and laying the foundations for the new Children's Centres (DfES, 2005b).

Conclusions

This chapter has painted a picture of the implementation of the first 260 SSLPs over a five-year period from 1999 to 2004. It has explored some of the strategic processes involved in implementing this major new initiative in serving disadvantaged children, families and communities and has identified some of the supports and obstacles that SSLPs confronted. For those staff in local authorities with the task of implementing the *Every child matters* agenda (DfES, 2003) and the establishment of Children's Centres, there are some lessons to be learned from the experience of SSLPs. The information presented on the process and experience of SSLP implementation is relevant to some key tasks that in the future face policy makers and practitioners seeking to cross existing professional, organisational and indeed conceptual boundaries.

References

Allnock, D., Tunstill, J. and Akhurst, S. (2006) 'Constructing and sustaining Sure Start Local Partnerships: lessons for future inter-agency collaborations', *Journal of Children's Services*, vol, pp 7–29.

Allnock, D., Tunstill, J., Akhurst, S. and Garbers, C. (2005) *Implementing Sure Start local programmes: An in-depth study. Part II: A close-up on services*, Sure Start Report 7, Part 2, Nottingham: DfES, www.surestart.gov.uk/_doc/P0001451.pdf

Anning, A., Chesworth, E., Spurling, L. and Partinoudi, K.D. (2005) *The quality of early learning, play and childcare services in Sure Start Local Programmes*, Sure Start Report 9, Nottingham: DfES, www.dfes.gov.uk/research/data/uploadfiles/NESS2005FR009.pdf

Atkinson, M., Doherty, P. and Kinder, K. (2005) 'Multi-agency working: models, challenges and key factors for success', *Journal of Early Childhood Research*, vol 3, no 1, pp 7-17.

Ball, M. and Niven, L. (2005) *Buildings in Sure Start Local Programmes*, Sure Start Report 11, Nottingham: DfES, www.surestart.gov.uk/_doc/P0001727.pdf

Brannen, J. and Moss, P. (eds) (2003) *Rethinking children's care*, Buckingham: Open University Press.

Cabinet Office (1999) *Modernising government*, London: The Stationery Office.

Cameron, A. and Lart, R. (2003) 'Factors promoting and obstacles hindering joint working: a systematic review of the research evidence', *Journal of Integrated Care*, vol 11, pp 9-16.

Cleaver, H., Barnes, D., Bliss, D. and Cleaver, D. (2004) *Developing identification, referral and tracking systems: an evaluation of the processes undertaken by trailblazer authorities*, London: DfES.

Cutler, T. and Waine, B. (2000) 'Managerialism reformed? New Labour and public sector management', *Social Policy Administration*, vol 34, pp 318-32.

DfES (Department for Education and Skills) (2003) *Every child matters: Change for children*, London: HMSO.

DfES (2004) *Every child matters: Next steps*, London: DfES.

DfES (2005a) *Sure Start: Our principles*, www.surestart.gov.uk/aboutsurestart/about/thesurestartprinciples2/

DfES (2005b) *Sure Start Children's Centres: Practice guidance*, www.surestart.gov.uk/_doc/P0001859.pdf

DH (Department of Health) (1997) *The new NHS: Modern, dependable*, London: HMSO.

DH (2001) *Valuing people*, White Paper, London: The Stationery Office.

Frost, N. (2005) *Joined-up working with children and families on the front line*, Totnes: Dartington Hall.

Garbers, C., Tunstill, J., Allnock, D. and Akhurst, S. (2006) 'Facilitating access to services for children and families: lessons from Sure Start Local Programmes', *Child and Family Social Work*, vol 11, pp 287-384.

Ghate, D. (2001) 'Family violence and violence against children: a research review', *Children and Society*, vol 14, no 5, pp 395-403.

Glass, N. (2006) 'Sure Start: where did it come from; where is it going?', *Journal of Children's Services*, vol 1, pp 51-7.

Glisson, C. and Hemmelgarn, A. (1998) 'The effects of organisational climate and interorganisational coordination on the quality and outcomes of children's service system', *Child Abuse and Neglect*, vol 22, issue 5, pp 401-21.

HM Treasury (2004) *Choice for parents, the best start for children: A ten year strategy for childcare*, London: HMSO.

Jack, G. (2006) 'The area and community components of children's well-being', *Children and Society*, vol 20, pp 334-45.

Kempson, E. and Whyley, C. (1999) *Kept out or opted out? Understanding and combating financial exclusion*, Bristol: The Policy Press.

King. J., Morris, L. and Fitz-Gibbon, C. (1987) *How to assess program implementation*, Newbury Park, CA: Sage Publications.

Kurtz, Z., McLeish, J., Arora, A., Ball, M. and NESS Implementation Study Team (2005) *Maternity service provision in Sure Start Local Programmes*, Sure Start Report 12, Nottingham: DfES, www.dfes.gov.uk/research/data/uploadfiles/NESS2005FR012.pdf

Lloyd, N., O'Brian, M. and Lewis, C. (2003) *Fathers in Sure Start*, Sure Start Report 4, Nottingham: DfES, www.surestart.gov.uk/_doc/P0001408.pdf

Meadows, P. and Garbers, C. (2004) *Sure Start Local Programmes and improving the employability of parents*, Sure Start Report 6, Nottingham: DfES, www.surestart.gov.uk/_doc/P0001088.pdf

Melhuish, E. (2004) *Child benefits: The importance of investing in quality childcare. Daycare Trust's Facing the Future Policy Paper No 9*, London: Daycare Trust.

Patton, M. (1990) *Qualitative evaluation and research methods*, Newbury Park, CA: Sage Publications.

Philo, C., McCormick, J. and Child Poverty Action Group (1995) '"Poor places" and beyond: summary findings and policy implications', in C. Philo (ed) *Off the map: The social geography of poverty in the UK*, London: Child Poverty Action Group.

Plewis, I. and Mason, P. (2005) 'What works and why: combining quantitative and qualitative approaches in large-scale evaluations', *International Journal of Social Research Methodology*, vol 8, pp 185-94.

Sanderson, I. (2002) 'Access to services', in J. Percy-Smith (ed) *Policy responses to social exclusion: Towards inclusion?*, Maidenhead: Open University Press, pp 130-48.

Schweinhart, L.J., Barnes, H. and Weikart, D. (1993) *Significant benefits: The High/Scope Perry Preschool Study through age 27*, Ypsilanti, MI: High/Scope Press.

Statham, J. (1994) *Childcare in the community: The provision of open access services for young children in family centres*, London: Save the Children.

Tilbury, C. (2004) 'The influence of performance measurement on child welfare policy and practice', *British Journal of Social Work*, vol 34, pp 225-41.

Tunstill, J. (ed) (2000) *Children and the state: Whose problem?*, London: Cassell.

Tunstill, J. (2003) 'Political and technical issues facing evaluators of family support', in I. Katz and J. Pinkerton (eds) *Evaluating family support; thinking internationally, thinking critically*, Chichester: Wiley, pp 25-45.

Tunstill, J., Meadows, P., Allnock, D., Akhurst, S. and Garbers, C. (2005a) *Implementing Sure Start Local Programmes: An integrated overview of the first four years*, Sure Start Report 10, Nottingham: DfES, www.surestart. gov.uk/_doc/P0001866.pdf

Tunstill, J., Allnock, D., Akhurst, S. and Garbers, C. (2005b) 'Sure Start Local Programmes: implications of case study data from the National Evaluation of Sure Start', *Children and Society*, vol 19, pp 1-14.

Tunstill, J., Meadows, P., Allnock, D., Akhurst, S. and Garbers, C. (2005c) *Implementing Sure Start Local Programmes: An in-depth study*, Sure Start Report 7, Part 1, Nottingham: DfES, www.surestart.gov.uk/_doc/ P0001450.pdf

Wilson, V. and Pirrie, A. (2000) *Multidisciplinary teamworking: Indicators of good practice*, Edinburgh: SCRE.

SIX

Living with Sure Start: human experience of an early intervention programme

Angela Anning and Mog Ball

Policy context

The introduction of Sure Start Local Programmes (SSLPs) in 1999 presented a significant shift in the way family life with very young children was regarded by central government in the UK. Hitherto this had been largely a private space in which intervention was not a normal occurrence unless some crisis of health, child protection or family failure had occurred. The SSLP approach, however, was to be universal, proactive and preventative, to change the way service providers and others worked with families and the way parents in deprived communities reared young children.

The intervention also reflected a general shift in conceptual models underpinning policy reforms in the US and UK. An ecological approach to understanding child, parent, family and community functioning had been influential. For example, Bronfenbrenner's (1979; Bronfenbrenner and Ceci, 1994) model of *child* development emphasised the historical/cultural influences on children's experiences of services and the psychological and structural factors shaping their *parents'* experiences. Belsky and Vondra (1989, p 157) described these influences and factors as:

> multiple pathways by which individual (parental personality or child characteristic), historical (parental development history) and social (marital satisfaction and social network support) as well as circumstantial factors (poverty, job dissatisfaction, ignorance about child development) combine to shape parental functioning.

At the *community* level, parenting, particularly of the first child, is regarded as a time of acknowledgement of position in the community. For young parents, producing children ensures the future of the community, and is highly valued (Benedict et al, 1989). Investment in the health and well-being of young children, particularly those seen as likely to be 'expensive' to the state, not only improves the child's life chances, but contributes to social regeneration. It may arrest the chain of adverse effects between poverty/social exclusion and poor life chances. Thus, SSLPs were to initiate a process that would gather momentum to improve the trajectories of whole communities in the long term (Oliver and Smith, 2000).

No reference was made to Sure Start in the 1997 Labour Party Manifesto. The initiative came direct from the Treasury and was unlike public policy generated in response to the demands of the electorate (see Chapter One). Moreover, the parents who were targeted were under no obligation – and might feel no need – to participate in any services offered. But the preventative approach did not come completely out of the blue. New Labour ideology acknowledged the interconnectedness of social and economic problems and the need to reflect this in reforming the workforce into more 'joined-up' approaches to delivering children's services (Blair, 1998).

What was new was the government's endorsement of the devolution of decision making about services to the front line in order to promote diversity and local creativity. In this sense SSLPs were a reflection of the general government imperative to modernise public services (DETR, 1999). Agents responsible for delivering them had been relentlessly criticised by the media for a decade. Notable examples included high-profile cases of failures in child protection systems, accusations of low standards in schools, and reports of the misuse of deceased children's body parts without parental consent for medical research. In 2002 Alan Milburn, then Secretary of State for Health, observed in a speech to the National Social Services Conference at Cardiff that the 'old style public service monoliths cannot meet modern challenges. They need to be broken up. In their place we can forge new partnerships that specialise in tackling particular problems local communities face'.

Some local authorities had robust histories of attempting to help families to avoid crises, and there was considerable experience of early intervention among voluntary organisations working within the field of family welfare. For example, the family centre model, involving a range agencies working collaboratively and delivering services to local families, had an established track record (Smith, 1996). Thus, the change in the day-to-day experiences of service reforms experienced by the providers and users of services with the arrival of SSLPs varied in intensity depending on the histories of institutions, workforces and services in any area.

Themed studies

The complex and varied nature of SSLP interventions reflected this multifactorial approach to early intervention. In response, the research design of the National Evaluation of Sure Start (NESS) was itself necessarily complex and multilayered. As part of the study of implementation (see Chapter Five), a series of qualitative *themed studies* were planned to provide snapshots in time of how SSLPs were operating and to explore critical issues.

Evidence in large-scale evaluations is sometimes, if not often, weighted against effectiveness evaluations provided by service users. Among other things, the themed studies served to provide important insights into the perspectives of key stakeholders (providers and users of services) within the SSLPs and offered a window on 'multiple pathways' (Belsky and Vondra, 1989) and day-to-day realities of the activities and interactions that were at the heart of SSLPs. The focus in this chapter then is on the *human experience* of local programme interventions, drawing on the qualitative evidence amassed in the course of conducting the themed studies.

The remainder of this chapter takes as its starting point the extensive changes experienced by providers and users of SSLP services in order to explore the *human experience* of SSLP interventions. These changes were evident in the amount of resources available for the delivery of services and provision of support for families; in the spaces where support and services were delivered; in the time and manner of their delivery; and in changes in conditions and expectations of the workforce. In what follows, each domain of change is considered in turn, drawing on the findings of diverse, content-specific themed studies. Full details of the studies can be found at <www.surestart.gov.uk> and they are referenced at the end of this chapter.

Overall, the evidence gathered in conducting these studies indicated that changes experienced by providers and users of services were mainly experienced as positive. Nevertheless, many professionals were unable to step outside their comfort zones to embrace radical changes in the way services were delivered and, in consequence, many services provided by SSLPs failed to reach many of the families for whom they were intended. These points are developed further in this chapter before drawing conclusions about fundamental flaws in the implementation of the programme.

Resources

By tradition, services for young children in the UK were seen as Cinderella services – undervalued and underfunded (Pugh, 2001). This reflected the longstanding unequal distribution of power, status and capital with respect to 'female' sectors of work; in this case those charged with responsibility for the education, care, health and well-being of young children and their parents. A good deal of energy had to be expended in lobbying local authorities, or raising funds as charities, in order to initiate or sustain resources for such 'female-related' services or initiatives. But suddenly, with the creation of SSLPs, the resources available were dramatically increased, at least in the case of the small geographic areas designated as local-programme areas. The exact amount of capital and revenue offered to each SSLP varied, but approximately £1 million in revenue a year was available for each programme, with an extra amount for capital expenditure. (For further discussion of costs, see Chapter Seven.)

Central government decreed the boroughs in which programmes would be situated, but 'local people' were supposed to decide on the physical boundaries of SSLP neighbourhoods. In reality, the decisions were made mostly by the local authority, often at chief executive or local political levels. On rare occasions, a 'competition' was instituted and managers of local services, sometimes in partnership with local people, could make the case for a particular neighbourhood being best positioned to deliver an effective programme.

With or without a competitive process, the area selection was often a cause of antipathies. Many working with young children and families felt that they had been without much support for years, but now that resources were flowing from central government, other interested parties were emerging to lay claim to them. One manager interviewed for the themed studies dealing with the quality of early learning, play and childcare reported that: 'Representatives of services and charities only come to the partnership boards when they want a slice of the cake. Then they don't deliver on the Sure Start services they promised us' (Anning et al, 2005, from field notes). Of course, for providers and users of services in locales not designated as SSLP areas, there was resentment about being excluded altogether.

In an attempt to ensure that the resources would reach the people who needed them most, government required that funds be administered by an SSLP partnership board that would include parents. The leaders who emerged from partnerships were those individuals with time and resources to put into developing the plan for the area – and in doing so they acquired a dominant position. Consequently, parents often felt marginalised (Ball, 2002).

Voluntary organisations were constrained in the amount of time they could spend on designing and setting up local programmes, as they had responsibilities to serve children and families in non-SSLP areas. There could also be competition over which of several charities working in an SSLP area should represent the 'voluntary sector' of the partnership board. In these struggles it was often small local groups – running simple, participatory parent and toddler and play opportunities – that got left behind.

Evidence from the themed studies showed that the nature of the partnership, and the relationship between the people on it, were the most important factors in getting the SSLPs planned and operational. Progress was fastest in local areas where members contributed materially to the design and development of the programme; where health trusts made their child health data available (see Chapter Nine); where education departments seconded staff; and where voluntary organisations sent staff to meetings accompanied by a parent who, thus supported, was able to contribute to the discussion. In other words, what made the process work was the willingness of partners to contribute to it.

The way resources were deployed soon established the profile of an SSLP in the area. Used to generate interest and family engagement in the programme were SSLP buildings, play buses and play areas, as well as notices of SSLP activities, together with SSLP events led by SSLP staff, sometimes in distinctive, 'branded' clothing, often with balloons, pens and welcome packs in SSLP colours to distribute. As one mother said, 'Everyone knows the Sure Start staff around here; you see them everywhere – when you're doing the shopping and just round and about. It makes a real difference' (Anning et al, 2005, p 105). Those who attended SSLP activities saw all these 'gifts', including the attention given to them and their children by the SSLP staff, as affirming their role as parents, while giving them recognition and status. Parents were attracted by activities that attracted their children – almost always the reason given for responding to an SSLP event – and resources made the events more inviting, including good-quality play equipment, food and entertainment (Anning et al, 2005).

From the outset, however, many parents raised questions about the focus of so many resources on young children only. They wondered why their older children, especially teenagers, did not receive the same attention. They queried why friends and families in adjacent neighbourhoods were excluded from these 'gifts'. Similar questions were raised by practitioners.

Parents also saw the benefits of practical experience in dealing with young children modelled by the SSLP practitioners; as one mother observed: 'No matter how much of a good parent you are, you look at someone else and how they do things and you think, "Oh, that's a good idea"'(Anning et al, 2005, p 119). Some users described how SSLPs had 'rescued' them from depression and family crises. Consider the testimony of one mother:

> After I had my first child I was very depressed. I thought I was going crazy, and I didn't know about any services. I didn't find out about Sure Start. They found me. I was splitting up with my husband. I was pregnant with my second child. I didn't have any friends or family. I was in a world of my own. I remember I was sitting at home, sitting around the sink half the day peeling vegetables and half the day wiping my son's bum, ironing my husband's shirts. Then the Sure Start worker came. She told me about their services. She was very pleasant. From that day the world changed for me. (Kurtz et al, 2005, p 72)

Parents with children with additional needs and disabilities were the most positive in their response. The mother of an 18-month-old with developmental delay was quickly linked with speech and language services and occupational therapy. As she appreciatively noted:

> Their help has been overwhelming. When children are different one doesn't know sometimes what is available and beneficial for a child. I'd never have found out about free nappies or sponsorship for a nursery place without the Centre staff. (Anning et al, 2007, p 82)

Clearly, for many parents living in SSLP areas, as well as for service providers and other stakeholders, the resources that became available with the onset of SSLP were unprecedented in scale. Personal experiences reported here attest to the immediate benefits these resources provided *to those parents who took advantage of them*. But as is made clear below, this was by no means broadly the case.

Changes experienced by the workforce

The reconfiguration of services central to the vision of SSLPs had implications for a wide range of workers, including day-care staff, playworkers, social workers, health visitors, midwives, family support workers and specialists such as speech and language therapists. Notably, however, there was no training to prepare them for the scale of changes they would experience. In large measure this was because the management required to coordinate and deliver the varied components of a programme had no precedent in the early years field. In consequence, local managers often were drawn from related specialist fields, such as family centres, day nurseries or health services, but few had project management experience on the scale that was required for managing as diverse and multifaceted an effort as an SSLP.

The actual providers of services had to face changes, including changes in line management, professional relationships, work location and partnerships with para-professionals, volunteers and parents. The expectation was that this previously low-paid and low-status workforce would be the engine of reform. Service providers assumed this responsibility out of enthusiasm and commitment to the idea of improving the life chances of disadvantaged children, but the assumption that the workforce could use the newly available resources effectively without extensive retraining might be seen in retrospect as naive.

Practitioners saw some changes as positive. Some enjoyed networking with other service providers and meeting new professionals. In the past staff such as family support workers and health visitors functioned as 'gatekeepers' to specialised services like speech and occupational therapy. They felt constrained from recommending such help for a small child because nothing suitable was available, or because there were long waiting lists. With the creation of SSLPs – and the resources made available through them – they could refer a client rapidly to specialist provision. Families with children with additional needs were particularly grateful that they could bypass bureaucratic procedures when seeking advice and practical support and could directly access specialist assistance when needed (Pinney, 2007).

But practitioners were sometimes caught between competing imperatives that challenged their professional judgements in the new approach. For example, there was tension between encouraging parents to find work, one SSLP mandate, and to be with their young children. One worker wondered:

> Why do parents have to go to work? It's against what the evidence suggests that up to three years children need to bond with one person. But yet we put our children in day nurseries at six months. It's a contradiction. (Meadows and Garbers, 2004, p 103)

Among the new challenges facing practitioners was the need to get out and market the local programme to families. Not everyone took to the 'selling' role, but some found they had hitherto underused skills. Multi-agency teamwork that involved changes in working roles and responsibilities could be stressful for staff, but they acknowledged that there were benefits for users. A single mother with a history of puerperal psychosis following her two previous births described how the SSLP team mobilised support for her when she was expecting her third child:

> The Sure Start midwife helped me get in touch with the obstetrician. She found out who specialised in depression, so I got the right person. The obstetrician and the Sure Start midwife got together, with the Sure Start family worker, the housing support worker from the housing association, my mental health worker and the head of midwifery. And they set up this thing so everyone was talking to each other and trying to set up a room in the hospital where I could go with the baby if I did get postnatal depression. So I knew all the things that were scaring me were taken care of. (Kurtz et al, 2005, p 71)

Another challenge in some areas was the employment of generic para-professionals. Professionals raised questions about their competence to diagnose and deal with more specialised conditions; about how much training they should be given before being allowed to work with families dealing with complex problems; and about how supervisions could be managed on a regular basis.

The challenges that many workers faced were inherent in the imperative to make many changes quickly in service delivery and in the redeployment of resources. And in all too many cases, it turned out, the time and energy professionals put into managing and effecting change detracted from the time and energy available for actually providing services to children and families.

Space

The visibility of SSLPs in neighbourhoods – and especially the generous resources available to them – increased greatly with the construction of new buildings and the conversion of existing buildings into Sure Start Centres. The first 260 programmes had at least £700,000 and sometimes as much as £1 million capital *in addition to* their non-capital funding. Eight-four per cent of programmes constructed a new building or undertook such a major conversion that it amounted to a new building. Programmes were encouraged to ensure that users could access programmes quickly and cheaply from their homes and that the settings for activities were welcoming.

The planning or construction of a building sometimes served to mobilise the local community. In the early stages, such building plans served to galvanise partnership boards and residents, but in many areas difficulties delayed the building process and led to disappointment. In one southern city a local community had become enthusiastic about converting a disused former public house into SSLP headquarters, but then the local authority refused to back plans already well advanced. Not surprisingly, local people felt bitter when they had to locate *their* centre in a place nobody liked, a disused school (Ball and Niven, 2005).

Pressure from local authorities was common in the case of buildings. Even strong alliances involving SSLP management, staff and parents proved unable to withstand it. Many managers described the capital process as a 'nightmare' (Ball and Niven, 2005). But once a centre was open, SSLP management was easier, not least because offices and services were conveniently located vis-à-vis community access and staff worked in close proximity. As one programme manager observed:

> We've achieved a wonderful level of joined-up working. Relationships between staff are very rich; everyone gives and gets a great deal from one another. Parents share in this – they have richer relationships with staff themselves. The Sure Start building sends a message that we complement and enhance one another. The agencies are not in competition here. (Ball and Niven, 2005, p 27)

Grand though many of the new centres were and pleasing as they were to staff, parents sometimes expressed a preference for older, more familiar spaces. But new buildings were generally not stigmatised, and parents were willing to come to them for help with matters like debt and domestic violence, which they wanted to discuss in confidence. Fundamentally, a centre could be experienced as sociable and collaborative if the building included facilities like a community café, but parents felt disempowered when spaces they anticipated would be for the community were requisitioned by professional staff. Moreover, both male and female users regarded them as feminised spaces, undermining male/father involvement (Lloyd et al, 2003).

Outreach and home visiting were required of all SSLPs, not least because young parents were often isolated, with few local contacts, and lacked confidence. In most programmes these home-based services were seen as the first step in persuading families to participate in SSLP group activities. Home visits provided a way for parents to get to know SSLPs on their own territory, as well as to discuss what help they or their children could use. In fact, often families were suspicious of professional visitors, seeing them as people who had come to tell them what to do. Parents were also anxious about child protection; fearing professionals would remove their children. Some SSLPs used para-professional visitors or trained volunteers in attempts to make home visiting informal. But parents objected to this strategy too, especially in black and minority ethnic communities, feeling that privacy and confidentiality might be breached by visiting members of their community (Williams and Churchill, 2006; Craig, 2007). It was in these communities especially that para-professional support with language or cultural awareness was essential.

Evaluations of successful early intervention programmes have shown that beneficial effects for children typically derive from a structured programme of activities offered in centres and/or the home (Schweinhart and Weikart, 1993; Olds et al, 2002). There was little evidence that what was being delivered during SSLP home visits, however, was informed by a detailed, explicit curriculum (Ball, 2006). Programme staff contended that time was too limited for such efforts and that SSLPs had too wide a mandate, population-wise, to service with intensive home visiting. Parents, too, felt that the demands made by young children prevented them from committing to eight-week parenting courses (Barlow et al, 2007, in press).

The changes in the spaces available in local communities for early years services meant that SSLPs had made these services more accessible and easier to use. This did not mean that families found it easy to make the change to using them, however. For many families established patterns of service use or non-use persisted. New services in new spaces meant developing new habits, and this was not easy.

Time

SSLP partnerships were promised that they would be funded by central government for 10 years. Plans were to taper up to full expenditure in years 1-3 and to taper down in years 8-10. The immediate reaction from those planning children's services was that they would have to pick up the bill at the end of that period. Many sceptics felt vindicated when, in 2004, the announcement was made that SSLPs would be replaced by a more widespread provision with much reduced resources that would be run by local authorities – Children's Centres.

Setting up SSLPs had taken far longer in many areas than anticipated (see Chapter Seven). Programmes building on established early years infrastructure could be fully functioning after three years, but those starting more or less from scratch took longer. Managers had to negotiate complex agreements with services and subcontractors and many felt that they could not get fully underway until their buildings were completed. Many SSLPs had not spent their capital by 2004. Once the transition to Children's Centres was announced, local programmes felt undermined and experienced difficulty persuading staff, already on short-term contracts, to stay. Staff felt demotivated and betrayed; the cohesion of staff teams was threatened; and often their hard-won collective knowledge and expertise were lost (Anning et al, 2007). The latter included understanding of the structural and systemic factors affecting proficient functioning, understanding of local networks and the ability to reference shared experiences with clients.

The new approach to professional working and engaging parents across all professional disciplines and levels placed a premium on openness, accessibility, informality, not being judgemental, and on listening, respecting and learning from parents' own experiences. Such an ethos could influence parents' own relationships with each other, with their children and families, as well as with the community at large. It took a long time to establish this orientation and the sudden reversion to a short-term policy jeopardised these profound developments (Williams and Churchill, 2006).

At the outset, the Sure Start initiative had seemed to offer the luxury of time as well as money to implement a radical change in the way professionals and users interacted. It turned out, however, that as soon as pressure was put on the time available, it was the sensitive, nurturing of family empowerment that tended to wither first.

Use

An intervention is only effective if it is used. As a universal intervention, SSLPs needed a critical mass of parents and children in their areas to make a long-term change to the social fabric. The remit was for programmes to engage all families with children under four in the neighbourhood. In fact, an SSLP judged proficient by NESS (see Chapter Nine) established regular, consistent and growing reach for 100% of all newborns, but only 26-50% of other targeted families. And only a small number of SSLPs achieved even this level of reach.

Proficient programmes continually tried to improve reach. Many programmes, however, relied on core groups of users, often families that attended several services a week. They did not try to attract and retain new users. Such programmes often offered services only during school hours, thus excluding working parents, particularly fathers. This choice was governed by convenience for providers rather than as a response to the realities of modern parenting. Although staff in maternity services reported high levels of job satisfaction, many of them did little to change their traditional modes of service delivery. The format of SSLP clinics was often the same as those offered at set times at general practitioner (GP) surgeries. When asked why they were not reaching families, staff from core services in SSLPs attributed poor attendance to the characteristics of users, citing lack of confidence and cultural or religious barriers rather than the characteristics of their services.

Too many families were left outside the loop of the intervention. Some simply did not want to be involved in activities that in their view replicated support systems they had already. As one parent commented, 'I already have my family around here to help me. I don't need to go to strangers for help' (Anning et al, 2007, p 83). Some were hostile to professionals intervening in their lives: 'I thought it was a bit of a cheek. I've already brought up two kids. I found it, like, interfering' (Anning et al, 2007, p 83). Some thought the services were for needy families and not for them; others that they were for cliques of better-off families and not for them. Those with limited English were daunted by a lack of interpreter support. Others reported that their lives were too busy or chaotic to allow them to attend services.

Parents with problems related to drug or alcohol abuse, mental health, domestic violence or criminality – the very ones whose children are most at risk – were reluctant to be drawn into 'systems'. They were frightened about being on anyone's list. They distrusted professionals, even SSLP ones. They were unwilling, too, to let para-professionals or volunteers into their homes. A great deal of time and sensitive, painstaking work was necessary to break down such barriers and to establish relationships with families manifesting this level of resistance, effort that often proved difficult to initiate when other, less needy, families were knocking on the SSLP door.

Overall, although individuals expressed delight at the impact of SSLP services on their health, parenting and well-being, poor reach figures overall, and particularly for those seen to be in the greatest need for support, inevitably impacted on the disappointing outcomes of this universal intervention programme, at least as detected in the early phase of evaluation (see Chapter Eight).

Conclusion

The SSLP mandate demanded a reconfiguration of the relationship between providers and users of services. This was a radical change and proved very difficult to make. It demanded a complete remodelling of the training and preparation of professional staff. There were not enough appropriately trained personnel available to deliver the major expansion of provision central to this well-intended initiative.

Sure Start Local Programmes were most likely to be effective when they built on pre-existing strengths, especially in locations in which agencies had a history of collaboration and where practice in the early childhood field was already of a high quality. Expectations of what could be achieved in the time available were unrealistic, especially given the historic underfunding and low status of work in this field.

Nevertheless, the SSLP approach appeared effective for families in which children had additional needs and disabilities. The model, based as it was on screening a whole population, diagnosing their needs and targeting families with appropriate 'treatments' did not work equally well with the general population. The poor reach figures demonstrated this better than anything else. But when SSLPs saw families as basically competent, regarding them as respected partners, they were more likely to create an atmosphere of collaborative endeavour to which families were attracted.

The take-home messages of the NESS themed studies highlight the extensive time it took to bring about substantive change in the way service providers worked with families and parents reared their young children. Despite the clarity of these messages, the time available for SSLPs to establish themselves and demonstrate efficacy was unrealistic to begin with and eventually inadequate.

References

Anning, A., Chesworth, E., Spurling, L. and Partinoudi, K.D. (2005) *The quality of early learning, play and childcare services in Sure Start Local Programmes*, Sure Start Report 9, Nottingham: DfES, www.dfes.gov. uk/research/data/uploadfiles/NESS2005FR009.pdf

Anning, A., Goldthorpe, J., Morley, A., Roberts, M. and Stewart J. (2007) *Understanding variations in effectiveness amongst Sure Start Local Programmes: Final Report*, Nottingham: DfES.

Ball, M. (2002) *Getting Sure Start started*, Sure Start Report 2, Nottingham: DfES, www.surestart.gov.uk/_doc/P0000121.pdf

Ball, M. (2006) *Outreach and home visiting services in Sure Start Local Programmes*, Sure Start Report 17, Nottingham: DfES, www.surestart. gov.uk/_doc/P0002376.pdf

Ball, M. and Niven, L. (2005) *Buildings in Sure Start Local Programmes*, Sure Start Report 11, Nottingham: DfES, www.surestart.gov.uk/_ doc/P0001727.pdf

Barlow, J., Stewart-Brown, S., Kirkpatrick, S. and Wood, D. (in press) *Family and parenting support in Sure Start Local Programmes*, Nottingham: DfES.

Belsky, J. and Vondra, J. (1989) 'Lessons from child abuse: the determinants of parenting', in D. Cicchetti and V. Carlson (eds) *Current research and theoretical advances in child maltreatment*, Cambridge, MA: Cambridge University Press, pp 153-202.

Benedict, R., Mead, M. and Bateson, M.C. (1989) *Patterns of culture*, Boston: Houghton Mifflin.

Blair, T. (1998) *The Third Way: New politics for the new century*, London: The Fabian Society.

Bronfenbrenner, U. (1979) *The ecology of human development*, Cambridge, MA: Harvard University Press.

Bronfenbrenner, U. and Ceci, S.J. (1994) 'Nature nurture reconceptualised in developmental perspective: a bioecological model', *Psychological Review*, vol 101, pp 568-86.

Craig, G. (2007) *Sure Start and black and minority ethnic populations*, Nottingham: DfES.

DETR (Department of the Environment, Transport and Regions) (1999) *Modernising local government: Guidance for the Local Government Act 1999, Best Value*, London: DETR.

Kurtz, Z., McLeish, J., Arora, A., Ball, M. and NESS Implementation Study Team (2005) *Maternity service provision in Sure Start Local Programmes*, Sure Start Report 12, Nottingham: DfES, www.dfes.gov. uk/research/data/uploadfiles/NESS2005FR012.pdf

Lloyd, N., O'Brian, M. and Lewis, C. (2003) *Fathers in Sure Start*, Sure Start Report 4, Nottingham: DfES, www.surestart.gov.uk/_doc/ P0001408.pdf

Meadows, P. and Garbers, C. (2004) *Sure Start Local Programmes and improving the employability of parents*, Sure Start Report 6, Nottingham: DfES, www.surestart.gov.uk/_doc/P0001088.pdf

Milburn, A. (2007) 'Reforming social services', Speech to the National Social Services Conference, Cardiff, November.

Olds, D.L., Robinson, J., O'Brien, R., Luckey, D.W., Pettitt, L.M., Henderson, C.R., Ng, R.N., Korfmacher, J., Hiatt, S. and Talmi, A. (2002) 'Home visiting by nurses and by para-professionals: a randomised controlled trial', *Paediatrics*, vol 110, pp 486-96.

Oliver, C. and Smith, M. (2000) *The effectiveness of early interventions*, London: Institute of Education, University of London.

Pinney, A. (2007) *A better start: Sure Start Local Programmes' work with children and families with special needs and disabilities*, Nottingham: DfES.

Pugh, G. (2001) 'A policy for early childhood services', in G. Pugh (ed) *Contemporary issues in the early years: Working collaboratively for children*, London: Paul Chapman Publishing in association with Coram Family, pp 9-24.

Schweinhart, L. and Weikart, D. (1993) *A summary of significant benefits: The High/Scope Perry Pre-School Study through age 27*, Ypsilanti, MI: The High/Scope Press.

Smith, T. (1996) *Family centres and bringing up young children*, London: HMSO.

Williams, F. and Churchill, H. (2006) *Empowerment in Sure Start Local Programmes*, Sure Start Report 18, Nottingham: DfES, www.surestart. gov.uk/_doc/P0002378.pdf

SEVEN

The costs and benefits of Sure Start Local Programmes

Pamela Meadows

The cost-effectiveness evaluation of Sure Start Local Programmes (SSLPs) is integrated with the implementation, impact and local context components of the National Evaluation of Sure Start (NESS) (see Chapters Two, Five and Eight). This chapter discusses the underlying principles of economic evaluation of social interventions, and briefly considers the difference between cost-effectiveness evaluation and cost-benefit analysis. It goes on to describe the relationship between the NESS cost-effectiveness work and related aspects of the evaluation. Included are discussions about which costs should be taken into account in addition to the expenditure of SSLPs themselves and how they might be measured, an overview of the expenditure of SSLPs, as well as factors related to expenditure levels. The chapter concludes by highlighting issues that will need to be considered once the longitudinal impact data become available.

What is economic evaluation?

Resources are almost always scarce and there are generally a number of alternative ways in which scarce resources can be used. If money is spent on one particular activity it cannot be spent on another. This is called the *opportunity cost* by economists because the use of resources in one way represents a missed opportunity to use them another way. Moreover, this alternative use of resources might produce better returns on investment or, in the case of social interventions like SSLPs, outcomes for children, families and communities. Within a market environment, prices act as a mechanism for allocating resources between competing uses, but in the absence of markets, alternative mechanisms need to be applied to ensure that resources for social interventions are allocated to the uses that derive the greatest benefits to society taken as a whole.

Economic evaluations of social interventions address three questions: (1) How much did a particular intervention cost? (2) What did that use of resources actually achieve? (3) Did the benefits from that use of resources exceed the costs? When the answer to the third question is 'yes', a fourth question is posed by those responsible for allocating resources: (4) Would an alternative use of the resources have achieved either a larger number or a higher quality of outcomes?

The systematic recording and comparing of the costs of an intervention with the outcomes achieved provides a valuable analytical framework to guide decision making by those who are responsible for allocating resources, at both a local and a national level (HM Treasury, 2003). The difference between economic evaluation and standard evaluations of process and impact is the stress on the importance of measuring costs as well as activities and benefits.

There are two broad approaches to economic evaluation. They both use the same information about costs, but focus on different outcomes. Generally speaking, cost-*effectiveness* evaluation examines intermediate outcomes over the short term, whereas cost-*benefit* analysis looks at final outcomes and spillover effects over a longer time period. Cost-effectiveness is easier to measure when an intervention is aiming to produce a single outcome that is measurable but difficult if not impossible to translate into monetary values (for example, achieving a particular health status or a reduction in the level of an indicator such as child abuse). It is also particularly useful when there is more than one way of achieving the same outcome so that the costs per measured outcome of the different methods can be compared. This explains the growing importance of cost-effectiveness analysis in the field of healthcare. However, as in the case of SSLPs where interventions have multiple goals and no single goal has clear priority, cost-effectiveness analysis may be much less revealing and cost-benefit analysis much more likely to be important (Gramlich, 1990; Layard and Glaister, 1994; Plotnik and Deppman, 1999; Boardman et al, 2005).

How the economic evaluation relates to the other elements of NESS

The cost-effectiveness evaluation of SSLPs has three separate but interrelated components: (1) analysis of the cost-effectiveness of the implementation, (2) analysis of the cost-effectiveness of the impact on children and families, and (3) cost-benefit analysis of the impact.

Cost-benefit analysis should include all outcomes, both positive and negative, direct, indirect and spillover, anticipated and unanticipated. The experience of evaluating early childhood interventions in the US has shown that unanticipated and spillover effects have produced the majority of the economic benefits (Olds et al, 1993; Barnett, 1996;

Karoly et al, 1998; Olds et al, 1998). Sure Start Local Programmes were likely to include both unanticipated effects and a large number of spillover effects. However, as far as the impact on the children themselves was concerned, the central framework for the economic evaluation of SSLPs was that it should be treated in the same way as education in school: investment takes place over a period of years during childhood and returns emerge once children enter adult life and start earning (Becker, 1993). Within this framework, individuals who invest in their human capital improve their productivity and receive a return in the form of increased probability of being employed and higher earnings in employment. Society as a whole earns a return from the investment in an individual's human capital from the increased overall productive potential of the economy, from the ability of more highly skilled workers to improve the productivity of their less skilled colleagues and from the reduced likelihood that the person with additional human capital will be dependent on out-of-work benefits.

At the time of preparing this chapter, very early 2007, it was not possible to undertake a cost-benefit analysis as the impact evaluation (on which it must rely for data on outcomes for children and families) was still in progress (see Chapter Eight). The emphasis of the evaluation to date has thus been on compiling information about costs and about how resources have been used.

Human capital theory and early childhood interventions

Traditionally, the analysis of the economic impact of the acquisition of human capital has focused on the period after school-leaving age, when taking part in full-time education or various forms of vocational training is a voluntary activity. It is also during this stage that people acquire the kind of qualifications that are known to be valued in the workplace, and are also regularly recorded in surveys, which makes them analytically straightforward. The analysis of the impact of primary education is generally confined to less developed countries where investment in primary schooling has to compete with other demands on scarce resources such as water supplies, basic healthcare or roads. Although economic theory suggests that returns to human capital investment are greater the younger the age at which the investment takes place, it is only recently that economists have begun to recognise that post-16 investments in human capital actually rely on the human capital foundations laid down earlier in childhood, and that without suitable foundations the later investment has very low returns (Heckman, 1998; Heckman and Lochner, 2000).

There are two reasons for focusing on human capital investments in early childhood. First, the earlier the investment takes place the longer the potential payback period and therefore the more likely that cumulative benefits will be positive. Second, later learning builds on the foundations supplied by early learning. If that early learning is not in place, then it is more difficult, if not impossible, to develop higher-level skills after the age of 16 that generate higher returns. Success or failure in the opening years of life may determine whether or not there is a foundation for later learning and, therefore, a person's lifetime earnings potential. Moreover, there is growing recognition that the level and quality of early childhood investments are not solely determined by the inputs from educational institutions, but that the family and community have central roles to play too (Leibowitz, 1974; Becker and Tomes, 1986; Hill and O'Neill, 1994; Haveman and Wolfe, 1995; Feinstein and Symons, 1999; Heckman and Lochner, 2000).

Sure Start Local Programmes should act to boost the human capital of the children in three separate ways: (1) by the direct provision of good-quality play, learning and childcare, (2) by improving the ability of parents to engage with their child's development, and (3) by improving the quality of the neighbourhood and thereby making it less likely that children and young people will be exposed to influences that adversely affect their life chances.

The analytical framework

The underlying conceptual framework for the economic evaluation of SSLPs is shown in Figure 7.1, which conveys that SSLPs do not operate in isolation from the other services for children and families that operate in the area. The main providers are from the statutory sector (that is, health services, particularly general practitioners [GPs] and health visitors), social services, early years education and childcare services, and from voluntary organisations (particularly support activities such as family centres or Home Start). The exact configuration of SSLP services reflected what was in place before the SSLP started. Thus, an SSLP in an area that already had a family centre run by a voluntary organisation would have been unlikely to develop a completely new family centre, and would be more likely to collaborate with the centre to enable it to provide additional or extended services, but an area without such a facility might do so.

Figure 7.1: Economic evaluation conceptual framework

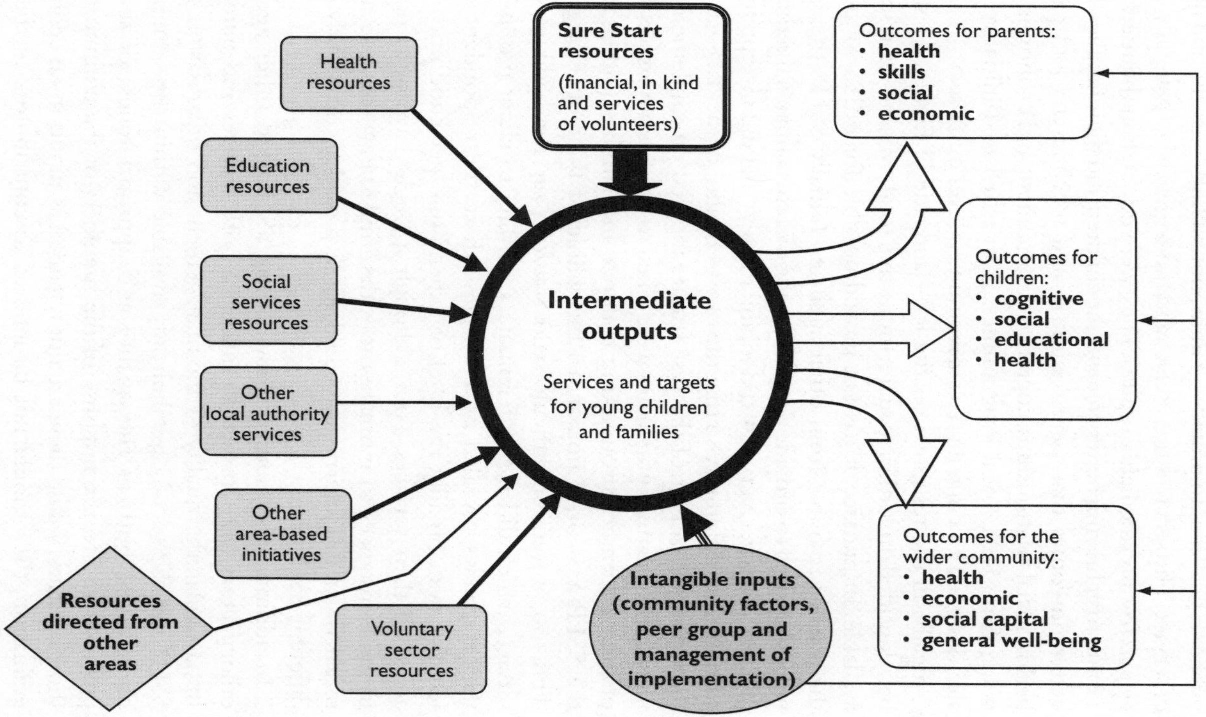

Outcomes for parents:
• health
• skills
• social
• economic

Outcomes for children:
• cognitive
• social
• educational
• health

Outcomes for the wider community:
• health
• economic
• social capital
• general well-being

Sure Start resources (financial, in kind and services of volunteers)

Intermediate outputs

Services and targets for young children and families

Intangible inputs (community factors, peer group and management of implementation)

Health resources

Education resources

Social services resources

Other local authority services

Other area-based initiatives

Voluntary sector resources

Resources directed from other areas

Sure Start Local Programmes and other organisations contributed to the services provided in each area. These services each had their own priorities and targets. The general purpose of targets for providers of public services was to provide an indication of both quantity and quality of service. The services themselves and the targets were generally called *outputs* (or intermediate outputs). They were not ends in themselves but a route to achieving better *outcomes* for children and their families. These better outcomes that were sought related to children's and parents' health, social relationships, cognitive development and economic well-being. Sure Start Local Programmes, as an area-based initiative, were also designed to contribute to community-level outcomes.

Ideally, all the resources on the left-hand side of Figure 7.1 should be identified in order to determine the total volume of resources available. In practice, it has not proved possible for NESS to identify the level of resource from other agencies. Initially, SSLPs themselves were supposed to provide this information in their financial returns. In practice, however, very few did so, and the few that did interpreted the requirement differently so that the overall quality of the data was poor. Subsequently, as part of the case studies focused on implementation, managers in statutory agencies were asked to provide a rough estimate of their expenditure on young children and families (either within the SSLP area or, if not, across the whole of their operating area). This, too, proved too difficult to do. Statutory services had budgets by service, which did not differentiate according to client group. Thus, the interviews revealed no examples where the respondent could identify, even broadly, the level of expenditure per child under four across all their services. Thus, although it might have been possible in some instances to estimate these, the implementation case studies revealed that this information could not be provided consistently across different SSLP areas.

In addition to resources provided by SSLPs and other agencies, other factors were known to influence both services and outcomes. In particular, the quality of the management and organisation of the SSLP and the social capital already available within the community contributed both to the quality and appropriateness of services provided and to the response of the members of the community to those services. While these are not regarded as inputs in an economic evaluation, they should not be ignored as contributors to the final outcomes observed.

The main potential quantifiable benefits of SSLPs are delineated in Table 7.1. These include benefits from the outcomes that SSLPs were expected to influence and spillover benefits, both to programme

Table 7.1: Sources of potential quantifiable benefits and additional costs

Beneficiary	Short term	Medium term	Long term
Child	Lower use of health services Greater use of specialist health services (–) Greater use of nursery education (–) Greater use of childcare (–) Greater use of play and library facilities (–) Lower use of social services	Lower use of health services Lower use of special education Lower use of social services Less involvement with criminal justice system Lower level of teenage pregnancy	Higher earnings Lower use of health services Increased time spent in full-time education (–) Reduced receipt of social security benefits (–) Less involvement with criminal justice system Lower level of early or unwanted pregnancy
Parents	Fewer unplanned pregnancies Lower use of health services Lower level of domestic violence Lower use of child protection services Increased earnings Improved skill levels Lower use of criminal justice system Lower receipt of social security benefits (–)	Fewer unplanned pregnancies Lower level of domestic violence Lower use of health services Lower use of child protection services Increased earnings Improved skill levels Lower use of criminal justice system Lower receipt of social security benefits (–)	
Local community	Improved access to public services Lower rates of crime Greater quality of daily life Improvement in property values Greater commitment to education and training	Improved access to public services Lower rates of crime Greater quality of daily life Greater commitment to education and training Improvement in property values Higher levels of economic activity and employment	Improved access to public services Lower rates of crime Greater quality of daily life Greater commitment to education and training Improvement in property values Higher levels of economic activity and employment
Wider society	Lower expenditure on health and social services Lower expenditure on social security Lower expenditure on criminal justice system Increased tax revenue	Lower expenditure on special education Lower expenditure on social services Lower expenditure on health services Lower expenditure on social security Lower expenditure on criminal justice system Lower costs to victims of crime Increased tax revenue	Lower expenditure on health Higher expenditure on education (–) Lower expenditure on social security Lower expenditure on criminal justice system Lower costs to victims of crime Increased tax revenue

Note: (–) = negative effect, ie a loss rather than a benefit.

participants and to wider society. Most of these spillover benefits were identified in previous evaluations of early childhood interventions (for a summary, see Karoly et al, 2005). Many of them were identified by chance, and many evaluations did not measure the full range of indicators because they were unexpected at the time the evaluation was designed. The NESS was fortunate in that these outcomes were found previously, so it was possible to build the measurement of these outcomes into the design of the evaluation.

Mainstream services and their costs

It is a key component of NESS that the outcomes for children and families in SSLP areas were not determined solely by the activities of the SSLPs. Rather, outcomes were presumed to be the result of a combination of SSLP and mainstream services. These mainstream services varied in their level, in their approach to service delivery and in their effectiveness.

The only practical option available to NESS was to use information about service levels rather than actual costs. Data gathered by the Local Context Analysis and implementation teams included information collected consistently from the first 260 SSLPs on the availability of mainstream services.

The Treasury's *The green book: Appraisal and evaluation in central government* (HM Treasury, 2003) emphasises the need to establish whether or not a new policy or programme is providing *additional* services, or whether it has replaced some pre-existing services funded from other sources (substitution) or has resulted in the diversion of resources from other related services or areas (displacement). This is a particular issue for regeneration and other area-based programmes. It is common for cost-effectiveness evaluation to take account of provision by other organisations. But other recent evaluations in the UK have encountered difficulties in attempting to measure such costs (Bertram et al, 2002) basically because current accounting practices across the public sector do not permit the identification of the true level of resources contributed to local services.

Resources used by SSLPs

The NESS analysis of resources used by SSLPs covered financial years 1999-2000 to 2003-04. This information derived from four sources: (1) regular financial information provided by SSLPs to the government Sure Start Unit (SSU), (2) monitoring information provided by SSLPs to the SSU, (3) information gathered by NESS implementation team surveys of SSLPs (see Chapter Five) and (4) information from the NESS implementation case studies and from the themed study related to SSLP buildings (see Chapter Six). Notably, none of these data sources were available every year on all 260 SSLPs covered by NESS, but the financial information and monitoring data were more than 95% complete, and no programme had missing information for every year.

Expenditure by operational year

In order to make analytically meaningful comparisons between different SSLPs at different stages in their 'lives', financial information based on financial years was analysed by programme operational years. Recall from Chapter One that programmes started their lives at different times such that a first operating year ranged from 1999-2000 to 2002-03. Any analysis of a particular financial year that did not take this variation into account could not produce a meaningful picture of expenditure. All expenditure analyses took such variation in programme life cycle into account, necessitating adjustment by the Gross Domestic Product (GDP) deflator to 1999-2000 prices to take account of the impact of inflation.

The establishment of SSLPs took time, not least because of the need both to engage the local community and to involve the agencies responsible for delivering mainstream services to children and families. With few exceptions, expenditure by SSLPs in the first two years of operation was well below that in the third, and around 1 in 10 programmes was not fully operational until the fourth operating year. Table 7.2 shows that the average expenditure in the first year of operation was approximately £150,000, whereas in the fourth year it was just under £700,000 per programme at 1999-2000 prices.

On average, the second-year expenditure was three times that in the first year. Third-year expenditure was 1.4 times that in the second year. For most programmes the increase between the third and fourth years was relatively modest, suggesting that it was reasonable to treat the third operating year as the year in which SSLPs were delivering the full range of services for the first time.

The data on average expenditure by SSLPs conceals great variation. Not surprisingly, this was particularly true for the first year of operation, with expenditure ranging from a low of less than £6,000 to a high of almost £750,000! Even by the third year of operation, when programmes were more likely to be delivering a full range of services, the range remained large – from around £250,000 to more than

Table 7.2: Average total expenditure by SSLPs by operating year (£, 1999-2000 prices)

	1999-2000	2000-01	2001-02	2002-03	2003-04	All
Year 1	90,684	188,203	144,396	**		150,858
Year 2		486,749	550,482	442,676	**	480,198
Year 3			722,100	657,287	600,916	639,174
Year 4				736,516	676,148	695,465
SSLPs of all ages*	90,684	285,084	380,456	600,486	715,334	

*Current year prices. ** There were only two programmes in this category. For reasons of confidentiality their information is only included in the total.
Source: SSLP financial returns

£1.5 million. By the third operational year, however, outliers were rarer. After adjusting for inflation, median expenditure was just over £629,000, with strong concentration around this figure, as half of all programmes spent between approximately £559,000 and £683,000 (see Table 7.3).

The fourth operational year showed a similar pattern. After taking account of inflation the median expenditure was just over £680,000, with half of all programmes spending between approximately £603,000 and £756,000. Even so, the gap between the lowest spending programmes (£296,000) and the highest (£1.2 million) remained large.

Thus, SSLPs functioned on very different scales even when they were fully operational. For fully operational programmes there was a strong clustering around spending about £700,000 a year, but approximately 20% of programmes spent significantly less and a similar proportion spent significantly more. There were likely to be quite marked differences in the level, range and quality of services provided

Table 7.3: Variation in total expenditure by SSLPs by operating year (£, 1999-2000 prices)

	Median	Lower quartile	Upper quartile	Minimum	Maximum	N
Year 1	120,310	68,117	205,611	0	749,186	252
Year 2	477,730	362,088	589,502	47,121	1,209,161	250
Year 3	629,255	559,363	683,877	238,949	1,523,471	249
Year 4	680,538	603,110	756,464	295,955	1,179,552	125

Source: SSLP financial returns

between programmes that spent more than £1 million a year and those that spent a quarter of that.

Expenditure per child

These differences in total expenditure did not just reflect differences in the number of eligible children served by SSLPs. Even when they were fully operational, large differences in expenditure per child existed between SSLPs (see Table 7.4). The average third-year expenditure per child was around £900 at 1999-2000 prices, but the minimum was around £350 and the maximum almost £2,500. These disparities did not appear to be based on differences in the level of existing services. Rather, they seemed to reflect different choices about services offered and scope of delivery.

Table 7.4: SSLP expenditure per child aged 0-4 by operating year (£, 1999-2000 prices)

	Mean	Median	Lower quartile	Upper quartile	Minimum	Maximum
Year 1	112	175	85	266	8	1,385
Year 2	650	624	456	802	57	2,865
Year 3	882	844	735	984	347	2,415
Year 4	926	856	717	973	365	2,319

Source: SSLP financial returns adjusted by GDP deflator

Programme size

The one clear pattern that emerged in expenditure levels related to economies of scale. Small programmes with fewer than 600 children aged 0 to 4 in their area spent more per head overall, more on non-service costs and more on each key service than did medium-sized and larger programmes. Large programmes with more than 800 children aged 0 to 4 living in the area consistently spent the least per child (see Figure 7.2).

The SSLP model of delivering services through small, freestanding local organisations working in partnership had the inevitable consequence that non-service costs (that is, management and administration, development and evaluation) were a relatively high proportion of total costs. Partnership working also imposed costs on other partner organisations that are largely hidden, but are still a consequence of the existence of SSLPs.

Figure 7.2: Expenditure per child at 1999-2000 prices by number of children covered by programme

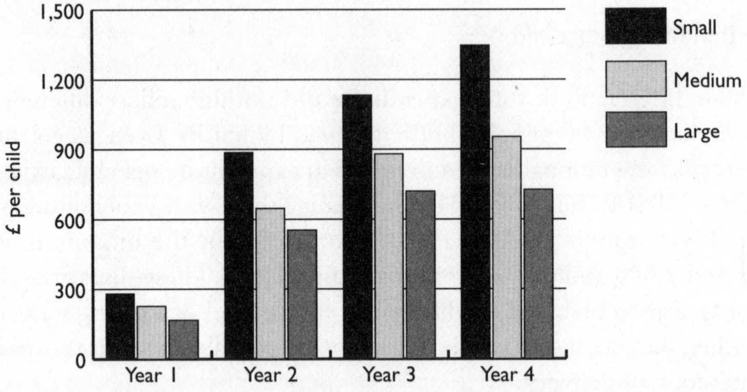

Note: Small programmes have fewer than 600 children aged 0-4, medium-sized programmes have 600-799 children and large programmes have 800 or more children.

By the fourth year of operation, small programmes spent £1,351 per head at 1999-2000 prices. Medium-sized programmes with 600-799 children spent £957 and large programmes spent £731. There was no evidence that larger programmes were providing fewer services. It seems likely that larger programmes provided services with larger groups or caseloads at lower average costs than smaller programmes.

Additional resources

Sure Start Local Programmes were encouraged, but not obliged, to seek additional funding from other sources. Some programmes did so and consistently recorded it in their accounts, whether the resources were received in cash or in kind. Many programmes included cash resources in their accounts but not resources in kind. However, others received additional resources either in cash or in kind, but the money did not flow through their accounts. This could happen, for example, when the lead agency allocated additional resources to the SSLP, perhaps in the form of an additional staff member, but the relevant expenditure only went through the lead agency's own accounts.

Almost all SSLPs received in-kind resources such as use of premises and support services for which they did not pay full charges. It was exceptional for any in-kind resources to be included in their accounts. Around half of all SSLPs had free use of premises belonging to other organisations. This was most common with clinics, libraries and schools.

Most programmes paid for their offices. Seven of 10 SSLPs were charged for finance and information technology services, and six of 10 paid for personnel/payroll and legal services.

Over the five financial years 1999-2000 to 2003-04, two thirds of SSLPs received financial resources to meet day-to-day operational costs in addition to their grant from the SSU. These resources came from partner organisations, other government initiatives and European Union programmes, as well as the National Lottery and charitable trusts. The amounts involved averaged around £50,000 or about 6% of an average programme's third-year expenditure. Sure Start Local Programmes classified their expenditure under a series of service headings, as detailed in Table 7.5.

To some extent the assignment by SSLPs of expenditure to different categories appeared arbitrary, and therefore apparent differences between programmes should be treated with caution. *Home visits* provided *support for parents*, for example, and thus were classified under either heading. Individual programmes sometimes changed the headings they used for the same activity, producing apparently large changes in the balance of services across years.

By the third and fourth years of operation, expenditure on play, learning and childcare amounted to around a sixth of all SSLP expenditure. Healthcare, outreach and home visiting, and support for parents each accounted for around a seventh (see Figure 7.3).

Capital expenditure

Each programme had an allocation of around £1 million for capital expenditure, irrespective of the number of children living in the area. What this meant was that although there was little variation in capital resources per *programme*, because of differences in programme size there

Table 7.5: Standard SSLP expenditure categories

Core services	Additional services	Non-service expenditure
Outreach and home visiting	Teenage pregnancy	Management and administration
Support for parents	Crime prevention	Development
Play, learning and childcare	Parental employability	Evaluation
Community healthcare		Other
Special needs support		

Figure 7.3: Proportion of third year expenditure on different service areas

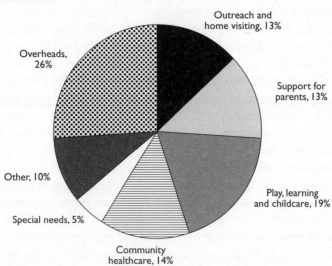

were significant differences in the capital available *per child*. However, the impact of this on the overall cost-effectiveness of SSLPs was unlikely to be large. This was because in looking at the overall cost per child per year, capital expenditure should be allocated over the lifetime of the asset. Most SSLPs' capital expenditure was on buildings, and buildings are conventionally assumed to have a life expectancy of 20 years. Thus, £1 million of capital expenditure spread over 600 children over 20 years yields £83 per child per year.

In fact, the central issue related to capital expenditure was the ability of SSLPs to develop and manage their capital programmes (see Chapter Six). The NESS themed study on buildings (Ball and Niven, 2005) showed that negotiations over sites, design, planning permission, commissioning and managing building projects all took significantly longer than expected. Some programmes in areas of high land values found it difficult to identify suitable sites for new buildings. Where buildings were shared with other organisations (for example, schools), this also added to the complexity of delivering a capital programme. Originally SSLPs' capital allocations were to be spent during the first three years of the programme's life, but in practice the time allowed was extended as very few proved able to complete capital programmes within this time period.

Issues for the next stage

Over the period covered by the evaluation, SSLPs spent an average of between £2,500 and £3,000 on each three-year-old child included in the impact evaluation; this figure includes capital expenditure. This is roughly equivalent to providing an extra year at primary school in expenditure terms. The next stage of the cost-effectiveness evaluation will use the evidence from the longitudinal impact evaluation to assess, where possible, the monetary value of the outcomes identified in the impact analysis to assess the extent to which there is a short-term return on the investment. However, the international evidence related to early childhood interventions suggests that returns that can have monetary values attributed to them do not generally emerge before children reach adolescence or early adulthood. This is not to say that there are no observable outcomes before this. Rather, the early outcomes that can be observed (for example, improved cognitive skills) cannot have immediate monetary values attributed to them (Karoly et al, 2005).

The main exception to this rule is the Elmira nurse home visiting programme (Olds et al, 1993), which produced small net savings for high-risk children by age four, mainly as a consequence of improved infant health because of better care in pregnancy and reduced prenatal smoking among single teenage mothers, and a lower incidence of child abuse (Karoly et al, 1998). The only other intervention in which the projected benefits have exceeded costs before the teenage years is the Home Instruction Program for Preschool Youngsters (HIPPY) in the US, and this calculation is based on the projected impact on lifetime earnings of the improvement in test scores at age six (Aos et al, 2004). While methodologically legitimate, calculations of this kind are based on previously observed relations between early indicators and both intermediate outcomes (for example, school-leaving qualifications) and longer-term ones (for example, employment probabilities and earnings levels). There is room for error at every link in the process, and there is also the risk that relations between a particular intermediate outcome and longer-term outcomes observed in one generation or location will not be the same for future generations or in other places (White, 1988). The Perry Preschool Project follow-up at age 27 had predicted that the lifetime earnings gain by participants would be $23,000 in 2003 dollars, whereas the follow-up at age 40 found that this was an underestimate of the trajectories the participants had followed during their thirties, and reassessed the value at $62,000 (Karoly et al, 2005; a standardised comparison based on Schweinhart et al, 1993; Barnett, 1996; and Barnett et al, 2005).

Early childhood intervention programmes that have had their costs and benefits analysed have generally had benefits that exceeded costs when the follow-up occurred at age 15 or later. Moreover, the consistent finding is that the longer the follow-up period, the greater the benefit/cost ratio (Karoly et al, 2005). In other words, projections of long-term benefits based on intermediate outcomes have consistently underpredicted actual outcomes achieved. However, it is also worth noting that meta-analysis suggests that the returns do not accrue to the government; rather, they accrue to participants themselves and to other members of society, most notably potential crime victims. The government's own benefits do not generally exceed the costs it has incurred (Aos et al, 2004).

Other important human capital indicators have been observed in other early childhood interventions that have followed participants into adulthood. These include higher rates of high-school graduation and higher college attendance rates. Several programmes have found higher employment rates, higher likelihood of being in skilled employment or higher earnings, even if these have not been analysed in a human capital framework (Karoly et al, 2005).

While recognising limitations, an important part of the next stage of the NESS cost-effectiveness evaluation is to identify short-term outcomes that are potential predictors of medium- and longer-term outcomes for children and families, particularly predictors of educational achievement – and therefore earnings potential in adulthood – and involvement with the criminal justice system.

References

Aos, S., Lieb, R., Mayfield, J., Miller, M. and Pennucci, A. (2004) *Benefits and costs of prevention and early intervention programs for youth*, Olympia, WA: Washington State Institute for Public Policy, www.wsipp.wa.gov/rptfiles/04-07-3901.pdf

Ball, M. and Niven, L. (2005) *Buildings in Sure Start Local Programmes*, Sure Start Report 11, Nottingham: DfES, www.surestart.gov.uk/_doc/P0001727.pdf

Barnett, W.S. (1996) *Lives in the balance: Age 27 benefit-cost analysis of the High/Scope Perry Preschool program*, Monographs of the High/Scope Educational Research Foundation, No 11, Ypsilanti, MI: High/Scope Press.

Barnett, W.S., Belfield, C.R. and Nores, M. (2005) 'Lifetime cost-benefit analysis', in L.J. Schweinhart, J. Montie, Z. Xiang, W.S. Barnett, C.R. Belfield and M. Nores (eds) *Lifetime effects: The High/Scope Perry Preschool Study through age 40*, Monographs of the High/Scope Educational Research Foundation, No 14, Ypsilanti, MI: High/Scope Press, pp 130-57.

Becker, G.S. (1993) *Human capital: A theoretical and empirical analysis with special reference to education* (2nd edn), Chicago, IL: National Bureau for Economic Research, University of Chicago Press.

Becker, G.S. and Tomes, N. (1986) 'Human capital and the rise and fall of families', *Journal of Labor Economics*, vol 4, pp S1-S39.

Bertram, T., Pascal, C., Bokhari, S., Gasper, M. and Holtermann, S. (2002) *Early Excellence Centre pilot programme annual evaluation report 2000-01*, DfES Research Report RR361, Nottingham: DfES, www.surestart.gov.uk/_doc/P0000401.pdf

Boardman, A., Greenberg, D., Vining, A. and Wiemer, D. (2005) *Cost-benefit analysis: Concepts and practice* (3rd edn), Upper Saddle River, NJ: Prentice-Hall.

Feinstein, L. and Symons, J. (1999) 'Attainment in secondary school', *Oxford Economic Papers*, vol 51, pp 300-21.

Gramlich, E.M. (1990) *A guide to benefit-cost analysis* (2nd edn), Prospect Heights, IL: Waveland Press.

Haveman, R. and Wolfe, B. (1995) 'The determinants of children's attainments: a review of methods and findings', *Journal of Economic Literature*, vol 33, pp 1829-978.

Heckman, J. (1998) 'What should be our human capital investment policy?', *Fiscal Studies*, vol 19, pp 103-19.

Heckman, J. and Lochner, L. (2000) 'Rethinking education and training policy: understanding the sources of skill formation in a modern economy', in S. Danziger and J. Waldfogel (eds) *Securing the future: Investing in children from birth to college*, Ford Foundation series on asset building, New York: Russell Sage Foundation, pp 47-83.

Hill, M.A. and O'Neill, J. (1994) 'Family endowments and the achievement of young children with special reference to the underclass', *Journal of Human Resources*, vol 29, pp 1064-100.

HM Treasury (2003) *The green book: Appraisal and evaluation in central government*, London: The Stationery Office.

Karoly, L.A., Kilburn, M.R. and Cannon, J.S. (2005) *Early childhood interventions: Proven results, future promise*, Santa Monica, CA: RAND Corporation.

Karoly, L.A., Greenwood, P.W., Everingham, S.S., Houbé, J., Kilburn, M.R., Rydell, C.P., Sanders, M. and Chiesa, J. (1998) *Investing in our children: What we know and don't know about the costs and benefits of early childhood interventions*, Santa Monica, CA: RAND Corporation.

Layard, R. and Glaister, S. (eds) (1994) *Cost-benefit analysis* (2nd edn), Cambridge: Cambridge University Press.

Leibowitz, A. (1974) 'Home investments in children', *Journal of Political Economy*, vol 82, pp S111-S131.

Olds, D., Hill, P. and Rumsey, E. (1998) *Prenatal and early childhood nurse home visitation*, US Department of Justice Juvenile Justice Bulletin, November, http://eric.ed.gov/ERICDocs/data/ericdocs2/content_storage_01/0000000b/80/25/63/24.pdf

Olds, D.L., Henderson, C.R., Phelps, C., Kitzman, H. and Hanks, C. (1993) 'Effect of prenatal and infancy nurse home visitation on government spending', *Medical Care*, vol 31, pp 155-74.

Plotnik, R.D. and Deppman, L. (1999), Using benefit-cost analysis to assess child abuse prevention and intervention programs', *Child Welfare*, vol 78, pp 381-407.

Schweinhart, L.J., Barnes, H.V. and Weikart, D.P. (1993) *Significant benefits: The High/Scope Perry Preschool Study through age 27*, Monographs of the High/Scope Educational Research Foundation, No 10, Ypsilanti, MI: High/Scope Press.

White, K.R. (1988) 'Cost analyses in family support programs', in H.B. Weiss and F. Jacobs (eds) *Evaluating family programs*, New York: Aldine de Gruyter, pp 429-43.

Part Four

The impact of Sure Start Local Programmes

EIGHT

Impact of Sure Start Local Programmes on children and families

Jay Belsky and Edward Melhuish

Sure Start Local Programmes (SSLPs) were intended to break the intergenerational transmission of poverty, school failure and social exclusion by enhancing the life chances for children less than four years of age growing up in disadvantaged neighbourhoods. More importantly, they were intended to do so in a manner rather different from almost any other intervention undertaken in the western world. What made them so different was their *area-based* nature, with *all* children under four and their families living in a prescribed deprived area serving as the 'targets' of intervention. This resulted in the need for a distinct approach to evaluation, one focused on sampling from all children under four and their families residing in SSLP areas rather than exclusively on children and families using specific SSLP services. This *intention-to-treat* design, the results of which are presented in this chapter, is very different from those employed in evaluations of more narrowly focused early interventions that assessed the functioning of only children/families known to use the centre- and/or home-based services provided.

An intention-to-treat design was required because SSLPs were designed on the premise that an area-based intervention would have both *direct* and *indirect* effects on children. Direct effects derive from services used by children, such as good-quality childcare or speech therapy. Indirect effects in the case of SSLPs come in two varieties, one mediated through parents and parenting and the other via the community. The latter, in particular, necessitated a research design in which all children in the community, irrespective of personal exposure to Sure Start services, were sampled for purposes of evaluating the impact of SSLPs. Indirect effects mediated by parents or parenting are ones that are considered to have an impact on the child by affecting the child's parent or parenting. For example, family support that seeks to prevent or reduce post-partum maternal depression can indirectly affect the child if it affects a mother's psychological well-being and, thereby, her parenting. Efforts to encourage non-punitive approaches to discipline can also indirectly affect the child.

But indirect effects can also be mediated via the community. Indeed, SSLPs, it will be recalled, placed great emphasis on community development (see Chapter One), based on the view that more cohesive communities would support families and benefit children. Children could be indirectly affected from this perspective, even if they or their parents never personally experienced a Sure Start service, through the effects upon the community in general. Consider, for example, the possibility that a child being cared for by a childminder might interact with other children whose linguistic abilities were greater or whose behaviour was more prosocial than would otherwise be the case because these other children had benefited directly from Sure Start services. Or, relatedly, consider the mother whose parenting might change, not because she ever participated in a Sure Start parenting support programme but because she had witnessed friends or other mothers in the community talking to their young babies or disciplining their children in ways she would not have thought to do herself, but now might imitate. In sum, it was because of such 'ripple effects' across the community that it was essential when evaluating the impact of SSLPs on children and families to sample from all the children under four and their families in the community, not just those who directly enrolled in one or more services.

SSLPs also differed from other early interventions in other ways that proved important in the evaluation of its impact on children and families. By design, and in contrast to more narrowly delivered early interventions, SSLPs did not have a prescribed 'curriculum' or set of services, especially not ones delineated in a 'manualised' form to promote fidelity of treatment to a prescribed model. Recall that each local programme was charged with improving existing services and creating new ones as needed without specification of *how* services were to be changed, although ideally these would have an 'evidence base'. This was a much broader mandate than virtually all other early interventions evaluated to date. This general and highly varied approach to early intervention contrasts markedly with most early interventions demonstrated to be effective, be they childcare based, like the Abecedarian Project (Ramey et al, 2000); home based, like the Prenatal Early Intervention Project (Olds et al, 1999), the Positive Parenting Program (Sanders, 2003) or Incredible Years (Webster-Stratton, 1993); or even a combination of centre and home based, like Early Head Start (Love et al, 2002). To our knowledge, there is only one thorough evaluation of a community-based intervention for young children and their families with a similarly loose structure to SSLPs. That is the Comprehensive Child Development Program (CCDP: ACYF, 1997) carried out in the US and its evaluation revealed no significant effect of the intervention.

Given the ambitious goals of SSLPs, it was clear that the ultimate effectiveness of SSLPs could not be determined for quite some time and that children growing up in communities with SSLPs would need to be studied well beyond their early years before a final account of the success of SSLPs would prove possible. Nevertheless, by studying children and families in SSLPs during infancy and the pre-school years, empirical inquiry might detect evidence of *early* effectiveness. It is the first phase of the National Evaluation of Sure Start (NESS) Impact Study that is reported in this chapter, a cross-sectional investigation of nine-month-olds and 36-month-olds and their families. In addition, a large number of children (and their families) are being followed longitudinally, beginning at nine months of age and then again when three and five years of age, but findings from this phase of the Impact Study are not yet available.

When NESS was launched in 2001, the general hypothesis guiding the Impact Study was that children and families residing in SSLP areas would develop and function better than those in comparison areas, with similar levels of deprivation, yet to receive SSLP services. Examples of better functioning might be less chaotic family environments, more cognitively stimulating parenting, better child language functioning or fewer child behaviour problems. Subsequent to the launch of NESS, an evaluation of Early Head Start (EHS) in the US, an early intervention programme for disadvantaged families providing high-quality centre-based childcare and/or family support through home visiting, indicated that different subpopulations of disadvantaged families were differentially affected by the intervention designed to enhance child and family functioning (Love et al, 2002). This new evidence, especially the finding that some children in the most at-risk families within a disadvantaged population were apparently adversely affected by the early intervention, required that the NESS Impact Study entertain the prospect that both positive and negative effects of SSLPs might be found.

This chapter presents findings related to the effectiveness of SSLPs in fostering the well-being of nine-month-olds (who are being studied again at ages three and five) and 36-month-olds (who were only studied once) and their families by comparing children/families in 150 of the first 260 SSLP areas with counterparts living in 50 communities that did not have up-and-running SSLPs at the time they were studied, but which were to have programmes shortly after data collection (that is, Sure Start-to-be communities). In a sense, then, these Sure Start-to-be communities, along with the children and families residing within them, could be conceptualised as 'waiting-list controls'.

The Impact Study addressed four questions pertaining to the effectiveness of SSLPs. First, did the use of services differ between SSLP and comparison communities, and did parents rate SSLP communities more positively? This compound question reflected the 'theory of change' of SSLPs, stipulating that enhancing services and fostering change in the community would benefit children and their families (both directly and indirectly). Second, did families in SSLP and comparison areas function differently? Third, did child health and development differ between SSLP and comparison areas? Because, as already noted, children can be affected directly (for example, by enhanced healthcare) or indirectly (by effects on parents), question four asked whether the effects of SSLPs on parenting mediated effects on child functioning. (For full details on all methods and results, see www.surestart.gov.uk/_doc/P0001867.pdf).

Research design

The research design called for comparing the functioning of all children under four and their families residing in 150 SSLP communities with those residing in 50 similarly disadvantaged communities that had not yet received a Sure Start programme, but had been selected to do so in the near future. Any such comparison must take into consideration pre-existing differences between the two sets of communities, implementing statistical controls for such differences before evaluating the effects of SSLPs. Such statistical controls would not have been necessary with a randomised clinical trial in which communities were *randomly* assigned to experimental (that is, SSLP) or control (that is, no SSLP) conditions. Because the government was not prepared to randomly assign SSLPs, this alternative approach was necessary.

Participants

Potential study participants living in SSLP areas and Sure Start-to-be (comparison) areas were identified from Child Benefit records and then a proportion randomly selected. Data collection proceeded in 150 SSLPs during 2003 and 2004 and in the 50 Sure Start-to-be communities during 2002 and 2003. Overall data were collected on

12,575 nine-month-olds and 3,927 36-month-olds and their families in the 150 SSLP communities, and on 1,509 nine-month-olds and 1,101 36-month-olds and their families in the comparison communities. Of the eligible children/families that could be contacted, the response rate was 84% for the families of nine-month-olds and 73% for the families of 36-month-olds. Selected demographic characteristics of the families of nine-month-old children are presented in Table 8.1, with comparable data on the 36-month-old sample in Table 8.2. Differences between the groups identified in the tables were statistically controlled before tests were conducted to identify potential effects of SSLPs.

Data collection

The families who agreed to participate in the study provided extensive information on child and family functioning during the course of a home visit, conducted by a specially trained fieldworker and typically lasting around 90 minutes. In the case of families with nine-month-olds, a professional survey-research field workforce under subcontract from the Office of National Statistics carried out the data collection. Visits to families with 36-month-olds, which included standardised cognitive and linguistic testing of children, were carried out by field staff specially hired and trained for this purpose by the Institute for the Study of Children, Families and Social Issues, Birkbeck University of London.

During the home visits, information was collected on demographic and background information that might influence outcomes and the predicted child and family outcomes. Information on the area characteristics of each community was also collected, so that their influence on the results could be controlled statistically.

Child, family and community control variables

A variety of child/family and community variables functioned as control variables in the analyses:

- *Child characteristics*: age, gender and ethnic origin.
- *Family demographic, socioeconomic and parental characteristics*: maternal age, maternal education, maternal work status, maternal occupational status, maternal cognitive difficulties, father's presence, father's occupational status household language, household income.
- *Area characteristics*: information on a variety of features of each community (for example, ethnic make-up, age distribution of the population, child health) collected by the NESS Local Context

Table 8.1: Selected background characteristics of families with nine-month-old children (percentages in brackets)

Characteristic	Sure Start group (n=12,575)	Comparison group (n=1,509)	p value
Child's ethnic origin			
White	9,208 (73.2)	965 (63.9)	
Mixed	636 (5.1)	94 (6.2)	
Indian	185 (1.5)	38 (2.5)	
Pakistani	920 (7.3)	131 (8.7)	
Bangladeshi	404 (3.2)	79 (5.2)	
Black Caribbean	182 (1.4)	26 (1.7)	
Other Black	577 (4.6)	93 (6.2)	
Other	399 (3.2)	66 (4.4)	
Not known	64 (0.5)	17 (1.1)	<0.001
Household language			
English only	9,938 (79.0)	1,090 (72.2)	
English and other languages	1,816 (14.4)	285 (18.9)	
Other languages only	808 (6.4)	129 (8.5)	
Not known	13 (0.1)	5 (0.3)	<0.001
Mother's age (years)			
≥20	10,696 (85.1)	1,267 (84.0)	
<20	1,677 (13.3)	221 (14.6)	
Not known	202 (1.6)	21 (1.4)	0.17
Equivalised income of household (divided into fifths)			
>£338 per week	2,503 (19.9)	261 (17.3)	
£217-338 per week	2,075 (16.5)	217 (14.4)	
£168-216 per week	2,561 (20.4)	270 (17.9)	
£126-167 per week	2,191 (17.4)	314 (20.8)	
<£126 per week	2,207 (17.6)	358 (23.7)	
Not known	1,038 (8.3)	89 (5.9)	<0.001
Mother's education			
Degree or higher education	2,092 (16.6)	242 (16.0)	
A level	2,794 (22.2)	299 (19.8)	
O level or General Certificate of Secondary Education	2,924 (23.3)	331 (21.9)	
Other	929 (7.4)	132 (8.7)	
None	3,694 (29.4)	485 (32.1)	
Not known	142 (1.1)	20 (1.3)	0.02
Mother's employment status			
Unemployed	8,462 (67.3)	1,039 (68.9)	
Employed, part time	1,395 (11.1)	142 (9.4)	
Employed, full time	2,593 (20.6)	308 (20.4)	
Not known	125 (1.0)	20 (1.3)	0.14

Table 8.2: Selected background characteristics of families with 36-month-old children (percentages in brackets)

Characteristic	Sure Start group (n=3,927)	Comparison group (n=1,101)	p value
Child's ethnic origin			
White	2,987 (76.1)	714 (64.9)	
Mixed	186 (4.7)	78 (7.1)	
Indian	43 (1.1)	32 (2.9)	
Pakistani	257 (6.5)	96 (8.7)	
Bangladeshi	106 (2.7)	57 (5.2)	
Black Caribbean	38 (1.0)	14 (1.3)	
Other Black	149 (3.8)	52 (4.7)	
Other	129 (3.3)	45 (4.1)	
Not known	32 (0.8)	13 (1.2)	<0.001
Household language			
English only	3,130 (79.7)	772 (70.1)	
English and other languages	663 (16.9)	263 (23.9)	
Other languages only	131 (3.3)	63 (5.7)	
Not known	3 (0.1)	3 (0.3)	<0.001
Maternal age (years)			
≥20	3,380 (86.1)	952 (86.5)	
<20	488 (12.4)	125 (11.4)	
Not known	59 (1.5)	24 (2.1)	0.37
Equivalised income of household (divided into fifths)			
>£338 per week	542 (13.8)	150 (13.6)	
£217-338 per week	957 (24.4)	195 (17.7)	
£168-216 per week	645 (16.4)	120 (10.9)	
£126-167 per week	655 (16.7)	167 (15.2)	
<£126 per week	651 (16.6)	269 (24.4)	
Not known	477 (12.1)	200 (18.2)	<0.001
Mother's education			
Degree or higher education	686 (17.5)	182 (16.5)	
A level	860 (21.9)	181 (16.4)	
O level or General Certificate of Secondary Education	964 (24.5)	256 (23.3)	
Other	345 (8.8)	116 (10.5)	
None	929 (23.7)	300 (27.2)	
Not known	143 (3.6)	66 (6.0)	<0.001
Mother's employment status			
Unemployed	2,575 (65.6)	693 (62.9)	
Employed, part time	508 (12.9)	147 (13.4)	
Employed, full time	733 (18.7)	212 (19.3)	
Not known	111 (2.8)	49 (4.5)	0.62

Analysis module (see Chapter Two) and measured prior to or at the onset of SSLPs were subjected to data reduction using factor analysis. Results were used to create composite factor scores reflecting dimensions of the community that could potentially influence the outcome measures. The labels of identified factors are listed in the left-hand column of Table 8.3, with associated component variables defining each factor listed in the right-hand column.

Child and family outcome variables

When it came to assessing potential effects of SSLPs, information was gathered through a variety of means (that is, parental report, observation, developmental assessments) on a variety of outcomes likely to be affected by SSLPs. These are listed below, with further details of the instruments used provided in Table 8.4, which highlights outcomes examined in the investigation of SSLP effectiveness:

- *Child physical health*: for nine-month-olds – birthweight, child ever breastfed, child breastfed through first six weeks. For both age groups – one or more accidents in the last nine (for nine-month-olds) or 12 months (for 36-month-olds), one or more hospital admissions due to injury in the past nine or 12 months. Scores for these outcomes were based on detailed reports by parents of the child's health history.
- *Child cognitive and language development (36-month-olds only)*: verbal ability; non-verbal ability. These measurements were obtained by means of standardised assessment of each child using subscales from the British Abilities Scales, specifically Block Building (non-verbal), Picture Similarities (non-verbal), Verbal Comprehension (verbal) and Picture Naming (verbal).
- *Child social and emotional development (36-month-olds only)*: conduct problems (that is, hyperactivity, aggression), prosocial behaviour, independence, emotional regulation and overall behavioural difficulties. These were all obtained by means of parental report.
- *Parenting and family functioning*: for nine-month-olds – maternal responsivity (observed), maternal acceptance (observed), household chaos (mother's report). For 36-month-olds – maternal responsivity (observed), maternal acceptance (observed), home learning environment, parent–child conflict, parent–child closeness, harsh discipline, father involvement (all mother report).
- *Maternal psychological well-being*: malaise, self-esteem.
- *Local area*: ratings by mother and by fieldworker.

Table 8.3: Local Context Analysis composites (derived from factor analyses)

Composite	Variables in composite
Ethnic population (Indian subcontinent) and young children	High % of population from Indian subcontinent
	High % of population children under 4 years old
	Low % of population aged 60+
Black population and number of working-age adults	High % of population Black
	High % of population working-age adults
Lone and teen mothers	High % of live births to teen mothers
	High % of live births to lone mothers
Deprivation	High % of 0- to 3-year-olds living in workless households
	High % of 0- to 3-year-olds living in households receiving Income Support
	High % of 4- to 17-year-olds living in households receiving Income Support
	High % of adults with no qualifications
	High % of primary-age children eligible for free school meals
Unemployment	High % of population unemployed and last worked before 1996
	High % of adults receiving Jobseeker's Allowance
	High % of children under 4 in households receiving Jobseeker's Allowance
Child illness/ disability	High number of cases of gastroenteritis per 1,000 children aged 0-3 years
	High number of lower respiratory infection per 1,000 children aged 0-3 years
	High number of cases of severe injury per 1,000 children aged 0-3 years
	High % of 0- to 3-year-olds receiving Disability Living Allowance
	High % of 4- to 17-year-olds receiving Disability Living Allowance
Infant mortality	High number of cases of infant mortality per 1,000 live births
	High number of cases of neonatal mortality per 1,000 live births
	High number of cases of perinatal mortality per 1,000 live births
School achievement: Key Stage 1 (KS1)	High % of children aged 7 achieving Level 2 KS1 English
	High % of children aged 7 achieving Level 2 KS1 Mathematics
	High % of children aged 7 achieving Level 2 KS1 Science
Household crowding	Low % households with up to 0.5 persons per room
	High % households with more than 1.5 persons per room
Council housing	Low % of households owner occupied
	High % of households council owned
Adult poor health/disability	High % of adult females with long-term illness (age standardised)
	High % of adult males with long-term illness (age standardised)
	High % of adults receiving Disability Living or Attendance Allowance
	High % of adults receiving Severe Disability Allowance or Incapacity Benefit

Table 8.4: Outcome variables

Outcome variable	Details
Services and community	
Mother's area rating	As place to live and raise children (Barnes McGuire, 1997)
Observer's area rating	As place to live and raise children (Barnes McGuire, 1997)
Total support services used	Out of 15 listed (NESS Research Team, 2005)
Total usefulness of support	Usefulness rating for each service used (NESS Research Team, 2005)
Maternal and family functioning	
Malaise	Defined in Rutter et al (1970)
Self-esteem	Defined in Bachman et al (1997)
Supportive parenting	Composite of observed 'responsivity' (such as praising, responsiveness, showing affection) and 'acceptance' (avoidance of scolding, spanking and restraining) (Caldwell and Bradley, 1984)
Negative parenting[a]	Composite of reported parent–child conflict and closeness (Pianta, 2001), harsh discipline (such as swearing, threatening, smacking) (Straus et al, 1998) and household chaos (disorganised, noisy) (Matheny et al, 1995)
Home learning environment[a]	Engaging in reading to child, taking to library, playing with numbers, singing and so on (Melhuish et al, 2001)
Involvement of father	Looking after child, feeding and playing (as reported by mother) (NESS Research Team, 2005)
Home chaos[b]	Disorganised, noisy, lacking regular routine (Matheny et al, 1995).
Child health and development	
Birthweight[b]	In grams
Duration of breast feeding[b]	In weeks
Frequency of accidents	During past year (or nine months for nine-month-old children)
Hospital admissions	During past (or nine months for nine-month-old children)
Social competence[a]	Composite of 'prosocial behaviour' (such as showing empathy, sharing) and 'independence' (such as working things out for self, choosing activities for self) (Goodman, 1997)
Behavioural problems[a]	Composite of 'conduct problems' (such as disruptive behaviour, fighting or bullying, temper tantrums), 'emotional difficulties' (such as worrying and anxiety, clingyness), 'hyperactivity' (restlessness, impulsivity) and 'general difficulties' (such as problems getting along with others, concentrating, behaving properly) (Goodman, 1997)
Verbal ability[a]	Language expression and comprehension abilities (English speakers only) (Elliot et al, 1996)
Non-verbal ability[a]	Spatial and number skills (Elliot et al, 1996)

Notes:
[a] 36-month-old children only.
[b] Nine-month-old children only.

- *Services*: total number of different types of services used, usefulness of services used.

Dependent variable data reduction

In order to reduce the likelihood that significant effects of SSLPs would emerge by chance (that is, ones that would 'masquerade' as actual effects of SSLPs), the number of outcome variables subject to statistical analysis was reduced by creating composites. To accomplish this, two factor analyses (with oblique rotation) were carried out on the 36-month data, one including parenting/family environment variables (that is, responsivity, acceptance, parent–child conflict, parent–child closeness, discipline, home chaos) and one including child socioemotional functioning (that is, conduct problems, hyperactivity, prosocial behaviour, independence, emotional regulation, overall difficulties). In each case, two clear factors emerged (eigen values >1.0), leading to the creation of a total of four internally consistent composite dependent variables:

- *Supportive parenting*: responsivity + acceptance
- *Negative parenting*: parent–child conflict + harsh discipline + home chaos − parent–child closeness
- *Child social competence*: prosocial behaviour + independence
- *Child emotion-behaviour difficulties*: conduct problems + hyperactivity + emotion dysregulation + overall difficulties

In addition, measures of child verbal and non-verbal ability and of parental acceptance and the home learning environment served as other outcomes for three-year-olds. The home learning environment was retained as a separate measure because two separate investigations, the study of Effective Pre-school Provision in England (EPPE) (Melhuish et al, 2001; Sammons et al, 2002; Sylva et al, 2004) and in Northern Ireland (EPPNI) (Melhuish et al, 2002), revealed this aspect of the child's family to be uniquely powerful in predicting children's development.

Statistical analysis

Two important issues need to be clarified regarding the statistical analyses undertaken to evaluate the impact of SSLPs. The first concerns missing data; the second the testing of across-the-board effects, also known as main effects, and subpopulation-specific effects, also known as interaction effects, by means of multilevel modelling.

Missing data and imputation

In gathering data from children and families, virtually all studies find that some proportion of information to be obtained cannot be gathered. This may occur for a variety of reasons, including insufficient time, unwillingness of research participants to provide the desired information, language translation difficulties, or even human error. Missing data pose data analysis problems; a single piece of missing data can result in the elimination of an entire case (that is, child or family) from a particular statistical analysis. It is important to note that cases with missing data are generally not randomly distributed in the population studied. Thus, if these cases are excluded from analyses because of missing information, this may lead to biased estimates, in this case of the effects of SSLPs.

There is a strategy to overcome this problem involving the 'imputation' of missing data. Imputation is based on the premise that tolerably accurate estimates of what a missing value would have been had it not been missing can be determined using all the data collected on all cases for whom data have been gathered. Taking an oversimplified example, knowing a person's age, education level, gender, working status and occupation enables a reasonably accurate prediction of salary, should salary information be missing, using information on all these variables obtained from respondents who also provided salary information. In this study, sophisticated and widely used multiple-imputation techniques were employed to overcome the possibility of biased findings resulting from non-random missing data (Rubin, 1987; Schafer, 1997; Schafer and Graham, 2002).

All statistical analyses to address the four questions posed earlier (on p 136) were carried out on two datasets. One dataset included only those cases for which 100% of the individual family-level background control variables were available. The second dataset included imputed data, affording a maximum sample size while reducing bias associated with incomplete data. This second dataset included all eligible individuals. Across all the data available, imputation of nine-month missing data resulted in an increase in approximately 3% of the data; the corresponding figure for 36 months was 6%. With respect to any specific dependent variable, imputed data were generated for between 10% and 41% of cases.

In reporting results and drawing conclusions, the greatest confidence is placed in significant findings that emerged in both sets of analyses, that is, analyses based only on cases with complete data *and* analyses that included imputed data. It is these results that are thus summarised in this chapter. In large samples such as that examined in the cross-sectional Impact Study, even small differences may be statistically significant. Moreover, when many tests are conducted, the number of significant findings that might emerge by chance increases. It is important, then, that all findings to be presented emerged at a rate greater than would be expected by chance relative to the number of tests carried out. Requiring a significant result to occur in both complete cases and imputed analyses to some extent counteracts the effect of finding significant effects by chance with many statistical tests being run.

With the relatively conservative strategy of relying only on those findings that emerged as statistically significant in both sets of analyses, a traditional criterion of significance $p<0.05$ (within either analysis) was adopted, often referred to as the '95% confidence level'. This means that if a result has a p value of less than 0.05, the result is taken as meaningful, in that it shows that there is less than five in a hundred possibility that the result in question had emerged by chance. Put another way, if p is less than 0.05, one can be 95% certain that the result is not simply a function of random variation, but reflects real differences within the sample (that is, the 'null' hypothesis is rejected).

Testing main and interaction effects: multilevel modelling

The first stage of data analysis was designed to assess the main or across-the-board effects of SSLPs on each dependent variable, after taking into account pre-existing differences between SSLP and comparison families and communities. A main effect represents the detection of a significant difference between SSLP and comparison communities on a measured outcome for the overall populations in those communities, having allowed for the background differences in the populations and areas.

Whether or not overall main effects of SSLPs emerged, analyses were also undertaken to determine whether specific subpopulations were differentially affected by SSLPs. Six demographic variables were chosen – because of their policy relevance – to define the subpopulations. More specifically, statistical interactions involving SSLP status and each of these variables were tested for each outcome measure after controlling for the child and family characteristics and significant local area characteristics: child gender (that is, boys, girls), maternal employment (that is, full time, part time, unemployed), maternal age at child's birth (that is, <20 years/teen, ≥20 years/non-teen), lone parenthood (that is, no partner living in home, partnered), household employment (that is, no adult employed/workless, adult employed) and income deprivation (that is, <£100 per week, £100-194 per week, >£194 per week). Households with incomes below £194 per week, representing 60% of England's median income at the time of data collection, are officially regarded as poor. The proportion of the sample below this official poverty line was 54.5%. The <£100 per week income figure identified the poorest group, representing 13% of the sample.

In order to determine whether across-the-board or subpopulation-specific effects of SSLPs on child development and family functioning were detectable, the data was analysed using multilevel models (Goldstein, 1995), a multivariate statistical procedure that takes into account the hierarchical nature of the data, with children and families nested within communities, some of which were SSLP communities and some of which were comparison communities. The analysis of each outcome controlled for pre-existing child, family or community factors. This procedure afforded an assessment of the effects of this set of variables – individually and collectively – on the outcome, and statistically controlled for effects of these (potentially confounding) variables before testing, subsequently, whether SSLP-specific effects existed (that is, significant differences between SSLP and comparison areas). This final and fundamental concern was addressed first by evaluating the overall effect of Sure Start and then, one by one, testing each of the designated interactions to determine whether subpopulations were differentially affected by SSLPs.

Results and discussion

The results of the cross-sectional Impact Study can be succinctly summarised in terms of answers to the four questions posed in the introduction to the chapter, each of which refined the general question, 'What was the effect of SSLPs, all other things being equal?' This is because answers to these questions were provided after taking into consideration (that is, statistically controlling for) the fact that families varied within and across communities and that communities in which children/families resided varied from each other as well – in ways that could influence the outcomes measured. To foreshadow what is to come, overall, only limited evidence of across-the-board SSLP impact was detected, but there were some subpopulation-specific effects. Table 8.5 presents the mean values and test statistics for all outcomes with significant SSLP effects, some of which can be regarded as beneficial whereas others are developmentally adverse. In all cases, the size of these limited effects, whether developmentally beneficial or adverse, is small.

Table 8.5: Imputed mean scores (and confidence intervals) of measures showing significant differences between SSLPs and comparison groups

Child's age group and sample subgroup	Outcome measure	Score estimate (95% confidence interval)		Difference between groups (95% confidence interval)	p value
		SSLP group	Comparison group		
9 months					
All participants	Home chaos	(n=12,575) 9.24 (9.01 to 9.42)	(n=1,509) 9.57 (9.35 to 9.79)	−0.33 (−0.48 to −0.18)	<0.001
36 months					
All participants	Mother's area rating	(n=3,927) 31.22 (30.15 to 32.29)	(n=1,101) 32.20 (30.98 to 33.41)	−0.98 (−1.61 to −0.34)	0.004
	Acceptance	2.82 (2.75 to 2.88)	2.69 (2.61 to 2.77)	0.13 (0.06 to 0.19)	<0.001
Non-teenage mothers	Negative parenting	(n=3,428) 33.10 (31.30 to 34.90)	(n=973) 34.70 (32.80 to 36.70)	−1.61 (−2.77 to −0.47)	0.006
	Social competence	24.35 (23.96 to 24.74)	24.08 (23.64 to 24.53)	0.27 (0.02 to 0.52)	0.04
	Behavioural problems	28.30 (27.22 to 29.38)	29.14 (27.91 to 30.37)	−0.84 (−1.51 to −0.17)	0.01
Teenage mothers	Verbal ability	(n=499) 39.10 (37.75 to 40.44)	(n=128) 42.17 (40.26 to 44.08)	−3.08 (−4.82 to −1.34)	<0.001
	Social competence	24.02 (23.57 to 24.46)	24.83 (24.21 to 25.45)	−0.81 (−1.40 to −0.22)	0.007
	Behavioural problems	31.13 (29.75 to 32.50)	29.08 (27.18 to 30.98)	2.05 (0.27 to 3.82)	0.02
Lone parents	Verbal ability	(n=1,378) 37.95 (36.94 to 38.95)	(n=379) 39.59 (38.21 to 40.97)	−1.64 (−2.78 to −0.51)	0.005
Workless household	Verbal ability	(n=1,520) 38.19 (37.02 to 39.36)	(n=452) 39.40 (37.92 to 40.87)	−1.21 (−2.30 to −0.12)	0.03

Did children/families in SSLPs receive more services or experience their communities differently than children/families in comparison communities?

Recall that the 'theory of change' underlying SSLPs stipulated that, by enhancing services and changing the nature of the community, the functioning of children/families would improve. Information obtained from interview respondents (that is, mothers) provided only limited evidence that services and communities were affected by SSLPs. Neither mothers of nine- nor 36-month-olds in SSLP areas reported greater (or lesser) use or usefulness of services than mothers in the comparison communities. In terms of the favourability–unfavourability of the community as a place to live and raise children, no effects of SSLPs were detected among families with nine-month-olds. Among families with 36-month-olds, however, mothers in SSLP areas actually rated their communities *less favourably* than those in comparison communities, a result certainly inconsistent with expectations. In summary, there was very little evidence that SSLPs achieved their goals of increasing service use and/or usefulness or of enhancing families' impressions of their communities.

Did families function differently in SSLP areas than in comparison communities?

Recall that children growing up in SSLP areas might have been affected by SSLPs both directly and indirectly. To determine whether SSLPs affected family functioning in ways that might be expected to influence child development, the Impact Study measured maternal well-being, reported and observed parenting, and household organisation.

Sure Start Local Programmes appeared to beneficially affect family functioning to a modest extent; the households of mothers of nine-month olds were less chaotic (for example, less noise, regular routines) and mothers of 36-month-olds were more accepting of their children's behaviour (that is, less slapping, scolding, physical restraint). There was a further benefit for non-teen mothers of 36-month-olds, who comprised the majority (86%), in that those living in SSLP areas showed less negative parenting than mothers in comparison areas. In sum, SSLPs appeared to enhance growth-promoting family processes somewhat, although many more family outcomes appeared to be unaffected by SSLPs than those few summarised here showing statistically significant effects.

Did effects of SSLPs extend to children themselves?

Because effects for family functioning may take time to influence children's development, it might be optimistic to expect SSLP-related effects on child functioning at this stage, when SSLPs had not been operating for a substantial amount of time. As it turned out, both beneficial and adverse effects of SSLPs on children were detected, although these were restricted almost entirely to 36-month-olds and varied across subpopulations. Once again these effects were limited, with many more child outcomes failing to reveal any effects of SSLPs than those few statistically significant effects summarised here. Nevertheless, because the limited findings form a coherent pattern, they were regarded as meaningful.

Three-year-olds of non-teen mothers living in SSLP communities exhibited fewer behaviour problems and manifested greater social competence than those in comparison communities. Adverse effects of SSLPs emerged in the case of children of teen mothers (14% of sample), however, as they scored lower on verbal ability and social competence and higher on behaviour problems than their counterparts in comparison areas. Children from workless households (40% of the sample) and children from lone-parent families (33% of the sample) also showed evidence of adverse effects of SSLPs, scoring significantly lower on verbal ability when growing up in SSLP areas than did their counterparts in comparison communities.

In sum, results suggested that within the sample of children from (mostly) deprived families living in deprived communities, those from *relatively* less (but still) disadvantaged households (that is, non-teen mothers) residing in SSLP areas benefited somewhat from living in these areas. In contrast, within these same deprived communities, children from *relatively* more disadvantaged families (that is, teen mothers, lone parents, workless households) appeared to have been adversely affected by living in an SSLP community.

How did effects on children come about?

In light of the evidence that SSLPs affected both parenting and child functioning, at least in the case of non-teen-mother families, it was of interest to determine whether effects of SSLPs on the child might have been a function of – that is, mediated by – effects of SSLPs on parenting (that is, SSLP → parenting → child development). Tests were carried out to determine whether the process of influencing the child was, in fact, indirect. In the case of non-teen mothers the data were consistent with this view: the beneficial effect of SSLPs on children's social competence and behaviour problems was (statistically) mediated by, that is, a function of, SSLP effects on negative parenting. In other words, when SSLPs functioned to reduce the level of negative parenting, children's social functioning was enhanced. Similar tests of mediation could not be made on other subgroups because none of the others showed evidence of SSLP impact on parenting and child outcomes.

Conclusions

The differential beneficial and adverse effects that emerged suggest that among the disadvantaged families living in the deprived SSLP areas, those parents/families with more personal, social and economic resources available to them were better able to take advantage of SSLP services and resources than those with fewer resources (that is, teen parents, lone parents, workless households). The finding that an intervention has produced greater benefits for the moderately disadvantaged than for the more severely disadvantaged has emerged in other evaluations (for example Early Head Start: Love et al, 2002). Possibly the utilisation of services by those with greater human capital left others with less access to services than would have been the case had they not lived in SSLP areas. This consideration suggests that special efforts may have been required to ensure that those most in need were not (inadvertently) deprived of assistance due to the way in which SSLPs operated. Special sensitivity (and related staff training) may also be required in dealing with the most disadvantaged families, as the adverse effects detected for them conceivably and inadvertently arose because they felt overwhelmed or turned off by the support offered by SSLPs, which might have been perceived as judgemental, such as the high-profile effort to reduce maternal smoking and increase breastfeeding.

It should be noted that the beneficial effects detected apply to more children/families than the adverse effects. There were many more children residing in families where the mother was not a teenager than in families in which the mother was a teenager at the time of the child's birth; there were more in households with an adult who was employed than there were in 'workless' households; and there were more in two-parent families than there were in families where the mother was a lone parent. However, because children from the most at-risk households are at greatest risk of school failure, drug use, crime and related problems that are costly to society, the possibility cannot be dismissed that the adverse effects detected and affecting fewer numbers of children could have greater consequences to communities and to society than the beneficial effects detected that affected more children/families.

In closing, it must be emphasised that the results summarised in this chapter reflected the cross-sectional study of SSLPs and comparison areas. The longitudinal follow-up of nine-month-olds at three and five years of age should provide additional evidence about whether, how and under what conditions SSLPs influenced children, parents and families. Obviously, only if the beneficial and/or adverse effects of SSLPs detected in the cross-sectional inquiry were maintained in the longitudinal follow-up would the results presented herein be truly meaningful. Moreover, it must be appreciated that, in the main, only limited evidence of effects of SSLPs, whether positive or negative, emerged and those that were detected were small in magnitude. The fact that SSLPs had been in existence for only three years when children/families were studied and perhaps not even entirely 'bedded' down and therefore not fully developed, further cautions against drawing strong conclusions from the first phase of the Impact Study designed to provide early insight into the effects that SSLPs might be having on children and families.

References

ACYF (Administration on Children, Youth and Families) (1997) *National evaluation of the Comprehensive Child Development Program*, available at: www.acf.hhs.gov/programs/opre/hs/comp_develop/reports/ccdp/ccdp00_title.html

Bachman, J.G., O'Malley, P.M. and Johnston, J. (1997) *Adolescence to adulthood: Changes and stability in the lives of young men*, Ann Arbor, MI: Institute for Social Research, University of Michigan.

Barnes McGuire, J. (1997) 'The reliability and validity of a questionnaire describing neighbourhood characteristics relevant to families and young children living in urban areas', *Journal of Community Psychology*, vol 25, pp 551-66.

Caldwell, B.M. and Bradley, R.H. (1984) *Home observation for measurement of the environment*, Little Rock, AR: University of Arkansas at Little Rock.

Elliot, C., Smith, P. and McCulloch, K. (1996) *British Ability Scales second edition (BAS II)*, Windsor: NFER-Nelson Publishing Company Limited.

Goldstein, H. (1995) *Multilevel statistical models* (2nd edn), London: Edward Arnold.

Goodman, R. (1997) 'The strengths and difficulties questionnaire: a research note', *Journal of Child Psychology and Psychiatry*, vol 38, pp 581-6.

Love, J., Kisker, E.E., Ross, C.M., Schochet, P.Z., Brooks-Gunn, J., Paulsell, D., Boller, K., Constantine, J., Vogel, C., Fuligni, A.S. and Brady-Smith, C. (2002) *Making a difference in the lives of infants and toddlers and their families: The impacts of Early Head Start. Volume 1: Final technical report*, Princeton, NJ: Mathematica Policy Research Inc, www.mathematica-mpr.com/PDFs/ehsfinalvol1.pdf

Matheny, A.P., Wachs, T., Ludwig, J.L. and Phillips, K. (1995) 'Bringing order out of chaos: psychometric characteristics of the Confusion, Hubbub and Order Scale', *Journal of Applied Developmental Psychology*, vol 16, pp 429-44.

Melhuish, E.C., Sylva, K., Sammons, P., Siraj-Blatchford, I. and Taggart, B. (2001) *The Effective Provision of Pre-school Education Project, technical paper 7: Social/behavioural and cognitive development at 3-4 years in relation to family background*, London: Institute of Education/DfES.

Melhuish, E., Quinn, L., Sylva, K., Sammons, P., Siraj-Blatchford, I., Taggart, B. and Shields, C. (2002) *The Effective Pre-school Provision in Northern Ireland Project, technical paper 5: Pre-school experience and cognitive development at the start of primary school*, Belfast: Stranmillis University Press.

NESS (National Evaluation of Sure Start) Research Team (2005) *Early impacts of Sure Start Local Programmes on children and families*, Sure Start Report 13, Nottingham: DfES, www.surestart.gov.uk/_doc/P0001867.pdf

Olds, D.L., Henderson, C.R., Kitzman, H., Eckenrode, J.J., Cole, R.E. and Tatelbaum, R.C. (1999) 'Prenatal and infancy home visitation by nurses: recent findings', *Future of Children*, vol 9, pp 44-66.

Pianta, R.C. (2001) *The Student-Teacher Relationship Scale*, Odessa, FL: PAR.

Ramey, C.T., Campbell, F.A., Burchinal, M., Skinner, M.L., Gardner, D.M. and Ramey, S.L. (2000) 'Persistent effects of early childhood education on high-risk children and their mothers', *Applied Developmental Science*, vol 4, pp 2-14.

Rubin, D.B. (1987) *Multiple imputation for nonresponse in surveys*, New York: Wiley and Sons.

Rutter, M., Tizard, J. and Whitmore, K. (1970) *Education, health and behaviour*, London: Longmans.

Sammons, P., Sylva, K., Melhuish, E.C., Siraj-Blatchford, I., Taggart, B. and Elliot, K. (2002) *The Effective Provision of Pre-school Education Project, technical paper 8a: Measuring the impact on children's cognitive development over the pre-school years*, London: Institute of Education/DfES.

Sanders, M.R. (2003) 'Triple P – Positive Parenting Program: a population approach to promoting competent parenting', *Australian e-Journal for the Advancement of Mental Health*, vol 2, www.auseinet. com/journal/vol2iss3/sanders.pdf, also available at: www.pfsc.uq.edu. au/02_ppp/ppp.html

Schafer, J.L. (1997) *Analysis of incomplete multivariate data*, London: Chapman and Hall.

Schafer, J.L. and Graham, J. (2002) 'Missing data: our view of the state of the art', *Psychological Methods*, vol 7, pp 147-77.

Straus, M.A., Hamby, S., Finkelhor, D., Moore, D. and Runyan, D. (1998) 'Identification of child maltreatment with the Parent–Child Conflict Tactics Scales', *Child Abuse and Neglect*, vol 22, pp 249-70.

Sylva, K., Melhuish, E., Sammons, P., Siraj-Blatchford, I. and Taggart, B. (2004) *The Effective Provision of Pre-school Education (EPPE) Project: Final report: A longitudinal study funded by the DfES 1997-2004*, London: DfES.

Webster-Stratton, C. (1993) 'Strategies for helping families with young oppositional defiant or conduct-disordered children: the importance of home and school collaboration', *School Psychology Review*, vol 22, pp 437-57.

NINE

Variation in Sure Start Local Programmes: consequences for children and families

Edward Melhuish, Jay Belsky, Angela Anning and Mog Ball

Sure Start Local Programmes (SSLPs) were true community interventions (see Barnes et al, 2006), in that all children under four and their families in an area were 'targets' of intervention. As discussed in Chapter One, community control was emphasised and was to be exercised through local partnership management boards. These boards brought together all stakeholders in the community concerned with children (that is, health services, social services, education, the private sector, the voluntary sector and parents). The placing of almost complete control with the community meant that there was very little specification of how to provide services, only what they should achieve. The programmes were to improve existing services and create new ones as needed, but there was no specification of *how* services were to be changed or what exactly was to be delivered – ends, not means. This is in marked contrast to focused early interventions that have been demonstrated to be effective, be they childcare based, like the Abecedarian Project (Ramey et al, 2000); home based, like the Prenatal Early Intervention Project (Olds et al, 1999); or the Positive Parenting Program (Sanders, 2003); or even a combination of centre and home based, like Early Head Start (Love et al, 2005).

While all communities selected were disadvantaged, such areas, including those selected for SSLPs, differed in important ways related to child and family well-being (Barnes et al, 2005). This area-level diversity is discussed in Chapter Two. Also, programmes' local autonomy, together with their diverse history and service provision, as well as diversity among lead agencies and professionals, resulted in wide variation across the programmes in what they did, how they did it, and in their implementation proficiency, posing a challenge for evaluation.

The preceding chapter highlighted the limited, but significant, across-the-board effects of SSLPs on family functioning, after controlling for child, family and area characteristics. Recall that mothers of nine-month-olds living in SSLP areas reported less household chaos and mothers of three-year-olds showed greater parental acceptance when compared with families living in similar areas that were yet to receive a Sure Start programme. In these analyses it was clear that great variation existed in the degree to which various programmes benefited children and families.

The extent to which interventions vary in effectiveness has been studied with regard to individual-level interventions such as parent training (for example, Kazdin et al, 1997; Hartman et al, 2003). Even generally effective interventions vary in their impact and illuminating the processes by which they prove to be more and less effective is critical for understanding not only how they achieve – or why they fail to achieve – their goals, but how their effectiveness can be increased. However, little research has been undertaken of community-level variation related to interventions. Thus, having discerned some general, even if limited and modest, intervention effects of SSLPs, the question arose: 'Does variation in the implementation of programmes account for variation in their impact on child/family functioning?' Elucidating the features of programmes that may account for variation in impact on children and families was undertaken in the evaluation of variation in Early Head Start implementation (Love et al, 2005), and we attempt to achieve similar goals as part of the National Evaluation of Sure Start (NESS) Impact Study.

Typically, evaluation studies regard the fidelity of implementation to the model of intervention as central to a programme's success. Fidelity concerns whether an intervention adheres to the originally developed protocol or programme or not. Criteria for fidelity typically include programmatic structure, the framework for service delivery, and the ways services are delivered. Using such criteria can facilitate the replication of an intervention over and over again (Bond et al, 2000) and, with highly specified interventions; fidelity is a cornerstone of the study of programme variation. When considering the case of SSLPs, however, local autonomy, coupled with a lack of specification of how aims were to be realised, resulted in a situation in which there was no specified model for traditional fidelity criteria to be applied.

In order to overcome this challenge, NESS developed an alternative to programme fidelity, which was proficiency in realising the basic Sure Start principles, as articulated in central government guidance documents provided to SSLPs (SSU, 2002). Eighteen characteristics were identified as being central to proficient programme functioning; theoretically, then, programmes that enacted these principles in their operations were expected to achieve SSLP goals – enhancing child and family functioning – more than programmes that failed to (see NESS Research Team, 2005a, for more details). In order to test this proposition, the NESS research team developed measurement scales so that each SSLP could be rated – quantitatively – on the extent to which it fulfilled each of the 18 principles (see Box 9.1). Collectively, these principles reflect the implicit and explicit 'theory of change' guiding SSLPs (see Weiss, 1995). As an example, benefits to children and families were expected to derive from successful efforts to (a) build functional partnerships among stakeholders, (b) empower service providers and parents alike and (c) facilitate family access to available services. In consequence, each of these implementation principles – and 15 others – was rated for each of the 150 SSLPs included in the NESS Impact Study. This exercise in measuring variation in implementation proficiency, then, was an attempt to move beyond the 'between-group' question addressed in Chapter Eight – Do children/families in SSLP areas function better than those in comparison areas? – to address the issue of potential determinants of variation in SSLP effectiveness.

Developing measures of programme implementation proficiency

The challenge of producing implementation proficiency measurements applicable across diverse programmes, with the same overall aims, required innovative methods. After conducting a pilot study, a wide range of quantitative and qualitative data gathered from diverse sources, including much data originally collected by the NESS Implementation module, were systematically collated, analysed and synthesised into summaries of programme characteristics, which allowed reliable ratings of domains of implementation proficiency to be made in quantitative terms. In addition, several measures of separate types of service provision and staffing were produced.

Scales for rating the proficiency of implementation

The 18 domains of implementation proficiency (seven concerning process, seven concerning progress and four concerning holistic aspects of implementation) were rated for each programme after careful review of information pertaining to each rating, assembled for each SSLP. Data sources that provided the information on which these ratings were made included original programme delivery plans prepared by each SSLP; an extensive survey of programme policies and practices supplemented by telephone follow-up to programme managers and others to gain additional information when required to clarify ambiguities; case study data where available; programme publications, publicity materials and organisational diagrams; SSLP local evaluation reports (see www.ness. bbk.ac.uk for some examples); NESS staff appraisals of local evaluations; and SSLP expenditure and monitoring data (on numbers of families using programmes) provided by the Sure Start Unit (SSU) within the Department for Education and Skills (DfES). Additional information used in making proficiency ratings came from structured telephone interviews conducted with key informants who had particular insight into the histories, implementation and functioning of the programmes, including Regional Programme Development Officers; chairs of SSLP management boards; and local authority Early Years Officers and NESS staff who worked with programmes on a regular basis, often supporting local small-scale evaluations undertaken by programmes themselves to help them in developing their services. In other words, any and all quantitative and qualitative information that all aspects of NESS had gathered over the course of several years on each programme was 'grist for the rating mill'. Although the quantity and quality of data on each programme was not exactly the same in all instances, for each programme there was more than enough raw data of one kind or another available to afford the reliable rating of the programme on each of the 18 criteria of proficiency. As already noted, for each of the 18 domains a seven-point rating scale was used (1 = inadequate, 4 = moderate, 7 = excellent) with explicit criteria specified for each scale point. Box 9.1 provides illustrative statements articulating the excellent end of each scale (see NESS Research Team, 2005a, for further details on criteria). Here is an example of the guidance criteria for rating the dimension of 'empowerment':

A good SSLP (rating = 5 on 1–7 scale) would have:

- users on the board;
- community volunteers;
- training for volunteers;
- a balance of voluntary and paid staff;
- built-in features to develop local people's involvement;
- clearly defined exit strategies for users;
- services that include self-help groups or other services run by users.

Box 9.1: 18 domains of SSLP implementation proficiency

Process

• **Partnership – composition**: the SSLP partnership board has a balanced representation of education, social services, health, voluntary and community organisations and parents.
• **Partnership – functioning**: the partnership functions well.
• **Leadership**: the SSLP has effective leadership/management.
• **Multi-agency working**: multi-agency teamwork is well established.
• **Service access**: there are clear pathways to access specialist services.
• **Staff turnover**: staff turnover is low.
• **Evaluation use:** the SSLP takes account of evaluation findings.

Progress

• **Services – quantity**: Service delivery reflects guidance for core services in family support, health, play, early learning and childcare.
• **Services – delivery**: the SSLP has a balanced focus on children, family and community.
• **Identification of users**: the SSLP has strategies for the identification of users.
• **Reach**: the SSLP shows a realistic and substantial involvement of families.
• **Reach strategies**: the SSLP has strategies to improve and sustain the use of services.
• **Services – innovation**: the SSLP shows innovation in service delivery.
• **Services – flexibility**: services accommodate the needs of a wide range of users.

Holistic

• **Vision**: the SSLP has a well-articulated vision relevant to the community.
• **Empowerment**: the SSLP procedures create an environment that empowers users and staff.
• **Communications**: communications reflect the characteristics/languages of the community.
• **Ethos**: the SSLP has a welcoming and inclusive ethos.

After creating the ratings of proficient implementation, a team was trained to search the information gathered on each of the 150 SSLPs for which impact data were available (see Chapter Eight) and to separately assemble information specifically pertinent to each of the 18 ratings in separate files. Subsequently, two trained raters, working independently, rated each programme on each of the proficiency dimensions after reviewing the relevant assembled material. Inter-rater agreement within one point averaged 87% (range 77% to 98%) between these two raters, with weighted Kappa averaging 0.8 (range 0.6 to 1.0), and indicating clearly that diverse qualitative and quantitative information on a community intervention could be reliably scored in quantitative terms. For all 18 ratings the full range of possible scores – from 1 to 7 – was used and the distributions across the 150 programmes approximated normal distributions. The distributions usually peaked between 3.0 and 4.0 (that is, moderate scores) and the means varied from 3.7 to 4.3 with standard deviations varying from 1.0 to 1.5. Clearly programmes were not judged, on average, as being excellent in their realisation of SSLP principles and there was substantial variation across programmes.

Variation in services and staffing in programmes

In addition to the raw data available on programmes providing sufficient information to afford reliable ratings of proficiency in realising SSLP principles, extensive information on actual service provision was also available. This afforded the quantitative scoring of four distinct types of services offered by programmes – so that it could also be determined whether variation in the types of service delivered might account for variation in programme impact on children/families. These were:

(1) child-focused services (for example, early education/care, outside play areas, and language/literacy schemes such as 'BookStart');
(2) parent-focused services (for example, helplines, health promotion, respite care, drop-in crèches);
(3) family-focused services (for example, family support, health services, family planning, toy libraries); and
(4) community-focused services (for example, welfare rights advice, credit unions, general practitioner [GP] surgeries, self-help groups).

These four major service categories were further subclassified as (a) inherited (that is, predating SSLPs), (b) improved (by SSLPs) or (c) new (SSLP-created) services. Thus, it proved possible to count the number of different services offered by a programme within each subcategory. In order to facilitate comparisons across different-size programmes, staffing numbers (that is, full-time equivalents) were converted to proportions of SSLP staff engaged in the four services that were present in all programmes of outreach, family support, health services, and play and childcare.

Producing measures of programme effectiveness

Given the availability of data on child and family functioning from the larger (between-group) Impact Study described in Chapter Eight, multilevel modelling was used to derive measures of effectiveness for each programme for a range of child and parenting outcomes. In the analyses of SSLP impact reported in Chapter Eight, particular outcomes showed significant variation, at the community level, among the 150 SSLP communities. These outcomes, of which there were eight, consisted of two nine-month parenting measures: *maternal acceptance* (that is, avoidance of scolding/spanking/restraining) from the HOME Inventory (Caldwell and Bradley, 1984) and *household chaos* (that is, the extent to which the household is disorganised, noisy, lacking regular routine) (Matheny et al, 1995); five 36-month parenting outcomes, *maternal acceptance*, *negative parenting* (a composite of reported parent–child conflict and closeness (Pianta, 2001)), *harsh discipline* (for example, swearing, threatening, smacking (Straus et al, 1998)), *household chaos*, and *home learning environment* (reflecting learning activities in the home, for example, reading, learning songs, playing with numbers) (Melhuish et al, 2001); and three child outcomes for 36-month-olds: *verbal and non-verbal ability* from the British Ability Scales, and *social competence* (composite of 'prosocial behaviour' from the Strengths and Difficulties Questionnaire: Goodman, 1997; and 'independence' from the Child Social Behaviour Questionnaire: Sammons et al, 2003). These child and parenting variables are used as outcomes in multilevel models to produce measures of SSLP effectiveness as described later.

The data analysed are hierarchical in that children and families are nested within communities. Multilevel modelling is a statistical technique that can take into account such hierarchical data structures and produce accurate estimates of differences between participants, between communities and between any comparison groups chosen. The technique of multilevel modelling also provides estimates of programme effects that are equivalent to programme 'effectiveness' scores for each programme for each outcome. These are equivalent to measures of the extent to which SSLPs produced outcomes better (or worse) than expected given child, family and community background characteristics.

Four questions concerning programme variation and impact on children/families

Having derived measures of implementation proficiency, services and staffing, as well as measures of overall programme effectiveness for parenting and child outcomes, the study sought to address four specific questions:

(1) Do implementation proficiency ratings collectively discriminate programmes varying in effectiveness?
(2) Do specific implementation ratings predict variation in programme effectiveness?
(3) Does service provision predict programme effectiveness?
(4) Do staffing patterns predict programme effectiveness?

In the remainder of this chapter, each of these questions is answered in turn and then some general conclusions are drawn.

Do implementation proficiency ratings collectively discriminate programmes varying in effectiveness?

To address this question, the statistical technique of discriminant function analysis (Huberty, 1984) was used. Specifically, the effectiveness scores for each SSLP across all eight parent and child outcomes listed above were averaged within a programme, separately for nine- and 36-month outcomes, and the distributions of the resulting composites of (nine- and 36-month) effectiveness scores were divided at the median to create two SSLP groups – one of more and one of less effective programmes (in terms of demonstrated impact on children/families). The question then became whether the 18 proficiency ratings, collectively, differed across these two groups' programmes. As it turned out, the 18 programme proficiency ratings significantly discriminated between groups of more and less effective programmes. For nine-month outcomes, improvement in correct classification beyond chance (that is, 50%) was 32% (p<0.001). For 36-month outcomes improvement in correct classification beyond chance was 35%. Importantly, the results of the discriminant function analysis based on all 150 Impact Study SSLPs, were fully replicated when the 150 programmes were randomly split into two halves and analyses rerun on both subsamples – after having defined half of the 75 as more and half as less effective using the same criteria articulated above for all 150 SSLPs.

These results clearly showed that variation in implementation proficiency mattered for programme effectiveness/impact. Moreover, they indicated that the reliably made ratings were themselves valid, having performed, at least collectively, as anticipated – by distinguishing more and less effective programmes. In other words, the turning of diverse pieces of qualitative and quantitative data into a series of quantitative ratings revealed that better implemented programmes exerted somewhat greater beneficial impact on the children/ families living within their boundaries than did other less effectively implemented programmes – and that this programme-variability effect was itself detectable.

Do specific implementation ratings predict variation in programme effectiveness?

It is one thing to determine that the 18 ratings collectively discriminated more and less effective programmes, but it is quite another to gain insight into which features of programme proficiency – that is, which of the 18 ratings – might be principally responsible for such an effect. To address the second question, then, the statistical technique of multiple regression was employed. The 18 ratings were used to predict each outcome in a hierarchical stepwise, forward entry, regression analysis, whereby the strongest predictor was entered first, followed by additional predictors if they yielded a significant increase in predictive power over and above the first-entered predictor. Given the substantial positive inter-correlation of the 18 ratings (mean 0.4, range 0.2 to 0.8) indicating that programmes that scored high on one dimension of proficiency tended to score high on others, any significant effect may reflect the overall impact of ratings. Therefore, whenever a particular rating proved significant, the regression was repeated adding the average of all 18 ratings (that is, ratings' composite) as an additional predictor. If this composite did not significantly affect the result of the first regression equation identifying individually powerful predictors, then the effect for an individual rating could be more confidently embraced. One individual rating significantly predicted one of the two nine-month parenting outcomes and this held when the composite rating was included as a predictor; the more an SSLP promoted *empowerment*, the more it enhanced maternal acceptance ($p < 0.01$). That is, in SSLPs in which both service providers and parents were being empowered, typically by diverse means, mothers in these programmes relied less (than would otherwise be expected) on harsh punishment and coercion, as observed during data collection visits to the home, than did mothers in other SSLP areas in which less empowerment was judged to have occurred.

With respect to outcomes for 36-month-olds, programmes rated higher on *identification of users* exerted greater positive impact on children's non-verbal ability ($p<0.01$) than other programmes, a result not changed by including the ratings' composite as a predictor. Programmes rated higher on *ethos* and lower on *service flexibility* exerted more positive impacts on maternal acceptance than did other programmes, but the latter result appeared to be an artefact of statistical suppression between these two highly correlated variables ($r=0.54$), as the latter proved unrelated to maternal acceptance when considered on its own. Moreover, when the composite rating was included as a predictor, the effect of *ethos* became insignificant, as did the composite itself, as a result of suppression between highly correlated predictors. Given the high correlation between *ethos* and the composite rating ($r=0.80$), the significant effect of *ethos* can be regarded as a proxy for a generally effective programme rather than an effect specifically attributable to *ethos*. Programmes exerted greater beneficial impact on maternal acceptance when programmes were rated higher on *empowerment*, which remained when the ratings' composite was included as a predictor. Finally, the outcome home learning environment was significantly predicted by the rating of *empowerment*.

Even though the results of this rating-specific regression analysis were not extensive, they did indicate that in some cases it was possible to pinpoint a feature of implementation proficiency that proved disproportionately responsible for a particular impact of SSLPs in this research into programme variation. In other cases, because proficient programmes proved to be, more or less, proficient across the board, with the same being true of programmes that were not particularly proficient, it proved impossible to attribute programme effects to a particular feature of the programme.

Does service provision predict programme effectiveness?

Having found that, at least in some instances, select features of programme proficiency could explain some variation in SSLP effectiveness, attention was turned in the third question to the some more refined particulars of service provision itself. The primary concern was with whether services were already in place when SSLPs began (that is, inherited services), whether existing services were improved and whether new services were created and how variation in each of these aspects of services affected variation in SSLP effectiveness with respect to child and family functioning. And this issue was addressed separately with respect to the different types of services that were measured – child focused, parent focused, family focused and community focused. The first analysis tested the relationship between an outcome and inherited (child, parent, family and community) services, and measurements of improved and new services were evaluated subsequently. In the hierarchical regression analyses, variables were allowed, within each stage, to enter stepwise with forward entry; thus variables only entered if they significantly improved prediction. For nine-month-olds, programmes that inherited more parent-focused services reduced negative parenting ($p<0.01$), more than did programmes that inherited fewer parent-focused services. For 36-month-old parenting, the more child-focused services were improved, the more maternal acceptance increased ($p<0.05$); recall that this latter effect reflects reductions in the amount of harsh discipline observed during the data collection home visit.

Do staffing patterns predict programme effectiveness?

Having addressed the issue of collective effects of proficiency across multiple dimensions, the particular importance of individual features of proficiency and of services offered, the final issue pertaining to programme variability concerned staffing. Staffing variables were analysed in the same way as service variables. Significant effects emerged for only one outcome, 36-month maternal acceptance. The greater the proportion of health services staff, the more maternal acceptance increased ($p<0.01$).

Discussion

It is important, for both theory and practice, to move beyond evaluation of the overall impact of an intervention and to identify processes that might account for variation in impact, as is increasingly recognised for parent training programmes (Reyno and McGrath, 2006). The study of programme variation reported in this chapter investigated why some SSLPs may have been more effective than others in promoting child and family well-being. Results reveal a limited – but significant and informative – degree of linkage between variation in programme implementation and impact on children/families, offering some guidance for practice. The methods adopted in this study are novel and might be applied to other interventions where implementation does not allow for the application of standard fidelity criteria. The strategy of inquiry adopted was based on the 'theory of change' approach to intervention evaluation (Weiss, 1995), which stresses the importance of developing interventions and assessing their implementation and impact in terms of their underlying theories or principles.

Whenever a high number of statistical associations are tested, as in this study between features of implementation and child/family outcomes, questions reasonably arise about the confidence that can be placed in the significant results that emerge. Examining the pattern of results partly addresses this issue and it seems noteworthy in this regard that all the significant relations detected between measures of implementation and of programme-specific impact were positive in nature (that is, higher implementation proficiency linked with more beneficial programme impact). If significant results reflected chance, some negative findings would be expected (for example, higher empowerment, less maternal acceptance). The probability of the detected results occurring by chance, then, is extremely unlikely, in that for eight significant findings the chance probability is 0.5^8, or $p<0.004$ (and this probability decreases further if the split-half replications of discriminant analyses are considered). This suggests that results reflect more than chance and so the findings of this study of within-group differences are consistent with the between-group study (presented in Chapter Eight): in both cases results show that SSLPs exert limited small effects, mostly (previous chapter) or exclusively (this chapter) in the desired direction, especially when they are implemented in ways more consistent with the overall programme philosophy (as operationalised in the 18 proficiency ratings).

Although detected relationships are not strong, it is encouraging that programmes scoring higher on implementation proficiency also scored higher on measures of programme impact on child and parenting. Collectively, 18 implementation-proficiency ratings differentiated more effective from less effective SSLPs for nine- and for 36-month-old child and parenting outcomes (which showed variation across the 150 SSLPs). In that proficiency ratings reflect adherence to the underlying principles in SSLP guidance, this result implies that programmes judged more proficient in putting guiding principles into practice were more likely to positively impact children and parenting. While it is not surprising that more proficient programmes are more effective, these results are important for two reasons. First, the systematic linkage between proficiency measurements, especially all 18 in the replicated discriminant function analysis, serves to validate the otherwise only face-valid measures, as noted earlier. Second, the proficiency findings illuminate the conditions under which an area-based programme like SSLPs can benefit children and families.

Recall that programmes tended to score similarly across all 18 ratings incorporating three broad aspects – what was implemented, the processes underpinning service delivery and holistic aspects of programme functioning. Proficiency in one domain goes with proficiency in other domains, and proficient implementation in general is more likely to produce better outcomes for children and families. For families, then, it matters not only what services are implemented, but also that they are proficiently delivered. This requires a clear vision, cogent means of communicating that vision and a welcoming ethos.

There appeared to be some effects related to specific programme features. More *empowerment* in programmes was related to greater positive impact on maternal acceptance for mothers of nine-month-olds; better *identification of users* was related to more positive programme impact on non-verbal ability of 36-month-olds; stronger *ethos* and better proficiency overall were positively related to greater beneficial impact on maternal acceptance of 36-month-olds; and more *empowerment* was related to greater success in fostering stimulating home learning environments for 36-month-olds. Although some readers may not be surprised by these findings, it seems instructive to note that a literature search failed to produce previous empirical evidence of the effects of such community-based programme implementation characteristics on children and families. Possibly this lack of evidence reflects the difficulties inherent in measuring such characteristics in multifaceted programmes like Sure Start. Clearly, then, this research offers innovative methods of measurement that could be adopted by others.

The finding that *empowerment* was related to two of the eight measures of programme impact on child and parenting outcomes, in particular two of the five parenting measures (nine-month-old maternal acceptance, 36-month-old home learning environment), suggests that strengthening programme activities relevant to *empowerment* should improve their effectiveness in influencing parenting. Important to appreciate is that *empowerment* in this study was not a self-report measure. *Empowerment* reflects a rating by trained experts of the extent to which procedures were in place in programmes that actually served to increase parent and staff participation and collaboration in decision making and programme activities. The programme characteristics that go with *empowerment* include community groups and parents being involved in the planning and delivery of services; parent representation; staff training opportunities; clear exit strategies for users; services to include self-help groups; evidence that staff and users constitute a learning community; and evidence of mutual respect for all parties.

The enhanced effectiveness for parenting may promote child well-being, given evidence from several countries that maternal acceptance is related to more competent child functioning (for example, Bradley, 2002) and research in the UK showing that the home learning environment has comparable beneficial effects (Melhuish et al, 2001; 2007; in press). Additionally, in that intergenerational continuity for behaviour problems is partly mediated by intergenerational continuity in parenting (Smith and Farrington, 2004), improving parenting is one way to disrupt cross-generational cycles of disadvantage, which was a central aim of the Sure Start initiative. Links between socioeconomic disadvantage and later maladaptive behaviour may be reduced given the evidence that adverse family functioning mediates the long-term link between socioeconomic status in childhood and susceptibility to crime in young adulthood (Fergusson et al, 2004).

Programme services and staffing were related to programme effectiveness only for 36-month-old parenting outcomes. Programmes with more inherited parent-focused services proved more successful in reducing negative parenting. Thus, some benefits that might appear attributable to SSLPs may actually reflect service history in communities. The fact, however, that more *improved* child-focused services predicted greater positive programme impact on maternal acceptance makes it clear that a new area-based initiative can promote positive change *when well implemented*. Finally, the fact that this same programme impact (that is, on maternal acceptance) was related to having a higher proportion of health-related staff is consistent with findings linking health-agency leadership to programme effectiveness (NESS Research Team, 2005b; Belsky et al, 2006).

The importance of integrating health services in multi-agency programmes is also evident in the finding that those more proficient in *identification of users* had greater positive impacts on non-verbal ability in 36-month-olds. Health-led programmes were better positioned to identify families with young children, because of easy access to birth records (from health services), enabling early use of services that may lead directly to stimulating experiences for children or, indirectly, via improvements in parenting. Also as health practitioners (midwives and health visitors particularly) already had established systems for visiting families with young children prior to Sure Start, they could probably 'hit the ground running' when the intervention provided resources to improve services. The NESS cost-effectiveness evaluation (see Chapter Seven) indicates that programmes led by health agencies became operational more quickly than those led by other agencies. Services that were implemented earlier by health staff (health visitors) with expertise in working with children aged 0 to 3 and their families were able to offer targeted treatment from birth and were therefore more likely to have a positive impact on parents, and ultimately their children.

Conclusions

No intervention is likely to be universally effective, and evidence of features of comprehensive interventions that promote child and family well-being is sparse. Hence it is critical to discover what elements of programmes account for variation in effectiveness in order to make programmes more effective. In order to inform practice, the programme variation study examined how implementation characteristics of a nationwide area-based intervention may influence variation in the impact on young children and their families living in disadvantaged communities. The resulting insights hold promise for practice and contribute to applied science by illustrating how diverse sources of often qualitative data can be quantified and subject to rigorous quantitative analysis.

It must be emphasised that other research indicates that it took around three years for these complex initiatives to approach full capacity in service delivery (see Chapter Seven), a period longer than originally anticipated by programme developers. Results from this inquiry underscore that some of these community programmes were better functioning than others, at least in terms of realising the underlying programme philosophy, and that this seems to matter with respect to their impact on children/families. This is an important message for the design of children and family services such as those to be delivered by Children's Centres in the UK and for other similar community-wide interventions, such as Stronger Families and Communities in Australia (FaCS, 2004). Also for the evaluation of such interventions, theoretically derived ratings of proficiency may be a fruitful alternative to established measures of fidelity or quality.

References

Barnes, J., Katz, I., Korbin, J.E. and O'Brien, M. (2006) *Children and families in communities: Theory, research, policy and practice*, Chichester: John Wiley.

Barnes, J., Belsky, J., Broomfield, K.A., Dave, S., Frost, M., Melhuish, E. and National Evaluation of Sure Start Research Team (2005) 'Disadvantaged but different: variation among deprived communities in relation to child and family well-being', *Journal of Child Psychology and Psychiatry*, vol 46, pp 952-62.

Belsky, J., Melhuish, E., Barnes, J., Leyland, A., Romaniuk, H. and National Evaluation of Sure Start Research Team (2006) 'Effects of Sure Start Local Programmes on children and families: early findings from a quasi-experimental cross-sectional study', *British Medical Journal*, vol 332, pp 1476-8.

Bond, G.R., Williams, J., Evans, L., Salyers, M., Kim, H.W., Sharpe, H. and Leff, H.S. (2000) *Psychiatric rehabilitation fidelity toolkit*, Cambridge, MA: Human Services Research Institute.

Bradley, R. (2002) 'Environment and parenting', in M. Bornstein (ed) *Handbook of parenting: volume 2* (2nd edn), Hillsdale, NJ: Lawrence Erlbaum Associates, pp 281-314.

Caldwell, B.M. and Bradley, R.H. (1984) *Home observation for measurement of the environment*, Little Rock, AR: University of Arkansas Press.

FaCS (Families and Communities Strategy) (2004) *Overview: Stronger families and communities strategy: National agenda for early childhood*, Canberra: Australian Government, www.facs.gov.au/sfcs

Fergusson, D., Swain-Campbell, N. and Horwood, J. (2004) 'How does economic disadvantage lead to crime?', *Journal of Child Psychology and Psychiatry*, vol 45, pp 956-66.

Goodman, R. (1997) 'The Strengths and Difficulties Questionnaire: A research note', *Journal of Child Psychology and Psychiatry*, vol 38, pp 581-6.

Hartman, R.R., Stage, S.A. and Webster-Stratton, C. (2003) 'A growth curve analysis of parent training outcomes: examining the influence of child risk factors parental and family risk factors', *Journal of Child Psychology and Psychiatry*, vol 44, pp 388-98.

Huberty, J. (1984) 'Issues in the use and interpretation of discriminant analysis', *Psychological Bulletin*, vol 95, pp 156-71.

Kazdin, A.E., Holland, L., Crowley, M. and Breton, S. (1997) 'Barriers to treatment participation scale: evaluation and validation in the context of child outpatient treatment', *Journal of Child Psychology and Psychiatry*, vol 38, pp 1051-62.

Love, J., Kisker, E.E., Ross, C.M., Constantine, J., Boller, K., Chazan-Cohen, R., Brady-Smith, C., Fuligni, A.S., Raikes, H., Brooks-Gunn, J., Tarullo, L.B., Schochet, P.Z., Paulsell, D. and Vogel, C. (2005) 'The effectiveness of Early Head Start for 3-year-old children and their parents: lessons for policy and programs', *Developmental Psychology*, vol 41, pp 885-901.

Matheny, A.P., Wachs, T., Ludwig, J.L. and Phillips, K. (1995) 'Bringing order out of chaos: psychometric characteristics of the Confusion, Hubbub and Order Scale', *Journal of Applied Developmental Psychology*, vol 16, pp 429-44.

Melhuish, E.C., Sylva, K., Sammons, P., Siraj-Blatchford, I. and Taggart, B. (2001) *The Effective Provision of Pre-school Education Project, technical paper 7: Social/behavioural and cognitive development at 3-4 years in relation to family background*, London: Institute of Education/DfES.

Melhuish, E.C., Quinn, L., Hanna, K., Sylva, K., Sammons, P., Siraj-Blatchford, I. and Taggart, B. (2006) *The Effective Pre-school Provision in Northern Ireland (EPPNI) Project: Summary report*, Belfast: Stranmillis University Press.

Melhuish, E.C., Sylva, K., Sammons, P., Siraj-Blatchford, I., Taggart, B. and Phan, M. (in press) 'Effects of the home learning environment and preschool center experience upon literacy and numeracy development in early primary school', *Journal of Social Issues*.

NESS (National Evaluation of Sure Start) Research Team (2005a) *Variation in Sure Start Local Programmes' effectiveness: Early preliminary findings*, London: DfES, www.surestart.gov.uk/publications/_doc/P0001868.pdf

NESS Research Team (2005b) *Early impacts of Sure Start Local Programmes on children and families*, www.surestart.gov.uk/_doc/P0001867.pdf

Olds, D.L., Henderson, C.R., Kitzman, H., Eckenrode, J.J., Cole, R.E. and Tatelbaum, R.C. (1999) 'Prenatal and Infancy home visitation by nurses: recent findings', *Future of Children*, vol 9, pp 44-66.

Pianta, R.C. (2001) *The Student-Teacher Relationship Scale*, Odessa, FL: PAR.

Ramey, C.T., Campbell, F.A., Burchinal, M., Skinner, M.L., Gardner, D.M. and Ramey, S.L. (2000) 'Persistent effects of early childhood education on high-risk children and their mothers', *Applied Developmental Science*, vol 4, pp 2-14.

Reyno, S.M. and McGrath, P.J. (2006) 'Predictors of parent training efficacy for child externalizing behaviour problems – a meta-analytic review', *Journal of Child Psychology and Psychiatry*, vol 47, pp 99-111.

Sammons, P., Smees, R., Taggart, B., Sylva, K., Melhuish, E.C., Siraj-Blatchford, I. and Elliot, K. (2003) *The Effective Provision of Pre-school Education Project, technical paper 8b: Measuring the impact on children's social behavioural development over the pre-school years*, London: Institute of Education/DfES.

Sanders, M.R. (2003) 'Triple P – Positive Parenting Program: a population approach to promoting competent parenting', *Australian e-Journal for the Advancement of Mental Health*, vol 2, www.auseinet.com/journal/vol2iss3/sanders.pdf

Smith, C.A. and Farrington, D.P. (2004) 'Continuities in antisocial behaviour and parenting across three generations', *Journal of Child Psychology and Psychiatry*, vol 45, pp 230-47.

SSU (Sure Start Unit) (2002) *Sure Start: A guide to planning and running your programme*, London: DfES.

Straus, M.A., Hamby, S., Finkelhor, D., Moore, D. and Runyan, D. (1998) 'Identification of child maltreatment with the Parent–Child Conflict Tactics Scales: development and psychometric data for a national sample of American parents', *Child Abuse and Neglect*, vol 22, pp 249-70.

Weiss, C.H. (1995) 'Nothing as practical as good theory: exploring theory-based evaluation for comprehensive community initiatives for children and families', in J.P. Connell, A.C. Kubisch, L.B. Schorr and C.H. Weiss (eds) *New approaches to evaluating community initiatives: Concepts, methods and contexts*, Queenstown, MD: Aspen Institute, pp 65-92.

TEN

How Sure Start Local Programme areas changed

Jacqueline Barnes

The Local Context Analysis (LCA) team of the National Evaluation of Sure Start (NESS) had two main tasks, the first of which was discussed in Chapter Two and involved describing the areas in which Sure Start Local Programmes (SSLPs) were situated. The second task, the results of which are summarised in this chapter, was to document change over time in SSLP neighbourhoods, based on the boundaries originally specified when SSLPs were first implemented, between 1999 and 2002.[1] This task was considered of great importance because extent of change over time *might* reflect a community-level impact of SSLPs, although it is not possible to attribute all, or even any, changes specifically to the presence of SSLPs – for two reasons. First, other area-based interventions (ABIs) were implemented in some portion of the majority of the first 260 SSLP areas being studied by NESS (see Chapter Three), making it impossible to attribute any change detected to SSLPs per se, rather than to overlapping initiatives, or to interactions between initiatives. Second, because no area-based data were gathered on truly suitable comparison areas that did not have SSLPs, and especially because NESS was never able to operate within the framework of a randomised controlled trial in which comparable areas were randomly assigned to SSLP or control treatments, it is impossible to draw strong inferences regarding any impacts of SSLPs on community characteristics (see Chapters One, Four and Eight). Documenting the extent of change in SSLP areas nevertheless provides important contextual information about SSLPs, information that has been integrated into the analysis of the impact of SSLPs on children and families (see Chapter Eight and Nine) and their cost effectiveness (see Chapter Seven).

In an effort to gain some insight into the *potential* meaning, impact-wise, of the changes that transpired within SSLP areas, data collected at the neighbourhood level by the NESS LCA team were also gathered for all of England so that the latter could function as a kind of benchmark on which change in SSLP areas could be compared. Such comparisons are presented in this chapter. Indeed, three core questions are addressed: (1) Between the fiscal years 2000/01 and 2004/05, did SSLP areas change in neighbourhood characteristics? (2) How did any such changes in SSLP areas compare with those occurring across all of England? (3) Among SSLP areas, what factors were associated with more or less change in neighbourhood characteristics?

With regard to question three, some of the factors considered were related to the extent of deprivation in the area, which interacts with the five types of SSLP neighbourhoods described in Chapter Two. The British government, in the 2005 pre-Budget report, indicated that one of their strategies to transform deprived neighbourhoods was to make them more 'mixed' in terms of housing and the socioeconomic status of resident families (HM Treasury, 2005). Thus, indicators of variability in housing, deprivation and ethnic background were also considered. As already noted, SSLPs were not the only ABIs implemented to enhance deprived neighbourhoods, either before or during the time period in question (NRU, 2002). Therefore, the presence of other such initiatives was also considered in an attempt to account for variation in community change in SSLP areas. In addition, some features of the SSLPs themselves were studied; principally the length of time they had been operating, the average amount spent per child and whether or not the lead agency was health. The latter was selected on the basis of findings from the NESS Impact Study suggesting that health-led programmes proved somewhat more effective in promoting child/family well-being than did SSLPs led by other organisations (Chapter Nine; NESS Research Team, 2005). Before presenting the analytic approach adopted to investigate change in SSLP community characteristics over time and resultant findings, obstacles that the NESS LCA team confronted in seeking to illuminate this issue are considered.

Challenges in chronicling community-level change

Investigation of change over time at the neighbourhood level is not straightforward, presenting many challenges. While many studies in the UK and elsewhere have followed children or groups such as those in one class or school over time to illuminate how they develop and change, relatively less attention has been given to change in spatially defined communities. Until 1990 or so, almost the only source of nationally available data in a standard format across the country, available at a small area level, was the decennial Census. Its strength lay in its standardised format; its main weaknesses were its relatively limited coverage and the infrequency of any updating (Noble and Dibben, 2004). Also the geographical units were prone to change from one Census to another, making any comparison over time problematic (see Chapter Three). Research assessing 'neighbourhood change' was effectively restricted to using either the Census, locally available data (for example, collected by a specific authority) or specially mounted surveys.

Lupton and Power (2004) note that there are no sets of monitoring data covering a consistent set of indicators for particular types of neighbourhoods over time, making it hard to assess neighbourhood trends. They identify some additional difficulties in making estimates of neighbourhood change beyond the limited range of data available – agreement about the concept of neighbourhood, what spatial delineators should be used, how to look at change from different perspectives and whether change should be conceptualised in relative or absolute terms.

Nevertheless, Noble and Dibben (2004) point out that that recent developments in data availability at the local level, particularly the growing volume of administrative data, are substantially increasing possibilities to chronicle neighbourhood change. While these developments, particularly the use of longitudinal administrative data, are at a relatively early stage, they should help to strengthen the evidence base. The increasing tendency to hold information electronically has led to the development of several national databases not previously available. This shift to more automated data processing of administrative data remains ongoing and geocoding, including standard geographical locators, gives scope for extracting consistent data across all parts of the country in a form also not previously available. Two recent examples are the Department for Education and Skills (DfES) Pupil Level Annual School Census (PLASC) from January, 2002, with individual records on all pupils in maintained schools, and recorded-crime data initially available at police-area level only, but later at Basic Command Unit (BCU) level. From 2004 these BCU data have been output to local area geographies, as police forces have moved to geocode recorded crimes in a consistent way (Noble and Dibben, 2004). However, the utility of these data depend on the same indicators being included each year, defined in the same way, which is not necessarily the case. For instance, definitions of drug crimes were amended part-way through the NESS work and indications of pupil achievement at age seven changed to reflect teacher ratings rather than formal test results.

In the time that NESS has been operating there has also been a rapid expansion of neighbourhood-level data for geographical areas smaller than electoral wards, previously the main way that most data were collated. The government's Neighbourhood Statistics website (neighbourhood.statistics.gov.uk) now provides a wealth of data at the lower super output area (SOA) level. Consequently, uniquely defined areas can be 'constructed' from output areas. Although these welcome developments came too late for the NESS LCA team to benefit from, it has still been possible to secure some information to fill the data vacuum described by Dorling and Rees (2003) regarding evidence about if, and how, neighbourhoods are changing, although it is limited in its scope to change in SSLP neighbourhoods rather than all neighbourhoods in England.

Beyond the issue of which data are available, the issue of neighbourhood definition remains. As several chapters in this volume make clear, these neighbourhoods were carefully defined by the SSLP partnership boards. Although a common strategy was used to define the neighbourhoods – areas where there were high concentrations of families with children under four, where enhanced and new services should be offered – the resultant areas vary both in size and population. Thus the following discussion of the average amount of change in SSLP areas is akin to looking at change in a group of children who vary in age from three of four years to late teenage years, and with different-sized families and social backgrounds, and needs to be read with that proviso in mind.

Method for studying change at the community level

The community-level indicators described in Chapter Two were collected annually, apart from those derived from the decennial Census, the Indices of Multiple Deprivation (IMD) and the geographical location of services. Statistical comparisons were made between levels of each indicator in the fiscal years 2000/01 and 2004/05, using paired *t* tests to evaluate whether changes were statistically significant. To determine whether there were significant differences in change in each indicator between SSLP areas and England, multilevel analyses were conducted in MLwiN, using the technique of iterative generalised least squares (IGLS) with Chi-square tests to estimate the parameters of the model (Goldstein, 1995). This made it possible to determine which changes were unique to SSLP areas rather than perhaps simply reflecting change in the whole of England. Appendix B of Barnes et al (2006) provides full details of the analytic method.

Correlation coefficients were calculated between the extent of change in each community-level indicator and continuous factors that might be associated with the amount of change. The latter included the months the SSLP had been in operation; the average amount spent per child in the year ending in March 2004; variability *within* SSLP areas on three dimensions: overall economic disadvantage, ethnic background of residents (white/non-white) and housing type (all derived from the 2001 Census; see Barnes et al, 2006, p 86); and the number of other ABIs covering all or part of the SSLP area. (For details of which initiatives these were, see Chapter Three and Barnes et al, 2006, pp 87-9.)

In order to determine which (if any) of these area characteristics was related to change once the initial level of the indicator and the extent of area deprivation (based on the IMD domains) had been partialled out, multiple linear regressions (using the 'enter' method) were calculated. These were done for those indicators that showed two characteristics: significant change over time; change that differed from change in England. All the continuous factors described above were included. One additional binary explanatory factor that might affect community change – whether the programme was health led – was added to the regression analyses.

Contextual sociodemographic and disorder changes

In order to provide a sense of change at the level of sociodemographic composition of the community, change in its population make-up is described and change in other contextual features such as the extent of family deprivation and the amount of crime, and disorder in local schools.

Population

Areas of deprivation experience high residential mobility. If there is substantial change in the population, it may have an impact on services available locally, especially if there is an increase in the target population – in the case of SSLPs the absolute number of children under four years and the proportion of the population that they represent. The aggregate data that could be used to address this issue that were available annually from the birth register and from the Department for Work and Pensions (DWP) database on the number of families receiving Child Benefit did not, unfortunately, include individual identifiers that would be necessary to determine whether the same families were still in the neighbourhoods; the data only reflected whether the number had changed and whether the relative proportion young children in the population had changed.

The SSLP areas included in the evaluation did, in fact, become home to more infants and young children over the five years of data collection. While there were on average fewer than 700 children under four living in SSLP areas based on the 2000/01 data, the average was close to 800 per area in 2004/05. The average number of live births per area increased between 2000 and 2004, as did the rate of births per 1,000 population (see Table 10.1). On average, the areas increased in terms of children under four years of age per 100 households and such young children a greater proportion of the area population. These increases were greater in SSLP areas than across England, making the areas even more likely to be home to young children than they were at the outset. The types of SSLP area labelled 'Indian subcontinent/ large families' (see Chapter Two for details) had the highest average number of children under four per 100 households at the outset and also experienced the greatest increase over time.

Family structure

On average, there were significantly more births to lone mothers in 2004 than in 2000 in SSLP areas, but this was also the case for England (see Table 10.1). Separating the SSLPs into the five types of communities described in Chapter Two, the increase was significant only in those SSLP areas classified as 'least deprived'. There was a significant reduction in the rate of births to mothers less than 18 years of age in SSLP areas, although again this change was equivalent to that experienced across England so that at both times of assessment the mean SSLP rate remained almost twice that of England (see Table 10.1). The reduction in infants born to mothers under the age of 18 was significant in only two of the five types of SSLP area, those classified as 'typical' and those having 'ethnic diversity'.

Deprivation

Although, on average, there were more young children in the SSLP areas over time, fewer were living in poverty (see Table 10.1). Moreover, a significantly greater decrease in the percentage of children under four years living in workless households was observed in SSLP areas than across England. Other indicators of deprivation also declined in SSLP areas to a greater extent than in England, specifically, the percentage of working-age adults receiving Income Support, the percentage of adults receiving benefits related to seeking employment (that is, Jobseeker's Allowance) and the percentage of children under four years living in a household in which an adult received Jobseeker's Allowance. But change in one indicator suggested increasing deprivation both in absolute and

Table 10.1: Significant changes in mean values of sociodemographic and disorder indicators in SSLP areas in rounds 1 to 4 and in England between 2000/01 and 2004/05

	SSLP mean 2004/05 n=260	Standard deviation	SSLP change 2000/01 to 2004/05	England 2004/05	England change 2000/01 to 2004/05	SSLP change versus England change
Number of live births[a]	201.1	69.9	+13.2**	607 (000s)	+34 (000s)	n/a
Number of births per 1,000 population	17.1	5.7	+1.1**	12.4	+0.7	n.s.
Number of children aged <4	773.3	255.1	+80.4**	2,271 (000s)	+75 (000s)	n/a
Number of children aged <4 per 100 households	16.3	6.9	+1.9**	11.1	+0.6	**
% population aged <4	6.6	2.1	+0.7**	4.6	+0.2	**
% population aged <16	25.7	5.8	+1.5**	19.7	+0.1	**
Number of births to lone mothers[a]	25.8	10.3	+0.8**	15.2	+0.7	n.s.
Number of births to mothers aged <18[a]	3.9	2.3	-0.4*	2.1	-0.2	n.s.
% children aged <4 in workless households	39.6	10.6	-4.6**	22.0	-1.2	**
% working-age adults receiving Income Support	14.2	5.2	-1.4**	6.4	-1.0	**
% eligible adults receiving Jobseeker's Allowance	5.0	2.3	-0.6**	2.6	-0.3	**
% children aged <4 in Jobseeker's Allowance households	3.9	1.9	-1.3**	2.3	-0.3	**
% children aged <4 in Income Support households	33.5	10.3	-5.5**	18.0	-2.3	**
% children aged 4-17 in Income Support households	30.7	9.5	-5.1**	15.5	-2.3	**
Burglary from dwellings[b]	23.3	13.7	-11.3**	15.2	-5.3	**
Violence against the person[b]	30.9	15.6	+10.2**	20.0	+7.5	**
% primary school permanent exclusions	0.03	0.05	-0.02**	0.03	+0.03	**
% of half days unauthorised absences, primary	0.53	0.26	-0.32**	0.43	-0.07	**
% of half days unauthorised absences, secondary	1.38	0.49	-0.33**	1.23	+0.14	**

Notes:
[a] Mean rate and change are based on the calendar years 2000 to 2004.
[b] Change is based on the fiscal years 2001/02 and 2004/05; data for 2000/01 were not available for all SSLPs.
** Change significant at $p < 0.01$

relative terms: the percentage of adults in receipt of Disability Living Allowance (DLA) increased more in SSLP areas than in England as a whole. This could either mean that more adults in the SSLP areas had health problems, or that more such individuals who previously did not receive the benefits that they were entitled to had succeeded in securing them.

Disorder

A mixed picture of changes in crime in SSLPs emerged across the period 2001/02 to 2004/05 (see Table 10.1). Burglary from dwellings, other burglary and vehicle crime declined significantly in SSLP areas, with the reduction in burglary from dwellings being significantly greater than that which occurred in England; and this was true of all five types of SSLP communities. The average amount of vehicle crime in SSLP areas was also lower, but the decrease was not different to that occurring across England. Somewhat in contrast, there was a significant increase in violence against the person in SSLP areas, greater than that which took place in England. This was evident in all types of SSLP areas, too, but the greatest average increase in violence occurred in those classified as 'typical'. Criminal damage and drug offences increased significantly in SSLP areas, but this was similar to the increase in England, not SSLP-specific changes.

Disorder and disruption in schools serving pupils resident in SSLP areas showed some positive changes in pupil behaviour (see Table 10.1). The average rates of both permanent exclusions and of unauthorised absences (that is, truancy) from these primary schools declined significantly from 2000/01 to 2004/05, with reductions proving significantly greater than those for primary schools across England, where exclusions rose marginally and unauthorised absences dropped only minimally. Exclusions from secondary schools attended by pupils living in SSLP areas also dropped, but at a similar rate to the reduction in England. Unauthorised absences, however, were reduced to a greater extent for the schools with pupils from SSLP areas than for all secondary schools in England.

In sum, with respect to contextual changes pertaining to community demographics and disorder, many changes chronicled suggested that communities were growing in terms of the number or proportion of children, improving in terms of less income deprivation, fewer births to teenage mothers, fewer young children living in homes dependent on benefits, less property crime and fewer severe behavioural problems in schools, although some indicators also suggested otherwise (for example, more violent crime). While some of these changes were greater than those taking place across England over the same five-year period, this was not routinely the case. For instance, the reduction of births to teenage mothers, while a target of work in SSLPs, was no different to change across England. Nevertheless, overall these changes indicate that the SSLP areas may have become contextually better locations for families and for service providers.

Child health and development changes

To demonstrate changes in children's well-being, which may be outcomes of the kinds of services enhanced or introduced by SSLPs, changes in infant health, emergency hospitalisations of young children, in the extent of identified special educational needs (SEN) and disability and achievement of children of all ages in school are presented.

Birth and the first year

On average, no change occurred between 2000 and 2004 in SSLP areas or in England in the mean proportion of low birthweight infants (that is, <2,500 grams) (see Table 10.2). In the case of SSLP communities classified as 'Indian subcontinent/large families', however, a significant reduction in such births did take place, although the mean rate remained highest in these areas. No evidence emerged, using data from Child Health System records – which were only available to NESS for about half the SSLP areas for each year under consideration – that median birthweight changed in SSLP areas (see Table 10.3). If anything, in fact, there was a trend for the median birthweight for infants born prior to reaching term (36 to 38 weeks) to be lower; this was also the case in England. There was no change on average in *perinatal* or *neonatal* mortality. There was, however, a significant reduction in the mean rate of *infant* mortality in SSLP areas from 2000 to 2004, but this change was similar to that for England (see Table 10.2). 'Indian-subcontinent' SSLP areas experienced the largest average decrease in perinatal and infant mortality, but they started with the highest level in 2000 and remained highest in 2004.

Emergency hospitalisations

The average rates of emergency hospitalisations of children under the age of four for lower respiratory infection and severe injury decreased significantly for those living in SSLP areas, in contrast to an increase in

Table 10.2: Significant changes in mean values of child health and development indicators in SSLP areas in rounds 1 to 4 and in England between 2000/01 and 2004/05

	SSLP mean 2004/05 n=260	Standard deviation	SSLP change 2000/01 to 2004/05	England 2004/05	England change 2000/01 to 2004/05	SSLP change versus England change
% of births <2,500 grams	9.3	2.7	-0.1	7.6	0.0	–
Infant mortality (per 1,000 live births)	6.7	6.7	-1.3*	5.0	-0.6	n.s.
Emergency hospitalisations, lower respiratory infection	21.9	10.7	-2.3**	18.6	+0.7	**
Emergency hospitalisations, severe injury	12.2	7.5	-3.3**	10.5	-0.1	**
Emergency hospitalisations, gastroenteritis	14.1	11.0	+1.2	9.7	+1.0	–
% aged 0-3 receiving DLA	1.1	0.5	-0.2**	1.0	0.0	n.s.
% aged 4-17 receiving DLA	4.0	1.0	+0.8**	3.0	+0.6	**
% SEN school action/school action plus[a]	22.2	5.2	2.1**	16.1	+1.6	**
% statement of SEN[b]	4.1	1.2	0.1**	3.2	+0.2	n.s.
% school-age children attending special schools[b]	1.6	0.6	0.1**	1.2	+0.1	n.s.
% achieving level 2+ for Key Stage 1 Writing[c]	73.4	6.8	-2.0**	82.4	-1.3	*
% achieving level 2+ for Key Stage 1 Mathematics[c]	85.7	5.0	+3.0**	90.9	+2.2	n.s.
% achieving level 4+ for Key Stage 2 English Final	67.7	7.6	6.1**	78.8	+4.2	**
% achieving level 4+ for Key Stage 2 English reading	74.4	6.8	6.7**	84.1	+4.6	**
% achieving level 4+ for Key Stage 2 English writing	51.6	8.9	5.1**	63.0	+3.6	**
% achieving level 4+ for Key Stage 2 Mathematics	64.1	7.9	2.4**	74.9	+1.9	n.s.
% gaining five or more GCSEs grade A*-C	38.5	9.5	5.5**	55.5	+2.4	**
% gaining no passes at GCSE	6.2	3.4	2.3**	3.8	+1.5	**
% ratio of 17-year-olds relative to 16-year-olds receiving Child Benefit	67.7	12.1	8.7**	75.8	+5.2	**

Notes:
[a] Change is from 2002/03 to 2004/05; comparable 2000/01 and 2001/02 data were unavailable due to changes in the definitions of special educational needs.
[b] Change is from 2001/02 to 2004/05; comparable 2000/01 data were unavailable due to changes in the definitions of special educational needs.
[c] Change is from 2001/02 to 2004/05; comparable 2000/01 data were unavailable at the pupil level, only at the school level.
* Change significant at p<0.05
** Change significant at p<0.01

Table 10.3: Median birthweight from 2000 to 2004 in SSLP areas in rounds 1 to 4 and England by weeks of gestation, based on data from Child Health System records

Weeks	SSLPs 2000 n=125	SSLPs 2001 n =128	SSLPs 2002 n =128	SSLPs 2003 n =138	SSLPs 2004 n =138[a]	England 2000 and 2004
			Median weight (5th and 95th percentiles)			
All	3,226 (2,543, 3,761)	3,217 (2,530 3,763)	3,216 (2,552, 3,732)	3,200 (2,518, 3,750)	3,210 (2,520, 3,760)	3,291, 3,271
36	2,668 (2,220, 3,150)	2,620.7 (2,181, 2,989)	2,689.1 (2,271, 3,259)	2,626.4 (2,203, 3,043)	2,630 (2,192, 3,105)	2,750, 2,720
37	2,929 (2,552, 3,293)	2,905 (2,588, 3,217)	2,907 (2,575, 3,256)	2,870 (2,541, 3,202)	2,894 (2,599, 3,268)	2,980, 2,960
38	3,121 (2,884, 3,340)	3,107 (2,880, 3,325)	3,108.0 (2,861, 3,372)	3,084 (2,845, 3,296)	3,105 (2,869, 3,332)	3,200, 3,180
39	3,258 (3,010, 3,490)	3,272 (3,052, 3,452)	3,263 (3,068, 3,452)	3,244 (3,046, 3,431)	3,255 (3,020, 3,491)	3,345, 3,320
40	3,415 (3,201, 3,628)	3,419 (3,235, 3,600)	3,421 (3,210, 3,659)	3,405 (3,185, 3,600)	3,418 (3,230, 3,611)	3,490, 3,470
41	3,567 (3,349, 3,823)	3,556.5 (3,329, 3,799)	3,565 (3,344, 3,807)	3,526 (3,268, 3,711)	3,540 (3,269, 3,777)	3,610, 3,600
42	3627 (3,218, 4,082)	3,632 (3,178, 4,124)	3,570 (3,184, 4,001)	3,646 (3,237, 4,044)	3,629 (3,182, 4,148)	3,660, 3,650

Note:
[a] Note that, while the number of programmes for which there are data are similar from year to year, they are not necessarily all the same programmes.

respiratory infection and virtually no change in severe injury in England (see Table 10.2). The mean rate of decrease differed depending on the type of SSLP area. Emergency hospitalisations of young children for lower respiratory infection only decreased significantly on average in the areas classified as 'most deprived', 'ethnically diverse' and 'Indian subcontinent' residents (see Figure 10.1). There was virtually no change in the rate of hospitalisations for gastroenteritis, which increased marginally both in SSLP areas and England.

Disability and special educational needs

Although there was a small but significant decrease in the proportion of children aged under four receiving DLA and no change in England, there was a significant increase in the average proportion of children aged four to 17 in SSLP areas in receipt of DLA, significantly greater than the increase in England (see Table 10.2). This increase was significant in all five types of SSLP areas, although greatest in those

Figure 10.1: Mean change in rates (per 1,000) of emergency hospitalisations of children aged 0-3 years for lower respiratory infection in five types of SSLP community and England (based on Hospital Episode Statistics)

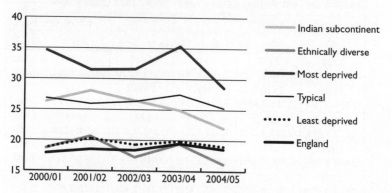

classified as 'least deprived'. The average percentage of children resident in SSLP areas and identified with SEN increased significantly, both for those with school action/school action plus (that is, levels one to four in the previous system) and those requiring statements. The percentage of children attending special schools also rose. Only the increase in SEN without a statement, however, was different from change in England (see Table 10.2).

Achievement

Little evidence emerged documenting change, including improvement, in the average achievement of children aged seven years living in SSLP areas between the 2000/01 and 2004/05 school years (see Table 10.2). Even though a significant increase in performance in mathematics at Key Stage One (KS1) emerged in both in SSLP areas and across England, there was no overall change in achievement in KS1 reading or comprehension and a small but significant decrease in writing achievement, which proved greater than the drop for England. To be noted, however, is that the method of assessment differed for the two time points, based on formal assessments in 2000/01 but on teacher ratings in the 2004/05 school year, due to a change in government policy.

A more positive picture emerged for older children. Formal Key Stage Two (KS2) assessment at 11 years revealed that the mean level of achievement of pupils living in SSLP areas increased for English final, English reading, English writing and Mathematics, with the increases in the three types of English attainment greater than those for England (see Table 10.2). There were significant increases in the percentage of SSLP residents gaining at least five good (A★ to C) passes at GCSE (examinations taken at age 16) and staying on at school after the age of 16, again greater than the England increases. At the same time, there was also a significant increase in the (relatively small) proportion of pupils in SSLP areas gaining no passes at GCSE, again greater than the increase in England.

Overall, then, there was little evidence that infant health had changed either in England as a whole or in SSLP areas, with the exception of those with more Indian subcontinent families. A positive change was evident in the lower rates of young children taken to hospital as emergencies and then hospitalised, for either lower respiratory infection or severe injury. The increase in the rate of children identified with SEN or disability that requires supporting by financial assistance could be perceived as positive – possibly better screening is in place – or negative, with more problems related perhaps to inadequate antenatal care.

Service activity changes

Sure Start Local Programmes were charged with enhancing local services, or adding new ones. Changes are presented here in the extent of provision for different types of childcare, in the ease with which health services could be accessed and in the activities of social services in relation to child abuse and neglect.

Childcare

Figures from Ofsted on childcare providers and places were only available at the national level from 2001 and from that time onward no evidence emerged of increases in the provision of childminders or places for children aged under eight in SSLP areas, the rates remaining substantially below those for England (see Table 10.4). There were significant increases in SSLP areas in the rates of both the providers of full day care and the places available, but the increases were significantly lower than those seen across England and mean rates of provision remained substantially lower in SSLP areas than England rates. In addition, looking at the five types of SSLP, there were no significant increases in areas with ethnic diversity or areas with greater Indian subcontinent populations. There were, however, substantial increases in the rates of crèche providers and places in SSLP areas, on average, and these proved larger than increases in England with rates of crèche

Table 10.4: Significant changes in childcare in SSLP areas in rounds 1 to 4 and in England between 2001/02 and 2004/05

	SSLP mean 2004/05 n=260	Standard deviation	SSLP change 2001/02 to 2004/05	England 2004/05	England change 2001/02 to 2004/05	SSLP change versus England change
Childminders per 10,000 0- to 7-year-olds	81.4	50.1	−1.2	152.4	−0.2	–
Childminder places per 1,000 0- to 7-year-olds	34.1	22.0	−1.3	68.6	+1.3	–
Full day care providers per 10,000 0- to 7-year-olds	16.4	12.1	+2.4**	26.3	+4.8	**
Full day care places per 1,000 0- to 7-year-olds	65.8	53.1	+12.7**	112.5	+26.7	**
Crèches per 10,000 0- to 7-year-olds	9.2	10.5	+2.5**	5.4	+1.1	*
Crèche places per 1,000 0- to 7-year-olds	15.4	18.8	+4.0**	9.4	−0.4	**

* Change significant at p<0.05
** Change significant at p<0.01

provision in SSLP areas in 2004/05 almost twice those of England (see Table 10.4).

Child health services

There was change in the level of provision of Child Health Clinics in SSLP areas between 2003 and 2004. The number of areas of a total of 260 with no clinic declined from 61 to 45 and there was a noticeable increase in the number of programme areas with four or five clinics within their boundaries, from just six to 26. The rise in provision of Child Health Clinics was reflected in a rising proportion of households living within one kilometre of a clinic. In the urban programme areas more than three quarters of households were in this position by 2004, an increase of 2% (with only 5% more than two kilometres distant from a clinic) although the proportion fell to half in the rural programme areas, with one-quarter of households more than two kilometres from a clinic, an increase of 5% from 2003.

Social service activity

From the outset of the evaluation it proved challenging to obtain accurate information about the extent of social service activity. Information relevant to the age group of interest to SSLPs, children under four years, was not routinely collated and many social service departments were only beginning to use electronic records, which might or might not have the accurate postcode information necessary to extract information about children specific to SSLP areas. This necessitated the compromise of collecting information about children aged under five years and under 16. Making accurate estimation even more difficult was the fact that the first full year of social service requests (2001/02) to the final year led to complete information for only just over half the SSLPs. With these caveats in mind, overall, no significant changes in social service activity were identified, perhaps due to both the reduced sample size and the large amount of variation among SSLPs. There was, nevertheless, a trend in SSLP areas for rates of referral of the under fives and under 16s to show upward movement, set against a decline in referrals in England. There were different patterns of change, however, across the five types of SSLP areas. Referrals of children under five had some fluctuation but no overall change in the 'least deprived' and 'typical' areas; there was more fluctuation from year to year in the areas classified as 'most deprived' and 'ethnically diverse'. However, rates of referral declined significantly (and were the lowest in 2004/05) in the areas with more Indian subcontinent residents and large families (see Figure 10.2). The same significant reduction in

Figure 10.2: Mean change in rates per 10,000 children aged under five of referrals to social services departments in five types of SSLP area between 2001/02 and 2004/05 (comparable England data not available)

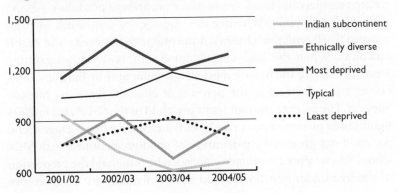

referrals in these areas was evident for referrals of children under 16. Thus, while there appears to have been more social service activity in some SSLP communities, this was not the case for all SSLPs.

Summarising, as observed in the case of community demographics, child health and academic achievement, there were changes in both positive and negative ways over time. On the positive side there was more of some kinds of childcare, and families were able to access health services more easily; on the negative side it was not possible to identify significant changes in social service support for families or the rate at which child abuse and neglect were identified.

Factors associated with change

It is one thing to chronicle change over time in SSLP areas at the community level and to compare such change with the benchmark of England, but something else to account for such change. This, of course, was one of the goals that NESS set for the LCA team. In this subsection, results pertaining to factors related to change across SSLP communities are presented. Considered first are factors related to the activities of the programmes themselves, followed by the presence of other local initiatives, finally focusing on whether or not the areas were more or less mixed in terms of the residents and the housing.

Months of SSLP activity spending and lead agency

Sure Start Local Programme characteristics predicted few changes at the community level. Therefore, those reported here need to be considered in the context of the large number of possible associations investigated, thereby calling attention to the prospect that some of these findings could reflect chance as well as actual causal processes. More months of programme operation predicted greater increase in crèche providers and less decrease in the proportion of adults receiving Jobseeker's Allowance. Whether the lead agency was health (or not) was associated with few changes, none of which involved child health outcomes. When the lead agency was health, however, programme areas were more likely to experience a reduction in burglary from homes and a decrease in the percentage of adults receiving Income Support. The average amount spent per child in the SSLP area in 2004 significantly predicted two child health outcomes: when average spend per child was greater, the percentage of children identified with SEN school action/school action plus increased by more; and the proportion of children under four hospitalised as an emergency for severe injury decreased by more. More spending also forecast a greater increase in full day care providers. Recall from Chapter Seven that higher spend per child was more typical of smaller than larger SSLPs.

Other area-based initiatives

The presence of other ABIs – ranging from none to six – was associated with an SSLP area's extent of deprivation. Once this was taken into account in regression analyses, some community-level changes were predicted by SSLP areas having more ABIs overlapping their patch. In particular, several improvements in school achievement and behaviour were related to this condition, including an increase in writing achievement at KS2, an increase in five or more good GCSE passes, a decrease in permanent exclusions and unauthorised absences from primary schools and a greater number of children staying on at school after 16. Only one effect involving academic achievement associated with numbers of ABIs operating in the SSLP area was in the reverse direction: greater improvement in mathematics achievement at KS1 was predicted by the presence of fewer ABIs in the area. More ABIs were also associated, although only at the trend level (that is, $p<.10$), with smaller increases in violence against the person, smaller decreases in children under four living in workless households, smaller increases in adults receiving DLA and greater reduction in adults receiving Jobseeker's Allowance.

Area variability

More variability in an area indicates a more mixed neighbourhood in terms of family economic status, housing and/or family ethnicity. When the SSLP area was more mixed, it appeared that some changes were more likely, some positive and others not. Greater variability with regard to economic disadvantage proved predictive of smaller decreases in the proportion of teen mothers (that is, aged <18 years) and in emergency hospitalisations for lower respiratory infection, but greater increases in the rate of crèche provision. When the area was more mixed in terms of housing, there was a smaller increase in the proportion of lone mothers making up the population, a greater decrease in children living in deprivation (workless households, Income Support households) and in burglary in homes and a greater increase in the proportion of children staying on at school after 16. A smaller increase in KS2 mathematics achievement and in the proportion of children identified with SEN (school action), however, was associated with more variability in the ethnic background of the area population. Areas with more variability in family ethnicity were also likely to show a greater increase in violence against the person and a smaller increase in the percentage of children gaining at least five good GCSE passes, but in such areas there were also smaller declines in writing achievement at KS1 and greater increases in KS1 writing achievement.

In summary, having partialled out the status of the areas at the outset and their level of deprivation, few changes could be attributable to SSLP activity; nevertheless, some positive changes appear more likely when a number of ABIs were present in addition to SSLPs, suggesting that they may have been more effective when supported by other groups, tackling regeneration and focusing in detail on schools. The belief that mixed neighbourhoods are advantageous is not clearly confirmed here, at least in relation to improvements in SSLP areas. There were some positive effects of more of a mix in housing (that is, more reduction in deprivation, more improvement in academic achievement). There were, however, some negative effects of a greater mix of ethnic background, such as more violent crime, and less educational achievement improvement.

Conclusions

Over the five-year period covered by the NESS analysis of the local contexts in which SSLPs operated, some improvements in SSLP areas were detected, although few could be linked in a straightforward way to SSLP activity, if only because many simply reflected national trends; certainly this is what many comparisons with the English benchmark suggested. Consistent with this reading of the data are the multiple regression results that failed to chronicle effects, in terms of predicting community change, of months of programme operation or amount spent by SSLP per child. Notable, nevertheless, was that even as SSLP areas increased over time in the proportion of children residing in the area, the proportion of children living in poverty declined. Some aspects of crime and disorder changed for the better, too, notably burglary and exclusions or truancy from primary schools. The fact that crimes typified by violence between people increased in SSLP areas to a greater extent than in England, and particularly in the areas with a mixed ethnic population, cannot be disregarded, however.

Also on the positive side was evidence of improvements in infant health in some types of areas, notably those with more residents from the Indian subcontinent, the only type of area also to show a significant reduction in the rate of children referred to social services. The reductions in emergency hospitalisations of young children for severe injury and for lower respiratory infection may have been a function of more families accessing routine healthcare within the neighbourhood, at GP surgeries or Child Health Clinics. It appears that increases in the health screening of young children occurred in SSLP areas over time, as the percentage of children identified with SEN or eligible for benefits related to disability increased across the five-year study period. The fact that the majority of the improvements in children's achievement involved older children tested at age 11 or 16 seems difficult to attribute to SSLPs in any simple way, as these programmes focused specifically on the under fours.

Some positive changes also emerged in childcare provision, particularly group care such as full day care or crèches. However, this increase still left SSLP areas with less full day care than other parts of the country and recall that childminder provision did not change. It was not possible, given the data available, to discern any significant changes in the activities of social services, perhaps due to so much missing information, but overall the trend was for increased rather than decreased activity with more children referred.

These comments notwithstanding, any conclusions about change in SSLP areas must be tempered by appreciation that much of the relevant data could not be obtained at the very beginning and very end of the investigation. There were several reasons for this. In some cases, particularly involving police and social service departments and child health systems, individual contacts at each local district were required, with lists of postcodes, digitised boundaries and details of the information required provided (see also Chapter Three). Also making it difficult to secure data on an annual basis were the following facts: responsibility for collating and thus sharing data in locales shifted during the period of inquiry; many localities proved to be short-staffed in this area; and poor data systems plagued many agencies.

In point of fact, problems remained even when national data were available from a single source. The responsibility for collating Hospital Episode Statistics changed to a different contractor halfway through the LCA team's work, resulting in problems with comparability; Ofsted was just starting to collate childcare information in 2000, so their data system in the first year was incomplete; national pupil achievement information was available only at the school level in the first year of research and, thereafter, the pupil level, meaning that the weighted estimates for the first year could not be used to study change over time. In 2003/04, the DWP altered its system, including the definition of some benefits, so data for that and the subsequent years had to be amended by them to allow cross-time comparison. Clearly, the kind of work carried out by the NESS LCA team in order to chronicle change over time at the community level and summarised in this chapter will continue to present challenges to researchers. Only when records are well maintained and nationally consistent data sources are available with indicators whose definitions are not subject to ongoing modification become the norm will the task of studying community change prove easier and probably more accurate.

Note

[1] Some SSLPs amended their original boundaries during their first year or so of operation. See Chapter Three for more detail about the implications of these changes for the evaluation.

References

Barnes, J., Cheng, H., Howden, B., Frost, M., Harper, G., Dave, S., Finn, J. and the National Evaluation of Sure Start (NESS) Team (2006) *Change in the characteristics of Sure Start Local Programme areas in rounds 1 to 4 between 2000/2001 and 2003/2004*, Sure Start Report 16, Nottingham: DfES, www.surestart.gov.uk/_doc/P0002266.pdf

Dorling, D. and Rees, P. (2003) 'A nation still dividing: the British Census and social polarisation 1971-2001', *Environment and Planning*, vol 35, pp 1287-313.

Goldstein, H. (1995) *Multilevel statistical models* (2nd edn) London: Edward Arnold.

HM Treasury (2005) *Support for parents: The best start for children*, London: The Stationery Office.

Lupton, R. and Power, A. (2004) 'What do we know about neighbourhood change?', Paper presented at the Urban and Neighbourhood Studies Research Network Understanding Neighbourhood Change Seminar 30 March, Westminster Central Hall, London.

NESS (National Evaluation of Sure Start) Research Team (2005) *Early impacts of Sure Start Local Programmes on children and families*, Sure Start Report 13, Nottingham: DfES, www.surestart.gov.uk/_doc/P0001867.pdf

Noble, M. and Dibben, C. (2004) 'Understanding neighbourhood change: challenges and potential for using and combining data at the neighbourhood level', Paper presented at the Urban and Neighbourhood Studies Research Network Understanding Neighbourhood Change Seminar 30 March, Westminster Central Hall, London.

NRU (Neighbourhood Renewal Unit) (2002) *Research summary No. 1: Collaboration and co-ordination in area-based initiatives*, London: Department for Transport, Local Government and the Regions.

Part Five
Conclusion

ELEVEN

Sure Start Local Programmes: an outsider's perspective

Sir Michael Rutter

This volume provides a most valuable, thoughtful account of both the origins of Sure Start Local Programmes (SSLPs) and what they have achieved so far. My assignment was to provide an independent assessment of the initiative as a whole, insofar as it can be judged at this rather early stage. I approach that task wearing the hat of a clinician who has throughout his career been concerned with preventive and therapeutic interventions, that of an epidemiologist concerned with the study of risk and protective factors for psychological outcomes, and that of a methodologist concerned with the critical examination of the efficacy and effectiveness of interventions. I examine the need for such an initiative, the evidence for this, the content of the provision, the design of the programme and the research evaluation and design, and conclude with an overview; during this critique I bring out positive elements of the initiative, as well as making critical comments.

Was there a need for a new initiative?

It is appropriate to start with the basic question of whether there was a need for a major new initiative. Of all the questions to be considered, that is the easiest to answer. Clearly, there was a *huge* need. The recently published UNICEF comparison of the well-being of children and young people in 21 industrialised countries (UNICEF Innocenti Research Centre, 2007) provides the stark conclusions that, despite being one of the richest countries, the UK is ranked bottom in terms of well-being assessment. Questions can be raised about the concepts and measures but the facts are indisputable. The UK is one of the worst countries with respect to child poverty, the proportion of children continuing in education and the rate of infant mortality, to mention but three relatively objective, quantifiable indices. The measures of children's social relationships and general well-being are inevitably rather 'softer' but they provide the same negative picture. The UK's bad international position is very similar to that of the US

– again one of the richest countries in the world (see Fitzgerald et al, 2006; Freeark and Davidson, 2006; Villaruel and Luster, 2006; Watt et al, 2006). Moreover, the evidence is clear that over the last 50 years or so mental health and psychosocial problems in young people have become much more common (Rutter and Smith, 1995; Collishaw et al, 2004). It could not be more obvious that something needed to be done to remedy this deplorable situation.

The government's response: the initiation of Sure Start Local Programmes

The government deserves high credit for both its willingness to recognise the challenge and its decision to provide major new funding to meet the challenge. A total of £542 million was made available to be spent over three years (see Chapter One). The intention was to provide a ringfenced budget equivalent to about £1,250 per child in the SSLP areas at the peak of funding, but with additional funds expected to be available for seven to 10 years. Although a trivial contribution from the Treasury's perspective (just 0.05% of public expenditure), it was truly new money (and not just relabelling of existing funds) and it served to transform services in the UK for pre-school children.

The evidence base for Sure Start Local Programmes

The government has been very forceful in demanding that other people's actions be judged on the basis of objective evidence. We need to ask, therefore, how the SSLP initiative measures up to that requirement. The government noted the evidence from a range of experimental studies in the US that early interventions could bring worthwhile benefits (see Chapter One). That evidence is indeed persuasive but Zigler (and Styfco, 2006), the father of the Head Start movement in the US, has pointed out that even the best interventions do not (and cannot) eliminate individual differences; that many of the evaluations have been undertaken by researchers uncomfortably close to the projects; that there are major differences between efficacy (that is, the benefits when the intervention is delivered by experts functioning in optimal services) and effectiveness (that is, the benefits when the methods are applied under the conditions of community-wide services); and that the need for interventions extends far beyond the pre-school years. Most crucially, he noted the 'tyranny of the mean' – in other words, the ignoring of the marked heterogeneity within groups.

The point about the need to provide services beyond the pre-school period is highlighted by the UNICEF report finding that the UK comes out particularly badly with respect to the rates of both teenage pregnancy and persisting in education beyond age 16. Pre-school interventions might have long-term beneficial effects but it is implausible that they would be sufficient to deal with the needs in later adolescence.

As noted in Chapter One, much credence was placed on the notion of 'critical periods' – the assumption being that the early years provided a special 'window of opportunity' because of the plasticity of brain development at that age. That represents a serious misreading of the research evidence (see Bruer, 1999). It is true that brain development undergoes particularly dramatic changes in these early years, but both animal studies and human studies (Nelson and Jeste, in press) have shown that experiences in adolescence and adult life can make a major impact (see Laub and Sampson, 2003). The early years are particularly important, not mainly because of any critical period effect, but because they come first and because early experiences tend to shape later experiences (see Rutter and Rutter, 1993).

Government statements on what it wanted SSLPs to achieve have lacked both consistency and precision. Clearly one key objective was to improve conditions for young children, but much emphasis came to be placed on its role in tackling child poverty and social exclusion (Tunstill et al, 2005). Several points need to be made with respect to these two goals. The first requires that SSLPs should be particularly effective in improving conditions for the most disadvantaged and, hence, should diminish the social inequalities. Undoubtedly, that is an important and worthwhile goal but cautions are necessary when dealing with universal interventions. Ceci and Papierno (2005) pointed out that, because it must be expected that people will differ in their ability to take advantage of the opportunities provided, effective universal interventions may inadvertently increase, rather than decrease, social inequities. The Early Head Start intervention in the US showed that there was a tendency for this to happen (Love et al, 2002).

The situation with respect to the expectations on child poverty is even more worrying. Although the government failed to meet its five-year target on the reduction of child poverty, a substantial worthwhile reduction was achieved (Commission on Families and the Wellbeing of Children, 2005). However, none of this reduction can safely be attributed to SSLPs. Rather, it stemmed from sensible changes in benefits. Presumably SSLPs were expected to bring further benefits through increasing the proportion of lone parents entering employment.

That is indeed a desirable goal because the UK is one of the worst countries with respect to the proportion of children living in families in which neither parent is employed. However, analyses have shown that, if parents are on the minimum wage, this would not lift children out of poverty (Hirsch, 2005; Harker, 2006). Moreover, to achieve future child poverty reduction targets would require a hopelessly unrealistic massive increase in parents coming into employment. Sure Start Local Programmes might help but the remedies required go far beyond that initiative. An increase in the minimum wage is essential; actions need to be taken to reduce gender inequalities in wages; and changes are needed in the arena of benefits. Most especially, steps need to be taken to deal with the special problems faced by families with three or more children (a particular concern with respect to some minority ethnic groups). In the rest of my assessment of SSLPs, therefore, I will focus on effects on child and family functioning rather than on the longer-term and more indirect effects on child poverty.

Content of Sure Start Local Programme provision

Sure Start Local Programmes were expected to provide five core services: (1) outreach and home visiting; (2) support for families and parents; (3) good-quality play, learning and childcare; (4) primary and community healthcare including advice about child and family health; and (5) support for children with specialised needs (see Anning et al, 2005). In addition, there was supposed to be improved coordination, streamlining and added value from existing services, and improved physical facilities to provide open access drop-in centres and high-quality play resources and part-time places for all three-year-olds whose parents wanted this. Discussion is possible on the details of these requirements but it may be accepted that they were generally in line with the research evidence.

Nevertheless, SSLPs differed from previous initiatives in five key respects, all of which were out of line with research findings, and likely to be severely damaging. First, SSLPs were explicitly planned to provide a service for seriously disadvantaged communities, and it was explicitly left up to each area to decide what it would do. The intentions were honourable in that they reflected recognition that successful interventions required a 'buy-in' from participants and not just an externally imposed intervention; and that they were meant to avoid the stigma of labelling high-risk families. Both these goals are important. There is good evidence that it is necessary to take active steps to ensure that families are being offered a service support and value what is on offer (McCall et al, 2003). That is not, however, at all synonymous with it being left entirely open to local areas to decide what to do.

The idea that changing a whole community in a desired direction should have benefits for families living there is a reasonable notion. Moreover, there is evidence that there are area effects on people's functioning (Brooks-Gunn et al, 1997; Sampson et al, 1997). The problem is that there is almost no evidence on what needs to be done to change communities suffering disadvantage. Accordingly, that aspect of SSLP was moving almost completely into uncharted territory.

A concern over an exclusively area target is that, although about half of disadvantaged families live in disadvantaged areas, half do not (see Chapter One). In short, even if successful, SSLPs would fail to reach half of all disadvantaged families.

In addition the area focus served to ignore the heterogeneity of disadvantaged families and the special needs of some. The Olds' interventions (for example, Olds et al, 1998, 2004a, 2004b) in the US, which had very similar goals to the SSLP initiative (see Rutter, 2006), took this explicitly into account by combining a universal programme with more targeted intervention elements. The aim was to avoid stigma but to provide special help for those who most needed it. It is a pity that SSLPs did not follow that model.

The second way in which SSLPs departed from accepted practice was that they made a virtue out of a deliberate lack of specification of *how* the goals should be met, and what sort of curriculum should be provided. In other words, there was to be no operationalisation of the programme. That runs completely counter to research findings. Olds et al (1986, 2004b), for example, provided a detailed curriculum to be followed but this did not involve a rigid mechanical approach because the content was tailored to the needs of individual families. Similarly, Fergusson et al's (2005, 2006) evaluation of an Early Start programme of home visitation in New Zealand emphasised the need for both curriculum specification and flexibility in individual implementation.

The third departure from research evidence concerns the lack of emphasis on professional skills, on supervision and on detailed monitoring. The Olds and Fergusson studies provide cases in point.

The fourth departure was the denial of the need for piloting. All interventions researchers regard this as essential and it is noteworthy that Norman Glass, the senior civil servant who was the main architect of SSLPs, argued (unsuccessfully) for the need to pilot carefully on a modest scale rather than zoom straight ahead into a very widespread implementation (see Chapter One). It can only be presumed that the political imperative to make a major splash far outweighed the need to ensure a really good intervention programme.

The fifth point is not so much a departure from the empirical evidence, but rather a failure to recognise the issue. The implicit assumption of the SSLP initiative was that it would improve overall parenting functioning as well as improve child development. The Fergusson et al (2006) evaluation of Early Start provides a caution in that connection. They found significant benefits for child-related outcomes but no effects on maternal mental health, family functioning, welfare dependency or exposure to stressful life events. Of course, the child benefits were worthwhile in their own right but it is striking that the gains did not include overall family functioning. A different focus of the intervention might have given rise to different findings but the message is that general benefits will not necessarily be forthcoming.

Research evaluations

It is said (see Chapter One) that one of the conditions imposed by the Treasury in funding SSLPs was that there should be a rigorous evaluation of the initiative. It is ironic, therefore, that the government ensured that this could not happen. Chapter Four provides a thoughtful, informed discussion of the variety of methodologies available to evaluate complex interventions and it is evident that there is no one perfect design. Randomised controlled trials (RCTs) have the major strength of eliminating social selection and of allowing statistical methods that are based on unbiased distributions. Of course, an individually based RCT would be quite inappropriate for an intervention targeted at areas rather than individuals. On the other hand, an RCT based on randomisation of areas would have been possible if government had not ruled out this possibility.

The undermining of the evaluation, however, went far beyond the rejection of an area-based RCT. There were four main features that seriously jeopardised a truly rigorous evaluation. First, the question of whether SSLPs were effective presupposes that there is a definable programme, but that was ruled out intentionally. Each local area was able to make up its own mind what it would do. Accordingly, there is no such entity as an overall SSLP. Rather, there is a large family of individual local programmes that share some common features but differ on others. The individual variation could be capitalised on if it was possible to measure it accurately but the lack of any defined curriculum and the lack of protocols makes that difficult.

Second, even if there was to be no randomisation of areas, comparisons could still have been undertaken if there were a substantial number of disadvantaged areas that did not receive an SSLP. That would have been possible if the government had stuck with the original notion of 260 SSLPs. Unfortunately, it was decided that the areas to receive SSLPs were to be increased to 524 before evaluation plans were under way. That particularly silly decision effectively torpedoed what might still have been a really good comparative evaluation.

Third, the evaluation was required to start immediately, without waiting for the SSLPs to 'bed down' and become properly established and well functioning. That runs completely counter to accepted research practice, and inevitably raises questions as to whether any lack of effects might be no more than a consequence of the evaluation being undertaken too early.

Fourth, government decision making was to be based exclusively on cross-sectional data (as reported in this volume), rather than longitudinal data that would be much more informative. Thus, in 2006, SSLPs were transformed into Children's Centres, with local authorities accountable for their management. For 2006/07, £1.7 billion was provided for these Centres, which became an integral part of the SSLPs. Was any of this based on a research evaluation of Sure Start? The answer has to be 'no' because, as this volume shows, the findings are inconclusive.

It has to be assumed that this governmental undermining of evaluation was political and deliberate (see Rutter, 2006). Of course, rigorous evaluations are only needed (and RCTs only justifiable) if there is genuine uncertainty on whether the intervention to be tested is effective. In this case, government had trumpeted the expectation that SSLP *would* drastically reduce child poverty and social exclusion and, therefore, that all disadvantaged areas should be able to benefit.

Research design

Chapters Eight and Nine well summarise the research design that was employed in the overall evaluation of SSLPs. In brief, a comparison was made between 150 SSLP areas where the SSLP had been instigated three years earlier and 50 comparison areas due to have the intervention later (as Chapter Eight puts it, a kind of 'waiting list' control). Outcomes were based on data for all families with nine- or 36-month-old children living in the area. Five key steps were taken to guard against artefactual differences:

(1) an 'intention to treat' design (rather than a focus on the families who had taken particular advantage of the services available);

(2) data analysis with and without imputation of missing data;

(3) determination of group differences both before and after adjusting for differences in background characteristics;

(4) the use of meaningful composite variables to reduce the likelihood of significant differences due solely to chance; and

(5) an assessment of whether variations in programme implementations were associated with differences in outcome.

As discussed in more detail in Rutter (2006), given the constraints imposed by government, this was as rigorous and careful an evaluation as could be undertaken. The research team are to be congratulated on their high-quality research. As a consequence, there is every reason to trust the research findings.

The key results may be summarised as follows. First, there was only one significant difference (out of 14) for nine-month-olds – a slightly lower rating on home chaos. For three-year-olds there was significantly less use of scolding, slapping and physical restraint. There was no evidence of any overall difference (for the better or the worse) with respect to children's behaviour or health. Second, the effects varied significantly by family characteristics: SSLPs were associated with significant benefits for non-teen mothers (who constituted 86% of the sample), but adverse effects for teen mothers (whose children scored lower on verbal ability and social competence and higher on behavioural problems). Children from workless households (40% of sample) and from lone-parent families (33% of sample) also showed adverse effects of SSLPs. Third, within the non-teen group, the benefits for the children were statistically mediated by more positive parenting. Fourth, where the independent ratings indicated better programme implementation, there were greater child benefits.

Three basic questions have to be asked about these results. First, are the differences and lack of differences likely to be valid for the sample studied? Because the quality of the research was so good and the methodological checks so rigorous, the answer must be 'yes'. Second, do the differences reflect a *causal* effect of SSLPs? Inevitably, the answer to that question must be much more cautious. As the researchers point out, the differences are solely based on cross-sectional findings and, in the absence (as yet) of longitudinal data, causal inferences must be extremely tentative. Nevertheless, their plausibility can be assessed to some extent by asking first whether there is a more plausible non-causal explanation (in my view there is not) and, second, whether internal analyses favour a causal inference. The relatively strong associations between programme implementation and child benefits suggest (but do not prove) some kind of causal effect.

The third basic question is whether the findings truly mean that SSLPs have only quite small beneficial effects for non-teen mother families and similarly small adverse effects for teen mother families. That is a very difficult question to answer. Because of the rigour of the methodological checks, it is most unlikely that either finding is due to chance. The reality of the adverse effect is supported by similar findings for workless and lone-parent households. The implication is that universal interventions often (perhaps usually) need to be combined with targeted ones. The main query is whether the findings (both beneficial and adverse) reflect the fact that it took quite some time for SSLPs to become properly established. Might the pattern look very different in a few years time? Maybe. On the one hand, structured interventions usually bring at least some early benefits. On the other hand, does the same apply to more complex multifaceted whole-community interventions? We do not know.

What should we conclude from the research as a whole? I have focused on the quantitative national comparative study, but there are also qualitative data of a more molecular variety – as described in other chapters. I draw three main conclusions from these qualitative data. First, a great deal has been learned about both the trials and tribulations, and the successes, of introducing and implementing community-wide interventions. Second, it is evident that both professionals and participating families have seen much that is good in SSLPs. Third, the government-imposed constraints will make it extremely difficult to differentiate among the SSLP elements that are definitely beneficial, those that are definitely unhelpful and those that are neutral in their effects. As Weersing and Weisz (2002) have pointed out, the crucial question in studies of all interventions is not so much whether overall they are better than doing nothing, but rather *which* elements serve to provide the benefits. The design of SSLPs has made that crucial objective impossible to achieve in any rigorous way. That constitutes a seriously missed opportunity.

Overview

In conclusion, let me summarise my assessment under four different headings. First, there is the role of government. On the one hand, it deserves very high credit for recognising the need to do something radical in order to deal with a serious challenge. Government also deserves high credit for providing substantial new funds to make SSLPs possible, and for appreciating that an investment in the pre-school years might bring worthwhile dividends. It is also necessary to appreciate that the overall focus of SSLPs was broadly in keeping with research evidence.

These are very important positives, but against them must be placed serious negatives. The ways in which the details of SSLP implementation were organised were completely out of keeping with the research evidence (as detailed above) and served to undermine its efficacy. Very little positive can be said about the planned programme implementation. It was really poor and it is to be regretted that more attention was not paid to the advice of academics who knew about prevention.

The conclusions on research are equally negative as far as government is concerned. Not only was there a failure to use the best designs, there was active interference with the possibility of rigorous evaluation. Moreover, in 2006 the government took actions in relation to SSLPs that completely ignored the tentative and inconclusive nature of the cross-sectional findings. It is impossible to avoid the conclusions that the government is determined to impose evidence-based practice on everyone else, but equally determined that evidence should never be allowed to get in the way of government policy.

The second heading concerns the role of Naomi Eisenstadt, who was given the responsibility of running the Sure Start Unit up to 2006. In my view, she comes out as having had a very positive effect on the enterprise as a whole. Of course, as she had to be, she has been loyal to the government throughout, but she has shown three crucially important qualities. First, in setting up the Scientific Advisory Group of the National Evaluation of Sure Start, she included people (such as myself but also others) whom she knew would ask awkward questions and who would be critical when that seemed to be needed. Both at an 'official' and at a personal level, she was firmly committed to getting the best advice that could be obtained. Second, while recognising the limitations of the research evidence available, she strove valiantly to use the findings (both positive and negative) to make SSLPs better. Third, in dealing with all concerned, she injected an intellectual and emotional energy to try to make everything work well. The government was fortunate to have someone of her calibre at the helm.

Third, there is the role of Jay Belsky, Ted Melhuish and the rest of a very strong research team. As already noted, the quality of the research (in all its varied elements) has been exemplary. I very much doubt that it could have been done any better. They have faced ridiculous government-imposed constraints but they have found good ways of making an impressive silk purse out of a sow's ear.

Fourth, there is the fundamental question of whether SSLPs have been worthwhile. Would the same money have been better spent another way? Given the uncertain nature of the research findings, it is impossible to give a firm answer to the question. I have raised a range of research queries but, as a clinician and as a researcher into risk and protective factors, my overall assessment is cautiously positive. Prior to the SSLP initiative, there was no doubt that the funding of services for the pre-school years was seriously inadequate. I am, therefore, optimistic that at least some good use will be made of these funds even if I remain concerned that the research has not been able to provide as much guidance as it could have done in the absence of governmental constraints. For the reasons given above, I am sceptical about the likelihood of SSLPs making much difference in alleviating child poverty but, if it succeeds in bringing about even a modest improvement in family functioning and child outcomes, that would be worthwhile. I am equally sceptical about the notion that good pre-school provision will obviate the need for interventions at a later age to deal with challenges and problems in adolescence. The UNICEF report (2007) makes it quite clear that the problems extend well beyond the pre-school years.

The key question for me, as a researcher, is whether the government will have learned any lessons from the experience of the implementation and evaluation of SSLPs. I would like to think that it has, but I am forced to admit that I doubt that it has the slightest interest in research evidence when dealing with its own policies.

References

Anning, A., Chesworth, E., Spurling, L., Partinoudi, K. and National Evaluation of Sure Start Team (2005) *Report 9: The quality of early learning, play and childcare services in Sure Start Local Programmes*. London: HMSO.

Brooks-Gunn, J., Duncan, G.J. and Aber, J.L. (1997) *Neighborhood Poverty, Vol. 1: Context and consequences for children*, New York: Russell Sage Foundation.

Bruer, J.T. (1999) *The myth of the first three years*, New York: The Free Press.

Ceci, S.J. and Papierno, P.B. (2005) 'Psychoeconomic consequences of resource allocation: what happens when an intervention works for those it was intended for, but works even better for others?', *American Psychologist*, vol 60, pp 149-60.

Collishaw, S., Maughan, B., Goodman, R. and Pickles, A. (2004) 'Time trends in adolescent mental health', *Journal of Child Psychology and Psychiatry*, vol 45, pp 1350-62.

Commission on Families and the Wellbeing of Children (2005) *Families and the state: Two-way support and responsibilities*, Bristol: The Policy Press.

Fergusson, D.M., Grant, H., Horwood, L.J. and Ridder, E.M. (2005) 'Randomized trial of the Early Start Program of Home Visitation', *Pediatrics*, vol 116, pp 803-9.

Fergusson, D.M., Grant, H., Horwood, L.J. and Ridder, E.M. (2006) 'Randomized trial of the Early Start Program of Home Visitation: parent and family outcomes', *Pediatrics*, vol 117, pp 781-6.

Fitzgerald, H., Lester, B.M. and Zuckerman, B. (eds) (2006) *The crisis in youth mental health: Critical issues and effective programs. Volume 1: Childhood disorders*, Westport, CN: Praeger.

Freeark, K. and Davidson, W.S. (eds) (2006) *The crisis in youth mental health: Critical issues and effective programs. Volume 3: Issues for families, schools and communities*, Westport, CN: Praeger.

Harker, L. (2006) *Delivering on child poverty: What would it take?*, London: HMSO.

Hirsch, D. (2005) *Financial support for children: Defining responsibilities and adequacy*, London: National Family and Parenting Institute.

Laub, J.H. and Sampson, R.J. (2003) *Shared beginnings, divergent lives: Delinquent boys to age 70*, Cambridge, MA: Harvard University Press.

Love, J., Kisker, E.E., Ross, C.M., Schochet, P.Z., Brooks-Gunn, J., Paulsell, D., Boller, K., Constantine, J., Vogel, C., Fuligni, A.S. and Brady-Smith, C. (2002) *Making a difference in the lives of infants and toddlers and their families: The impacts of Early Head Start. Volume 1: Final technical report*, www.mathematica-mpr.com/PDFs/ehsfinalvol1.pdf

McCall, R.B., Ryan, O.S. and Plemons, B.W. (2003) 'Some lessons learned on evaluating community-based, two-generation service programs: the case of the Comprehensive Child Development Program (CCDP)', *Journal of Applied Developmental Psychology*, vol 24, pp 125-41.

Nelson, C.A. and Jeste, S. (in press) 'Neurobiological perspectives on developmental psychopathology', in M. Rutter, D. Bishop, D. Pine, S. Scott, J. Stevenson, E. Taylor and A. Thapar (eds) *Rutter's Child and Adolescent Psychiatry* (5th edn), Oxford: Blackwell.

Olds, D.L., Henderson, C.R. Jr, Tatelbaum, R. and Chamberlin, R. (1986) 'Improving the delivery of prenatal care and outcomes of pregnancy: a randomised trial of nurse home visitation', *Pediatrics*, vol 77, pp 16-28.

Olds, D.L., Henderson, C.R. Jr, Cole, R., Eckenrode, J., Kitzman, H., Luckey, D., Pettit, L., Sidora, K., Morris, P. and Powers, J. (1998) 'Long-term effects of nurse home visitation on children's criminal and antisocial behavior', *Journal of the American Medical Association*, vol 280, pp 1238-44.

Olds, D.L., Kitzman, H., Cole, R., Robinson, J., Sidora, K., Luckey, D.W., Henderson, C.R. Jr, Hanks, C., Bondy, J. and Holmberg, J. (2004a) 'Effects of nurse home visiting on maternal life course and child development: age 6 follow-up results of a randomized trial', *Pediatrics*, vol 114, pp 1550-9.

Olds, D.L., Robinson, J., Pettitt, L., Luckey, D.W., Holmberg, J., Ng, R.K., Isacks, K., Sheff, K. and Henderson, C.R. Jr (2004b) 'Effects of home visits by paraprofessionals and by nurses: age 4 follow-up results of a randomized trial', *Pediatrics*, vol 114, pp 1560-8.

Rutter, M. (2006) 'Is Sure Start an effective preventive intervention?', *Child and Adolescent Mental Health*, vol 11, pp 135-41.

Rutter, M. and Rutter, M. (1993) *Developing minds: Challenge and continuity across the lifespan*, Harmondsworth: Penguin Books; New York: Basic Books.

Rutter, M. and Smith, D. (1995) *Psychosocial disorders in young people: Time trends and their causes*, Chichester: Wiley.

Sampson, R.J., Raudenbush, S.W. and Earls, F. (1997) 'Neighborhoods and violent crime: a multilevel study of collective efficacy', *Science*, vol 277, pp 918-924.

Tunstill, J., Meadows, P., Akhurst, S., Allnock, D., Chrysanthou, J., Garbers, C., Morley, A. and National Evaluation of Sure Start Team (2005) *Report 10: Implementing Sure Start local programmes: An integrated overview of the first four years*, London: HMSO.

UNICEF Innocenti Research Centre (2007) *Report card 7: An overview of child well-being in rich countries: A comprehensive assessment of the lives and well-being of children and adolescents in the economically advanced nations*, Florence: UNICEF.

Villaruel, F.A. and Luster, T. (eds) (2006) *The crisis in youth mental health: Critical issues and effective programs. Volume 2: Disorders in adolescence*, Westport, CN: Praeger.

Watt, N.F., Ayoub, C., Bradley, R.H., Puma, J.E. and LeBoeuf, W.A. (eds) (2006) *The crisis in youth mental health: Critical issues and effective programs. Volume 4: Early intervention programs and policies*, Westport, CN: Praeger.

Weersing, V.R. and Weisz, J.R. (2002) 'Mechanisms of action in youth psychotherapy', *Journal of Child Psychology and Psychiatry*, vol 43, pp 3-29.

Zigler, E. and Styfco, S.J. (2006) 'Epilogue', in N.F. Watt, C. Ayoub, R.H. Bradley, J.E. Puma and W.A. LeBoeuf (eds) *The crisis in youth mental health: Critical issues and effective programs. Volume 4: Early intervention programs and policies*, Westport, CN: Praeger, pp 347-71.

Index

buildings for Sure Start Centres 105-6, 126

C

Campbell, D. 65-6
capital expenditure 125-6
causal effects: lack of analysis 204-5
Ceci, S.J. 199
Census data 29, 32, 49, 52, 53-4, 57, 59-60
  and 'neighbourhood change' 174-5
centre-based service delivery 87, 90
chaotic household *see* household chaos
Chicago Child-Parent Centers 7
child abuse 8, 9
Child Benefit Office records 29, 50, 57
child development
  conflicting policies 103-4
  research evidence and early child development 6-7, 97
  critical periods in child development 8, 9, 199
  as SSLP outcome 136, 143, 149, 202
  and community change 182, 183-5
  and proficiency of implementation 156-69
  SSLP targeting of deprived areas 27-8, 33-6
child health 7-9, 17-18
  and area characteristics 141
  and implementation proficiency 168-9
  as SSLP outcome 136, 140, 141, 142
  and community change 181-5, 188, 190-1
  SSLP targeting of deprived areas 27-8, 33-6, 52
child health clinics
  ease of access 37, 38, 53
  levels of service provision 186, 191
Child Health System data 181, 183
child poverty
  levels in SSLP areas 31, 42
  reduction as government aim 199-200, 207
child protection services 9, 17, 51
child-focused services 160-1, 165, 168
Childcare Act (2006) xi
childcare provision xi
  access in SSLP areas 1, 38, 51, 52, 91
  and access to other services 80, 91-2
  and community change 185-6, 188, 189, 191
  crèche facilities 91-2, 185-6, 189, 191

Childcare Unit (DfES) x
children
  identification of households with young children 45, 50-2, 178
  proportion of children under four in SSLP areas 29
  UK rating in well-being assessment · 197-8, 199
  see also Impact Study: impact on children and families
Children Act (2004) 17
Children's Centres *see* Sure Start Children's Centres
children's services 79, 89-92, 186-8
  see also joined up services for young children
Climbié, Victoria 17
cognitive development as outcome variable 140
collaborative working *see* interagency collaboration
commissioning new services: parental input 88
communication and implementation 159
community policing 74
community and SSLPs ix, 5, 9-10
  community-based services and implementation 79-92
  community benefits 98, 133, 134
  community change evaluation 173-92
  challenges to 174-6
  change factors 188-90
  community development approach 9-10, 12, 133
  community-focused services and variation in impact 160-1, 165
  local partnerships 12-13, 155, 158, 159
  maternal rating of communities 148
  targeting of deprived neighbourhoods 25-43
  dangers of 201
  profiling communities 45-60
  see also neighbourhoods
complex interventions and evaluation 70-4, 156, 202-3
Comprehensive Child Development Program 135
Comprehensive Spending Review (CSR)(1998) vii-viii, 3, 4-6, 10-11
conditional parents 87
conflicting policies 103-4
Connell, J.P. 72
consultation and service delivery 80, 87, 88

T

take up levels in SSLPs 108-9
targeting deprived neighbourhoods
  25-43, 201
targets
  shared targets 83
  see also outcomes for individual
    children
teenage mothers
  and community change 178, 189
  and impact of SSLPs 141, 147, 149,
    150
tenure type as area characteristic 141,
  189
themed studies 99-100, 101, 121, 126
'theory of change' approach 136, 147,
  157, 166
Tilley, N. 68, 69-70
time pressures on SSLPs 107, 109
travel to work distances 53-4
Treasury *see* Her Majesty's Treasury
trust and SSLP implementation 84
'typical' SSLP subgroup 41, 42, 180
'tyranny of the mean' 198

U

unanticipated effects of programmes
  114, 115
unemployment in SSLP areas 31-2, 42,
  141, 147, 149, 178, 199-200
UNICEF report 197, 199, 207
United States
  research on early years interventions
    6-7, 127
  see also Head Start programme
universal interventions: drawbacks 199,
  201
US National Institute for Mental
  Health (NIMH) 71-2
users *see* service users

V

variability within areas as change factor
  189-90
verbal and non-verbal ability
  and early interventions 8
  and measurement of implementation
    proficiency 161, 167
  as outcome variable 140, 142, 143,
    147, 149
vision 159, 167
voluntary sector viii, 98, 101, 158
Vondra, J. 97

W

'waiting-list controls' 136
Weersing, V.R. 205
Weiss, H.B. 71
Weisz, J.R. 205
work journeys data 53-4
workforce
  experience of change and SSLP
    working 99, 103-4, 107
  lack of reach 108-9
  and SSLP implementation 84-5
  and measuring implementation
    proficiency 159, 165, 168
'workless' households 31-2, 141, 147,
  149
  and benefits trap 199-200
  and community change 178, 189

Y

young mothers *see* teenage mothers

Z

Zigler, E. 198